To Chris,

Thanks so much for your
help in getting this project
rolling.

all my best,

Ted

PRAISE FOR MONEY SMART

"Boy do I wish I'd had this book fifteen years ago!"

—**RAFAEL MAGALLAN**, RETIRED DIRECTOR OF PUBLIC POLICY,
THE COLLEGE BOARD

"*Money Smart* is a realistic guide for anyone to who hopes to attain financial freedom. It turns seemingly overwhelming and incomprehensible financial topics into easy-to-understand strategies and simple how-tos that will empower anyone to take control of their own financial well-being and success."

—**LYNN WILLIS**, COMMUNITY BUSINESS MANAGER,
TANGLEWOOD CONDOMINIUM RENTALS

"I have been investing for many years, and *Money Smart* has changed my approach. Many thanks to Ted Hunter."

—**DENNIS PECORELLA**, OWNER, DENNIS BARBER SALON

"The money rules and spending rules have already helped me put the brakes on my impulsive shopping. *Money Smart* is a great read, one section pulls me to the next, and Ted Hunter's take on money is aligned with a spiritual sensibility."

—**TIFFANEY ARROUZET**, OWNER, ADDICTED TO MASSAGE

"This book is something people badly need. I loved that it was so easy to read and understand."

—**CAROL GRENNAN**, PRICING COORDINATOR, AVIS BUDGET GROUP

"*Money Smart* is a treasure trove of useful information. If you follow the author's advice, this book will change your life for the better. I'll be giving it to family and friends."

—**KEN CARTER**, RETIRED OWNER, CURTIS TURNER REALTORS; FORMER EXECUTIVE MEMBER, MORRIS COUNTY BOARD OF REALTORS

"I will keep it and refer to it for many years to come and give it to the important people in my life. It's a reminder that common sense rarely fails. This principle, mixed with a goodly amount of learned knowledge, makes for a workbook that I wish I had long ago."

—**MELANIE MAKEUP**, OWNER, ILLUSIONS BY MELANIE

"This is a game changer. In clear, concise steps, Ted Hunter lays out the strategy for you to take control of your finances and save money."

—**CHRIS BAILEY**, SYSTEMS TECHNICIAN, AT&T

"I was taught long ago to 'run the numbers' and verify what people say. I ran the numbers presented in the graphs, charts, and examples in this book and they are solid. The advice is sound and timely. *Money Smart* will help ease anxiety in an uncertain time."

—**RANDY HURSH**, OWNER, CHECKER CAB COMPANY, DAVIS, CA

MONEY
$MART

MONEY $MART

How to spend, save, eliminate debt,
and achieve financial freedom

by TED HUNTER

Georgea Books

Published by Georgea Books, Sacramento, California

Money Smart is part of the Smart Books Series.

Georgea Books publications are available at special quantity discounts. For inquiries about use as sales promotions, premiums, or in courses and training programs please e-mail us at sales@georgeabooks.com. For information regarding permission to reprint material from this book, please e-mail your request to permissions@georgeabooks.com.
www.GeorgeaBooks.com

Library of Congress Cataloging-in-Publication Data

Hunter, Ted, 1940-
 Money $mart : how to spend, save, eliminate debt, and achieve financial freedom / by Ted Hunter.
    p. cm.
"America's manual for smart personal money management ."
Includes index.
ISBN 978-0-9843877-0-0
1. Finance, Personal. I. Title. II. Title: Money smart.
HG179.H86 2010
332.024--dc22
                    2010031732

Printed in the United States of America

CONTENTS

Acknowledgments

It has been exactly two years and six months since I began this project and, finally, the book is ready to go to the printer. When I started, I had no idea what a huge job I had taken on. As it turned out, I sure needed help and I am very grateful for the support I received.

First I would like to thank my daughter-in-law, Gabrielle Hunter, for all that she has done. By the end of the first year I could see I needed help; a project manager and early editor, someone with the right background and aptitude for what I now realize was a very challenging job. It was obvious to me that Gabrielle would be an outstanding candidate for the job. Gabrielle, in turn, had recently established her own company to provide exactly the kind of support I needed. The problem was that I have always felt that mixing family and business was a bad idea, as did Gabrielle. So we talked and decided to make an exception and do it, but on one condition. If either of us ever felt it was hurting our relationship, the collaboration was to be ended immediately. Well that never happened and Gabrielle has just been fabulous at the job. Gaby, I can't thank you enough.

The next person I wish to thank is my brother, Ron, someone I greatly admire. When I produced the first version of the book in November 2008 and gave it to a group of people to read, I discovered that there was almost no feedback on the content of the book, just on the writing style and organization. Everyone seemed to just accept the information and advice I had provided as correct and complete. This was *not* good. There had to be errors and omissions regarding the content. Fortunately, I knew of someone with the business, financial, and life experience necessary to watch my back and double-check what I had to say. Thank you so much, brother, for being there for me, as always, and for being so very good at all that you do. It has meant a lot.

I would also like to thank my editor, Susan Suffes. Susan, you have been a delight to work with and have helped us so much in insuring that the critical messages of this book have been delivered in the best possible way.

I also owe a big thanks to my eldest son John for his advice, expertise, and effort in making all the graphs in the book, and to my son Dan for creating the user software on my website.

Lastly, I wish to thank the many professionals who have double-checked or helped me in areas where I needed it. I'd like to extend a special thanks to several individuals in particular. My thanks to Don Guthrie of Davis, California, for his assistance on chapter twelve, "Buying and Selling a Home." It is a subject I know well. The problem was that it's been thirty years since I worked in that field and I had to assume that I'd lost touch with the subject some and that some aspects had changed. Don was terrific in filling in some key holes and insuring that what I had to say was reasonably thorough and fully up to date. Thanks, Don. Much appreciated.

Finally, I wish to thank Doris Keller of Sacramento, California, for her assistance on the subject of paying for an education, a subject she knows so well from her long career assisting on such matters. Also, thank you to my attorney, Dave Jorgenson of Maui, Hawaii, on the subjects of legal matters and estate planning. Thanks, guys.

It's Time to Take Control of Your Money

Over the past few years I've watched in dismay as millions of people who believed in the established financial system saw their dreams for financial independence vaporize in a sea of financial mismanagement. I witnessed friends and family members from a wide range of ages and backgrounds negatively affected by their lack of knowledge about money and by the vulnerability this creates. I saw that the financial turmoil that showed up in early 2008 had barely begun to bring to the surface the depth of the incompetence of the financial services industry and the vast majority of its alleged "experts." I saw, with great clarity, the depth of the myths, and, in some cases, the outright lies that had been told about money and the damage they had done. Worst of all, I realized that all of this would just continue to happen unless something was done, and so I decided to do something about it.

In *Money Smart*, I explain what you need to know to be successful with money in a comprehensive and easy-to-understand way. I cover how to spend money, save it, get out of debt, buy or sell a home, buy a car, invest, and achieve financial freedom. You'll learn how to make financial decisions that will be in your own best interest and not in the interest of others. Whether you're a high school dropout or you hold a PhD in economics, this book is for you.

Why listen to me? For one thing, over the last twenty years I've called, and taken advantage of, every one of the major highs and lows of both the stock and real estate **markets**. Further, like you, I've had my share of financial ups and downs. Everything I did with money—and what money did to me and for me—gave me invaluable experiences that had nothing to do with financial experts or their advice.

I discovered that being money smart isn't complicated. It doesn't require advanced courses in finance or expensive seminars. All it really requires is a basic understanding of the true fundamentals of successful personal money management. But looking at all that's been happening with money, I realized that this straightforward formula has gotten lost. It's time to find it again. That's what *Money Smart* is all about.

My Personal Financial Education

One day, many years ago, my father sat me down and told me he signed me up for a paper route as an addition to my other existing business ventures. (I already was a junior door-to-door salesperson, had a lawn-cutting service in the summer, and worked as a trapper in the winter.) Dad said that from then on, if I wanted anything I had to earn the money myself. He would feed me and provide a roof over my head, and that was it. Dad was true to his word. Did I resent it? Nope. I went and did what I had to do. I learned a heck of a lot very quickly, I can tell you; I had no choice. Through trial and error and with a decent amount of common sense, I quickly piled up many life lessons. To this day I go back to the basic lessons I learned from those experiences. They are the foundation for all I do when it comes to money. By the way, it was sixty years ago when I added that paper route. I was *nine*-years-old.

My father never gave me another penny until I went to college and he paid part of my tuition. I worked my way through Syracuse University where I earned a BA in economics and business. As an undergraduate I held jobs as a dishwasher, a rock bandleader, and a YMCA counselor. After spending two years in the Army as a military police officer, I had a very successful thirteen-year career with the International Paper Company and Johnson & Johnson as one of the pioneers in large-scale computer-based business systems design and implementation.

In 1977, a friend and I started a real estate brokerage company from scratch. We grew it to five offices with over one hundred agents and we ran it for ten years. By the mid-1980s I was a multi-millionaire. I drove a Porsche and owned a penthouse on New York Harbor. I would stand on my balcony at night looking out at the Statue of Liberty, its reflection shimmering on the surface of the water. During the day I went to NYU Film School, on my way to becoming the next "great" independent filmmaker. Life was good.

Sounds great, huh? Well it didn't stay that way. Despite my success, I did not yet fully understand the real estate market. On the contrary, I had become a full-fledged card-carrying member of the real estate industry and, like the rest of them, had bought into "the system" hook, line, and sinker. At that point the real estate cycle turned, and turned hard. In less than four years, everything I had built was gone, along with my very last cent.

The real estate market crashed because it was badly overpriced. I looked back at the history of the market and saw that it would have been possible to predict this market adjustment. I studied other markets, like the stock market, and saw that all markets cycle through periods of substantial overpricing and underpricing. And at that moment I got it! I *saw* the cycles of both the real estate and financial markets and understood what they meant and how I could use that knowledge. I realized I had been foolish to believe that you "always invest for the long run" and that the correct approach was to buy when the market was underpriced and sell when a market was overpriced. From that day on I've played all the major moves of both the real estate and stock markets to my personal benefit.

Taking advantage of my newfound insight, I entered the stockbrokerage industry and became a "hired gun" stock investor for about thirty affluent private clients. The 1990s couldn't have been a better time to invest in the stock market. Better yet, I beat the market most of the time, making my clients a heck of a lot of money and bringing myself back from the dead.

How I've Called the Markets

In 1991, when I began my career as a stockbroker/investment advisor, my friends and business acquaintances were aghast. "The stock market is a disaster!" they cried. "Why would you do that?" they demanded. To me, the answer was crystal clear. We were at the low end of that market's cycle and I saw it. In hindsight, I doubt you could find a better point in the last fifty years to have entered the stockbrokerage industry.

By the end of 1999, I saw that the stock market was again terribly overpriced. I sold my investment business and the majority of my **stocks** and told my clients to get out of the market because they were unlikely to make a penny there for many years to come. At that moment the **DOW** was at about 10,900 and the **NASDAQ** (mostly the **tech stocks**) at about 4,000. The markets peaked several months later.

In the winter of 2000, I saw that the real estate cycle was favorable and I put a lot of my available money into a fairly expensive house. The rest went into **fixed-income investments** and into building a small wholesale company.

In the fall of 2005, I sent an e-mail to my friends and family, telling them that the real estate market was now very badly overpriced. I estimated it was likely to peak in the summer of 2006 and then drop at least 30%–35%, especially on the coasts, over the next three years or so. As I predicted, the market peaked that next summer.

Also in the fall of 2005, I saw the Asian real estate market was lagging behind the U.S. real estate market so I reinvested some of my money in a luxury oceanfront condo in Thailand. In the spring of 2006, I sold the U.S. house at the peak of the market for 92% more than its purchase price.

In the summer of 2008, I sold the Thai condo for a three-year net profit of 58%, less than ninety days before the world markets began to nosedive. As I was essentially 100% in cash (short-term **CDs**) and not wishing to be such an extremist, I reluctantly put 10% of my assets into the stock market in February of 2008. The bad news, you know. The market dropped by about 30% that year. The good news was that I only lost 22%, beating the market by 8%. The great news is that the loss was only on 10% of my overall assets as I was 90% in cash and CDs.

This modest re-entry into the stock market also reinforced a lesson. I had thought that I could probably select some winning exceptions in a badly overpriced market. Not so. The good stocks may drop less (and they did) but a falling market takes almost everything with it.

By October 2008 the DOW dropped to 10,000 from a high of 14,000 in the fall of 2007, and the "buying opportunity" drums began beating again in financial circles and in the financial media. I cautioned my family and friends that the stock market was still overpriced, and the best bet was to continue to stay out of the market. Five months later it dropped to 6,600.

So there you go. Over twenty years ago I learned the hard way to understand markets and their cycles. Since then I have called them to my benefit. My bottom line strategy is, again, really very simple. When something is underpriced, buy it. If it's fairly priced, maybe buy it. But if it's noticeably overpriced, sell it and invest elsewhere. These are not decisions you will have to make every day. You may only make them a couple of times in a decade. The important thing is that you must remain aware of where things stand and act when it becomes necessary to do so.

There is a lot more to being money smart, however, than knowing when to buy and sell stocks and real estate. Being money smart means spending your money wisely and seeing to it that money plays a positive role in your life. Most of all it means taking control of your finances and never turning that control over to anyone else.

In this book I use terms such as *investment, stocks, bonds, mutual funds* and so forth. There is a glossary (beginning on page 351) that explains the terms I will be using. If you haven't had the opportunity to learn these terms you might want to take a few minutes and read the glossary before you proceed.

It's Time for You to Take Control

We are living in very challenging financial times. Most people have suffered painful losses in their long-term savings. For the millions who have lost their jobs—or even their homes—the challenge is greater yet. There is no easy answer. In the short run, some things may go badly despite your best efforts. However, there are many tactics you can employ to survive now, minimize further damage, and then prosper as you move forward. The first step is to understand what went wrong both on a national and personal level.

The old adage, "Understanding the problem is 90% of the solution" couldn't be truer than here, so I'll start by looking at how these problems began and showcase the myths and, in some cases, the outright lies you've been told and will continue to be told. Separating truth from fiction is as important as knowing what to do about it.

By the time you finish *Money Smart* you will have gained both an excellent fundamental education in successful real world money management and the practical tools you need to put it to use. You will have opened the door to true success regarding the spending, saving, and investing of your money. You'll be able to insure that money is adding to, and not taking away from, the quality of your life.

PART ONE

PUTTING MONEY INTO CONTEXT

CHAPTER ONE

You Can Manage Your Money Better Than Anyone Else

Sixty years ago, personal money management was a fairly simple thing. People cashed their paychecks every Friday and set aside the cash needed for the upcoming week. They went to the bank to put some money in a savings account and, if they had one, to pay the mortgage. There were no credit cards, very little personal debt, and few investments. If you wanted to buy something, you saved for it. Most workers didn't have to save for retirement, as the company they spent most of their lives working for provided an adequate pension plan.

In the 1950s the affluence of the country increased, the middle class expanded, and television arrived as a fixture in most households. Together these factors fueled a dramatic shift, and the consumer-driven society began to grow. If people wanted something like a car, they no longer needed to save for it; they could just take out a loan. And they did. "Living well" and "having it now" became more and more commonplace.

The ground was fertile for the banks' budding new venture, the personal credit card. The credit card industry was introduced, began to flourish, and ultimately exploded. Living in debt and beyond one's means became an accepted and normal part of our culture and financial lives.

By the 1980s, the increased mobility of the workforce broke the relationship between the workers and their companies. People no longer stayed with the same company for life. They needed a portable retirement plan. At the same time, the economy was becoming increasingly global, and U.S. companies found it harder to compete, especially under the burden of the huge retirement programs that were in place.

It was during this same time that the **401(k)** was born, providing the answer both parties so badly needed. Companies began to replace their retirement programs with new 401(k) plans in which the company provided limited matching funds.

Soon thereafter, the dot-com explosion and increased corporate leveraging (use of corporate borrowing power to ramp up profits) combined to fuel the greatest stock market boom in history. Employees were more than receptive to shift away from company pensions and toward their own personal retirement plans. They saw the tremendous gains to be made in the stock market and believed they would make more money that way. Wall Street was now connected to Main Street. Over *70 million* new company-sponsored 401(k) accounts were opened by the end of the 1990s, and in this way the average American became a stock market investor for the first time since just prior to the Great Depression.

Throughout the last half of the twentieth century, as these dramatic changes regarding personal money management continued to unfold, American habits shifted. Most people now carry credit cards and loans for all kinds of things from cars to furniture. Nearly half of all

Americans now carry crushing debt loads—many before they've even turned twenty-one! The cost of a college education has also exploded and, along with it, so has debt. With company retirement plans rapidly becoming a thing of the past, each of us is now responsible for his or her financial future. With all these changes and stresses I don't need to tell you that money has become one of the major causes of unhappiness in our society today.

The incredible growth of middle-class affluence, along with the financial complexities Americans now face, have created an urgent need for a fundamental education in personal money management. Learning from our parents' example simply isn't enough anymore. The massive personal debt and high foreclosure rates so common today are symptoms of this lack of basic education and of the vulnerability it has created. Our educational institutions have failed to respond to this growing need. As a result, people remain adrift when it comes to managing their money and planning for their futures.

As you were growing up, how much did you learn about money, either in school or at home, that truly readied you for the real world? I graduated from a well-regarded university with a major in economics and a minor in business. Yet I was taught little or nothing I could use regarding money management. Fortunately, I had already learned much of what I needed to know from real-world experience while growing up.

Over time the financial services industry and the financial media grew exponentially to satisfy the new needs for expertise and advice regarding personal money management. They were more than happy to provide advice on financial management to the newly wealthy middle class.

On the surface this all seemed to be a good thing. It was not.

Who Should Manage Your Money?

In the absence of a formal money education, maybe you turn to the financial media, a massive group of magazine and newspaper writers and columnists, company and online newsletters, TV show hosts, and a never-ending supply of books and their authors. If you do, you're hit with a non-stop overload of highly repetitive and often flat-out bad information. With the overload of data facing you, it probably seems like there are only two alternatives: Either you throw up your hands and simply live day to day and hope that it all works out in the future, or you turn over your financial decisions—and your future—to "financial experts."

Over the last several decades, a large and highly lucrative industry of financial and investment experts—including stockbrokers and financial advisors—has gone mainstream. Maybe it seems very appropriate to get some expert help when it comes to both your financial education and decisions. Unfortunately, this will not solve your problems. On the contrary, the advice of these experts will often add to them.

For the most part, financial services experts are trained in and excel at sales and marketing, asset gathering, and commission generation—but not a lot else. They tend to attribute the success of their investment decisions to their own good judgment, not recognizing the larger forces at play on the market. Over the last forty years, as this new industry expanded its superficial analysis of the stock market, its advice became accepted as genuine investment expertise when, in truth, it was anything but. The vast majority of these experts truly believed that market growth just goes on forever. It doesn't. But to keep you believing that it will, the experts in the financial services industry and the media have built a system founded on four myths. It's time you heard the truth.

Myth #1: "Money Management Is Very Complicated"

You've heard, over and over again, from every area of the financial industry, that money is a very complex subject and you must master a huge amount of information if you wish to succeed financially. The underlying message is this: You'll have to read an awful lot of books, study markets in great detail, and have an aptitude for investments or you will get into trouble. Make your own financial decisions? Not a good idea.

This is just not true. There is no reason why you can't understand the subject of money management by investing a very modest amount of time—just as you are doing now by reading this book.

Myth #2: "Let Us Handle Your Finances Because We Do It Better Than You Can"

We have all participated in one of the greatest financial disasters in history. I am not just talking about the recent banking crisis, which is only a part of it, but something much larger. I'm referring to a destruction of personal wealth on a scale never seen before.

Most who invested in the stock market, and many who own a home, have been following the investment advice of people who for the most part have no real-life track record of investment success in anything other than an up market. The experts likely didn't learn about modern money management or how to invest successfully either. They didn't need to, as the soaring stock markets of the 1990s and the tens of millions of new 401(k) accounts made everybody a winner. They literally couldn't miss. There was no need for them to truly learn how to invest, especially in a down market.

The results have been devastating. According to *Time Magazine* (October 19, 2009), "At the end of 1998 the average 401(k) balance was $47,004. By the end of 2008 the average balance was down to $45,519 ($33,375 after adjusting for 26.7% inflation)." Add to this the fact that millions of families have now lost their homes as well. How can people possibly retire on $33,000? Or even two or three times that amount? Well, they can't. This, by and large, is what has happened by entrusting the experts with your financial future.

Why would you accept that these unproven strangers are capable of making your financial decisions? Would you let someone fix your teeth without proof that the dentist knew what he was doing and could provide a record of doing it successfully? Would you allow a doctor to operate on you without such proof? Would you hire someone to build a house, repair a car, or even fix a leaky sink without some knowledge of his qualifications and records? Of course you wouldn't. Yet you've been lulled into accepting financial experts at face value, *something you must no longer do*! Ask yourself:

- What proof of a real-world track record of success has a financial professional shared with you regarding his or her *personal* performance or that of their firm?
- Has your real estate agent shared how well she has done with her real estate investments?
- What about all those financial "experts" dominating the financial media? How have their investments fared?

If you have a stockbroker or financial advisor, ask him to provide, in writing, how he's done on *100%* of his own personal investments over the last ten years. Also request the ten-year performance on 100% of his firm's investment recommendations in writing. I'll bet you won't get either one. It's information they seldom wish to divulge. Most firms flat out will not allow their people to provide such information to the public in writing. So, I ask you: On what basis are you to pick someone to advise you? How can you trust the person without any physical proof that he is good at what he does? And even if the "experts" do provide something, it is very unlikely to be a true picture, as they will usually just select a portion of their results—information carefully chosen to show success.

What about the **mutual fund** industry? Did you know that year in and year out, about 80% of the managed mutual funds fail to beat the overall average of the stock market? What does that tell you about all those fund managers? Further, do not assume that you or any financial professional can reliably pick one of the 20% of the funds that will beat the market, especially since those funds are often not the same ones each year.

If you look under the covers of the managed mutual fund industry, I believe that what you will find are waves of huge unnecessary fees that deeply damage returns and a norm of nothing short of utter investment incompetence. I consider the managed mutual fund industry to have been, without question, just a disaster for the hard-working people of this country. A detailed explanation of why I say these things is provided in chapter eleven, "Evaluating Your Investment Alternatives," in the section on investing in mutual funds, **index funds**, and **ETFs**.

Mutual fund managers, supposedly the cream of the financial advisor crop, are paid millions to manage billions. If about 80% of them can't beat the average of the market in a given year, what makes you think the other professionals can? Do not use a stockbroker or an employer-provided financial advisor to pick your investments. They will almost certainly underperform what you can do on your own—and that's even before the hit you'll take from the fees and commissions involved.

If you dig into it far enough, I am confident you will find that the vast majority of the financial experts performed no better than the markets performed and that many of them did worse; that they, in fact, cannot invest your money any better than you can.

You will also find that the system has built this myth so successfully that the majority of the people in the financial services industry truly believe that they *are* good at it and invest their own personal money under the belief that it is true.

Myth #3: "Always Invest for the Long Term"

The implication here is that the markets will always do well over the long run; therefore, so will your money. But talking about the "long run" fails to consider a very critical point. How long are we talking about? If it's fifty years or more, then maybe that's so. But what matters is not fifty years; what matters is your personal time horizon. When it comes to a shorter time horizon, to say that you will always win is simply not true. And even with a very long period of time you would certainly have done far better if you had been out of the market during periods of major overpricing.

Over the last one hundred and ten years, U.S. stock has on average been valued at (bought and sold at) a little over sixteen times company earnings. This comparison of stock price to company earnings is called the price/earnings ratio (**P/E**). While the market has fluctuated a great deal over time, it has continued to fluctuate around this same average price. For this reason it is logical to consider it a good approximation of fair market value.

The following two graphs show what happened over those years. In the first graph, the solid line shows the pricing history of the market—what the market actually sold at; the dashed line shows fair market value over that time. The second graph covers the same time period and shows the difference in percent between the actual price/earnings ratio and the average, or fair, ratio to which it always eventually returns. The general patterns you see have held true since the inception of the market and I believe they will remain true into the future.

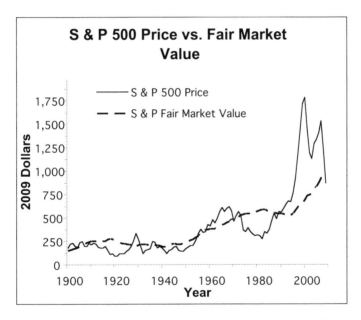

Source: Schiller, R. J. 2009. Information Site for Irrational Exuberance, www.econ.yale.edu/~schiller

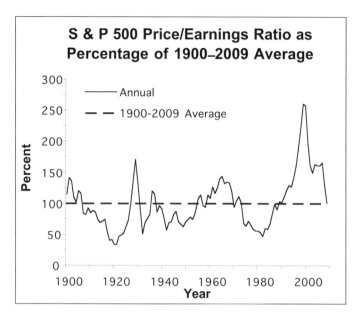

Source: Schiller, R. J. 2009. Information Site for Irrational Exuberance, www.econ.yale.edu/~schiller

As you can see, the problem with the industry's simplistic "invest for the long run" solution is that the market goes though long periods of substantial over- and underpricing. This, in turn, creates long periods of time when you are pretty much guaranteed to lose money, and other times when you are pretty much guaranteed to make money. Look at 1902–1920, when all people did was lose money for eighteen years. Look at 1966–1981, when investments again lost money for another sixteen years. As I write this book in late 2009 we have a loss, after adjusting for **inflation**, of about 25% since 2000. Together, that's at least twenty-six out of the last forty-four years—and counting—that the market has not made money. On the flip side, look at 1983–2000, where the market was surging upward and you were pretty much guaranteed to win.

The people and companies that make up this industry are in a trap. As the one-hundred-year-graph demonstrates, everyone should have been selling stocks, not buying them, in 1999–2000 and 2007–2008. During periods when the stock market is overpriced, a logical alternative is to shift, usually for years, to other markets, such as fixed-income investments or, perhaps, real estate. For the financial industry, this cyclic pattern poses a problem, as they make a lot more money when *your* money is in the stock market. The industry solved its problem, and created yours, with the adoption of their underlying working formula, which tells people to always keep investing in the stock market.

If you point out this information to a professional in this industry, the almost universal response you will get is that nobody can time the stock market. You'll be told that if you left the market for just a couple of years out of, say, every thirty, you'd miss all the gains. Heck, they can even show you that if you were out of the market for just forty days in your life you could miss it all. Is that true? Yes, that's probably so, but it is also irrelevant!

No, you cannot time the market. It's impossible to predict ahead of time when the stock market will go up or down—which days, weeks, months or even years. Nobody can. But you sure as heck can tell when a market is badly overpriced. If you stop buying and start selling what you own when the stock market becomes badly overpriced, and then start buying when the price becomes reasonable again, as it eventually does, you will usually do quite nicely. You'll do a lot better than if you'd remained invested in stocks the whole time. This is not timing the market; it is simply buying and selling based on price.

Said another way, the whole purpose of investment is to make money. Unless you invest exclusively in high-**dividend** investments, which few people do, the *only* way you can make money is by selling something for more money than you paid for it. Failing to sell substantially overpriced investments and failing to buy at no more than fair value—failing to buy low and sell high—totally undermines any success you might otherwise have achieved.

Look at how overpriced the market was in 1999 and 2000 in the graph that compares the **S&P 500** price to fair market value. This was not a time to add money. It was a time to sell stock investments, which is exactly what I did then. I moved my money to real estate and fixed income (CDs). Do you think Warren Buffet buys overpriced assets? How do you think he became the richest man in the world? He loves buying stock from "Mr. Market" as he calls it—but only when the price is right. In the fall of 2008 he was quoted in a *New York Times* article as saying that his personal account had been *exclusively* in fixed income, but since the market had dropped 3,000–4,000 points he was again starting to do some buying. I guess I wasn't the only one in fixed income at that time.

Myth #3 is so insidious and persuasive, so universally sold and accepted, that most financial professionals believe it themselves—and even invest their own money based on it. This is just what I did as a real estate professional before going bankrupt and learning my lesson. Unlike you, however, the financial professionals have been able to offset their losses with the billions of dollars in commissions and fees they have been paid and for which far too frequently they have not rightfully earned.

By now you may be asking yourself; "Is there no way to invest successfully? Isn't there a better alternative?" Yes, there is, and I explain it in chapter five, "The 10 Rules of Investing Successfully"; in chapter ten, "When to Invest"; and chapter eleven, "Evaluating Your Investment Alternatives." On my website, www.MoneySmartOnline.com, I also provide links to some of the better sources of information on this topic.

Myth #4: "It's Okay to Live Beyond Your Means"

The success and affluence enjoyed in this country are wonderful things. However, there has been a belief held by tens of millions of people that it is okay to live beyond their means, to own and enjoy what they have not yet earned. Most of these same people also bought into Myth #3, thereby greatly escalating the problem. They didn't sell their stock market investments in 1999–2000 when they should have. On the contrary, they projected the future value of those investments using unrealistically high rates, then repeated that same thinking when it came to the value of their homes, rationalizing that everything would come out just fine in the end.

I truly hope you are not one of the many people who bought into the destructive mindset that it's okay to live beyond your means. Your parents may not have taught you otherwise or set a good example. The endless impact of advertising, in all its forms, has undoubtedly been an enormous negative influence. Should you be in this situation, living beyond your means and in debt, I hope that by now you have come to understand how important it is that you stop living this lie. It's time to create a successful future for yourself and the people you care about.

I explain how you can turn your situation around in the next five chapters, culminating with chapter seven, "Getting Out of Debt."

The Real Estate Industry:
Pulling Your Home Out from Under You

The following graph shows the eighty-year price history of the U.S. residential real estate market, adjusted for inflation, as compared to building costs and average family income. Just like the stock market, the real estate market also enters significant time periods when it is substantially over- or underpriced. Buying when the market is badly overpriced is a recipe for disaster.

We recently hit one of those periods and hit it hard. Waves of money shifted from the troubled stock market into the real estate market and eventually caused prices to rise to unsustainable levels. The overpricing that resulted was made even worse when lending standards were irresponsibly loosened at the same time. It turned out to be the worst period of real estate overpricing in the last one hundred years.

Without an understanding of **market cycles** and how they were playing out at the time, millions of people made decisions that could not have been worse. They sold out of the stock market after it fell and then bought into an overpriced real estate market. It serves as a dramatic example of the incredible damage that occurs when people do not understand market cycles and the fair value of a market.

As for the experts, most had absolutely no idea how overpriced the market had become and most of those who did sure didn't say so. Do you know of any real estate professionals, especially in the regions that had become most grossly overpriced, who told their customers it was not a good idea to buy a home in 2005, 2006, or the first half of 2007? I don't.

Like all commissioned salespeople, real estate agents are always faced with a personal need to sell. Had they understood the current pricing versus the actual value of the market and done the right thing by it, their income would have dropped quite a bit for a period of years. Because they either did not understand or chose to ignore this absolutely critical information, they failed their clients and the financial futures of millions of families were destroyed.

Almost all who bought during that time were virtually guaranteed to lose a lot of money. Millions more borrowed on equity that was only temporary as a result of the overpriced real estate market. A few years later, as the overpricing began to correct substantially, people discovered that they owed more than their home was worth.

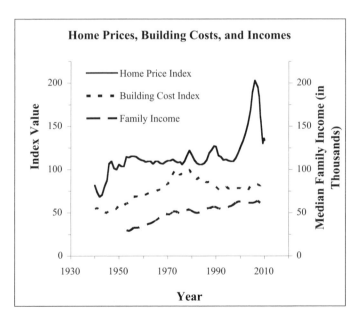

Sources: Schiller, R. J. 2009. Information Site for Irrational Exuberance, www.econ.yale.edu/~schiller; U.S. Census Bureau. 2009. Income: Historical Income Tables – Families, www.census.gov/hhes/www/income/histinc/incfamdet.html

In the winter of 2009, the drums started to beat that the real estate cycle reached the bottom and would soon begin to rise. Once again, this may be what the real estate industry wished to sell. Nevertheless, that advice flies in the face of market, investment, and historical realities. Visit www.MoneySmartOnline.com to see where I maintain a current estimate of where we are in both the real estate and stock market cycles. That information, along with this book, will help to insure that you can make more informed decisions in the future.

The Experts Aren't Watching Out for You

With rare exception, the financial media just repeats the financial industry mantra when it comes to investing in the stock market. In 1999 and 2000, when the stock market was about 100% overpriced, their advice continued to be, "Keep investing for the long run." It should have been "Sell!"

In 2007 and all the way through 2008, it was the same terrible advice. And where were they during the real estate market of 2005–2006? If they had advised people not to buy and not to use all of their **home equity** when the markets were overpriced (as I did), it would have made an enormous difference for millions of people who may not have lost their homes and life savings.

Even after all that has happened, most of the financial services industry still doesn't appear to have learned very much. A common advertising tactic adopted in response to the recent financial crisis goes something like this: "Have things gone badly for you? Has your financial advisor let you down? Call us. We're different! We'll take care of you! We'll see to it that your investments are protected and your money is working for you going forward."

All I can say is, wow! They, like most all the others, failed their clients, losing a lot of them in the process. Now that you know the truth I hope that *you* are no longer buying their story.

As for the financial media, it also failed to adequately analyze and understand the market forces of the day. They just kept buying into the industry mantras to "keep investing for the long run" regarding both the stock and real estate markets. This failure was amplified by overly focusing on the marketability of their spokesperson and the job of making money. If the talent didn't have strong real-world experience and success with money, it didn't matter so long as the public liked them.

As for the financial media's specific investment advice, here are several examples that should give you some food for thought.

Jim Cramer (the *Mad Money* show) has been arguably the financial media's most popular stock investment expert for the last ten years or so. Here are some interesting excerpts from the article, "Cramer's Star Outshines His Stock Picks" from *Barron's* on February 9, 2009, regarding his stock investment recommendations:

> In 2007, when we questioned Cramer's performance, he told viewers we were know-nothings and assured them his *Mad Money* picks had "killed" the S&P 500. The only regrettable thing about any of this is that CNBC and Cramer won't meaningfully discuss how his advice pans out.

Cramer's recommendations underperform the market by most measures. From May to December of last year, for example, the market lost about 30%. Heeding Cramer's Buys and Sells would have added another five percentage points to that loss, according to our latest tally.

Other careful, honest examinations of the CNBC star showed the same underperformance—including several independent studies by finance researchers, and a 2007 review by *Barron's* that found the only way to reliably profit from Cramer's stock picks was to short them. (**Shorting a stock** means to temporarily borrow some of that stock to sell it—betting that the price will drop—so you can later buy back the stock you owe at a lower price and pocket the difference.)

As to the financial media's annual lists where they select the "Best Mutual Funds to Go With for 2010" and so forth, it's quite common for about half of their chosen top performers to disappear from their lists within three to four years. Do you want to switch funds every three years? I sure don't.

Sometimes it just gets ridiculous. Take *Smart Money* magazine. At the start of 2007 the publication ran a featured article where they picked their thirty-five best stock funds. In March of 2010 their cover story was "The 15 Best Funds to Complete Your Comeback" where they selected their "fifteen best" stock funds. How many of their thirty-five chosen best funds of 2007 do you think made their list for 2010? Are you ready? Try one. *One* fund! The other thirty-four were gone!

What You Can Do

You—and only you—must be in charge of your money.

The fact that neither the real estate industry nor the financial media, much less the financial services industry, can provide any kind of reliable information should serve as a huge warning. Only you must determine how you spend, save, and invest your money from now on. In the chapters to come, I'll show you how to make your own financial decisions that will usually turn out to be a lot better than what the "experts" have done or will do. Best of all, those decisions will be in your own best interest.

I believe that the best approach to learning about money is to break it into three steps. In this book I cover the first two steps. The first step shows the *fundamentals* of personal money management. The second outlines the *actions* you must take to put the fundamentals to use. Once you have learned these two things you will have mastered almost everything you need to known on a day-to-day basis about managing your money.

The third step is what I call "just-in-time" subjects. There are a number of financial subjects you may or may not need to know more about in your lifetime, depending on your particular circumstances. To learn this information in depth before you need it is more than just a waste of time; it is a recipe for systems overload.

A list of these "just-in-time" subjects is provided at the end of the book. If, and when, the need arises, visit my website, www.MoneySmartOnline .com, to learn more about each topic. I maintain a set of up-to-date links and references for each of these subjects and I include websites, books, and articles that can provide the information you require at the moment you need it. All of the links and resources have been chosen to be among the best of what's available.

This "just-in-time" information strategy and resource is designed to eliminate the pressure to know all of this information until and unless you have an imminent need for it. It is the key to insuring that money management remains relatively uncomplicated so that you can, indeed, understand it and make all of your own financial decisions.

Small Changes, Large Returns

A lot of financial progress can be achieved with a modest amount of effort. You will see that there are a number of changes that have the potential to give you up to $100,000 or more in your life. I'm not talking $100,000 total; I'm talking as much as $100,000 *per change*. In fact, most of you are sitting there at this very moment with a number of such opportunities!

Better yet, the rewards are not just financial. How much does money influence your life in how you spend your days, where and how you live, your relationships, and your overall happiness? Most people live a life that is far less than they wish for because they do not really understand money and how to use it.

In the next chapter, "Your Goals and Dreams," you will start the process of setting financial goals and achieving them. This is your life and, as always, the choices are yours. Whatever personal goals you choose, it's time to get money smart.

CHAPTER TWO

Your Goals and Dreams

What are your hopes and dreams, your goals and desires? Yes, this can be a difficult question but you are very unlikely to get the things you wish for unless you first identify those wishes. Only after you have clearly identified what it is you want from your life can you make good decisions regarding money and the role you want it to play.

Make a list of the major goals you wish to achieve, with the highest priority items at the top. Consider what you wish to be, what you wish to do, and what you wish to have. Include such things as what you wish to work at and for how long, where you wish to live, becoming debt-free, getting married, starting a family, a college education, things to do with your health and energy, self-improvement, daily happiness, personal relationships, use of your personal time, giving to others, etc. Also list the major purchases you wish to make, such as a house, a better car, a special vacation, a new TV, additional education, etc. Your list of goals is the foundation for building a meaningful and effective plan. Don't limit yourself only to large goals, but strive to make the list as comprehensive as possible.

As you do this exercise, do not shortchange the things you would like to do during your life. Far too often we concentrate on what we want to have or accomplish, when what we end up doing is so often the real key to having a happy and satisfying life. Consider if you want to add some experiences to your list such as a special vacation or other adventure.

Finally, if you are married or share your life with another, each of you should start by writing your own list and identifying your own personal goals and dreams. After you've finished, you then need to share your lists of goals and dreams with each other, as many of your key goals will undoubtedly need to be bought into by both parties in order to succeed.

Here is a list of possible goals to help jump-start your imagination.

List of Possible Goals and Dreams

- Acquire medical insurance
- Build a good emergency cash fund
- Eliminate all debt
- Find a great life partner
- Pay for a wedding
- Buy a home (or a better home)
- Have a child
- Save 20% of your income before taxes
- Live on one salary
- Achieve financial freedom
- Live somewhere else
- Change careers

- Start a business
- Invest in real estate
- Reduce financial pressures and worries
- Make two extra mortgage payments a year
- Own your home free and clear
- Help others more
- Pay for your children's college education
- Go back to school
- Acquire long-term health care insurance
- Buy a car
- Fund home improvements
- Buy a new TV
- Purchase new furniture
- Improve my health and/or appearance (be specific)
- Spend more time with family and friends (again, be specific)
- Learn something new, i.e.: photography, martial arts, interior design
- Spend more time on a sport or hobby
- Take a special vacation. (Think big as well as small, as this is your whole life we're talking about. Have you always wanted to go to Tahiti, take a cruise to Alaska, visit Yellowstone or the Grand Canyon, spend a week in wine country, or travel in outer space?)
- Attend a special event such as the Indy 500, the Super Bowl, the Olympics, the Oscars, the Burning Man Festival, or New Year's Eve in New York City

- Do something really different you always wanted to do like take a race driver's course, learn to fly a plane, skydive, or act in a play or movie
- Take the time to write down your life story. Add pictures or edited home movies
- Do something very indulgent like eat in one of the finest restaurants in the world, spend a night in one of the world's best hotels, buy an Armani suit or an awesome designer dress

Once you have completed your list, consider each item in the context of your life now. You may already be working on some goals, while others may be far in the future. Starting with the highest priority items at the top, write each goal on a separate piece of paper and identify the steps involved in achieving the goal. If the aim is to become a registered nurse, you may need to go back to school. This could involve attending some courses in preparation, taking the SAT exam, researching and applying for various programs, and ultimately completing the education. List the steps required to achieve each goal underneath that goal and assign a realistic completion date next to it. Do this for each objective, as best you can, giving special attention to adding a date next to the goal. Listing the steps and a target date is what makes it a plan, otherwise it is just a list of wishes.

Get a degree (June 2014)
- Learn about available programs
- Take prerequisite courses and/or exams
- Apply for programs
- Complete the education

Fit into my old jeans (December 2011)

- Eat well, make gradual changes—no soda, whole grains
- Exercise—a walk a day to start
- Take the stairs

This new plan will change, sometimes dramatically, over the course of your life, but it is the foundation for the detailed financial plans that you will be developing in future chapters. I recommend coming back to your list once each year (on your birthday or on New Year's Day usually works well) to bring it up to date.

As you do this exercise, do not lose sight of today for tomorrow. Look around you at all the people who spend far too many years of their lives overly caught up in working for tomorrow. Today is your life as much as tomorrow is, and the right plan is one that creates a balance between the two. In addition to this balance, there are four other things that are likely to greatly influence the life you choose. They are:

1. What Money Means to You
2. The Goal of Financial Freedom
3. Don't Sell Yourself Short
4. Plan for the World of Tomorrow

What Money Means to You

What does money mean to you? You need to make money to pay for the basics of life, but I'm sure you want a lot more than just the basics. But why do you want what you want? This may not be as simple a question as it seems. Let's look at some of the things that may have influenced you up to now.

In an average day you see, hear, and absorb over six hundred sales messages. You have been subjected to this almost every day of your life. That's over *four million* attempts to influence how you spend your money by the time you turn twenty-one. TV, radio, magazines, billboards, and the internet are just some of the sources, and the product pitchmen are a lot more abundant than you think. How about the celebrities who are paid to use or wear a particular product, or the companies that have paid for you to see their merchandise in the movies and TV shows you watch? Just think about it. If you are hit with six hundred messages a day, that's over two-hundred-thousand a year. If just one in a thousand works on you, you have been influenced over two hundred times in the last year alone.

Worst of all is the underlying message so often embedded in all of this advertising: You need whatever it is they're selling to be success-ful, attractive, and happy. Successful people live in big fancy houses, drive the right cars, live the "good" life, and wear the right clothes. Material acquisition is the road to happiness. This message is sent every day during almost every TV show or movie; in TV, internet, and print advertising; and in a lot of the magazine and internet articles you read. Think about what a massive assault it has been and how much influence it has. Billions of dollars are spent on advertisements, often delivered in a very sophisticated way, every year. Those billions of dol-lars are working, otherwise the advertisers wouldn't keep spending the money. These messages not only tell you what to buy; they tell you to buy *now*. Do it and the future will be fine. You deserve it! Unfortunately, the path of instant gratification is a never-ending quest that seldom leads to a satisfying life.

Think about what you've spent money on recently. Why did you buy what you did? Why do you want what you want now? Why that car, that pair of sport shoes, that vacation? Was there a "hidden" psychological game pulled over on you?

Start analyzing the commercial messages you receive. I believe you will soon begin to spot what is going on. The minute you do, you will regain control of how you spend your money and, more importantly, how you spend your life. This will be a magic moment because you will realize that only you can decide what will make you happy.

Do not lose sight of the fact that money is a means to an end and not an end in itself. Be fully aware that every expenditure is a trade that requires you to give up something else. If you buy another watch, that money will not be available to save toward your next car. It's a trade-off. From this moment on be consciously aware of the trades you are making. Sometimes a trade is small, but sometimes it can be huge. Trades are more than just swapping one possession for another. Sometimes it is a fundamental quality of life trade, things such as your health, your relationships, or enjoying how you spend your day. An example might be that you decide to buy a nicer house but are now trapped in your current job, or perhaps the new house created a longer and more tiring commute leaving you less free time to spend as you choose.

So carefully think through what money really means to you, about what you want, why you want it, and what you are willing to trade to get it.

The Goal of Financial Freedom

Save your money so that someday you can retire and live the "good life." This idea has become entrenched in our society as the cornerstone of long-term financial and life planning. Well, right here and now, I ask you to challenge that idea. For most people it is a bad goal and a misguided life plan.

Why should you have to wait until you are sixty-five before you can live the life you wish? Who says you must wait until you may be too old or too sick to enjoy so many things in life to the fullest? Instead, replace the R-word, *retirement*, with two new ones: *Financial freedom*. This is the goal to pursue.

Achieving financial freedom means being able to work at what you want, when you want, live where you want, and to have it a lot sooner than sixty-five. You absolutely can make this happen. If you don't think so, the only person standing in your way is you.

There are two ways to accomplish financial freedom: Either possess the money you need to be totally free to do whatever you want; or possess enough money to be able to earn less and live a better life a heck of a lot sooner. The second approach will get you free faster. (You can always plan toward total freedom and change your mind along the way.)

Say you're forty-five and you have saved reasonably well but aren't at a point of total freedom. The family income is $6,000 per month after taxes and the family needs $5,000 per month after taxes for living expenses. Your savings and investments can provide $2,000 per month after taxes. This means you now need to make only $3,000 per month more after taxes to live on. This leaves you a lot of options. If you're a two-income family, one of you can stop working. Or you can shift jobs or careers, work part-time, or end a brutal commute. You could also choose to stop working for a couple of years to do something you've always wanted to do or explore something you've always wanted to see. You can move your life closer to the life you want and do it long before you are sixty-five.

Even if you're in your twenties, this point is no less relevant. Why should you accept the idea that you must live a life that is less than you want it to be for the majority of your time on earth? The younger you start, the bigger the win. How does partial freedom by your mid-thirties and total freedom by age forty-five sound? The sooner you reject the accepted idea of total retirement and focus instead on financial freedom, the easier and faster it will be to achieve.

There is also another issue to consider. To completely stop working may be a bad idea. Having something to do is a key part of who you are and of what life can be. Why not spend some of your time doing something rewarding that you really enjoy doing?

Do you really believe you will like being fully retired? If so, that's fine. Just don't lose sight of the fact that you always have another possibility, financial freedom, and that you can make financial freedom happen a lot sooner than you think.

Maybe you think you're not capable of reaching your goal. If so, there's something you need to know. You're wrong.

Don't Sell Yourself Short

Far too many people set their goals and dreams lower than they should, settling for a life far less than they could enjoy. It is often too easy to convince yourself you can't achieve what you'd really like to accomplish. If you find yourself doing this, or suspect that you may be, take a close look at those who are successful. Often you will find you have just as much going for you as they do or did before they became successful.

The self-undermining arguments that you may tell yourself are potentially endless. They may be that you must have money to make money, that you need the right connections or the right education, that you need to be a whiz at business, or that you can't do it because you tried before and failed. None of these things is true.

Many people believe that they're not smart enough to be successful beyond a certain level. This is also usually just not true. What is intelligence? Is it your IQ? How well you did in school? Are the people with the highest IQ the most successful in life? The people who graduate at the top of their class? It may surprise you, but study after study is repeatedly unable to find any significant correlation between IQ and success in life. To the contrary, these studies find that other factors usually dominate when it comes to both career and life success. Here are some of the most important factors from one such study by Robert J. Sternberg's, (1996), *Successful Intelligence: How Practical and Creative Intelligence Determine Success in Life*.

He finds that successful people:

- Motivate themselves
- Learn to control their impulses
- Know how to make the most of their abilities
- Complete tasks and follow through
- Are initiators
- Aren't afraid to risk failure
- Make mistakes, but not the same mistake twice
- Don't procrastinate

It's an interesting list, isn't it? What you are seeing is that many things together make up "intelligence" and lead to success. Academic intelligence is just one of them. What about people skills? Artistic ability? Mechanical aptitude? Common sense? Street smarts? All of the things listed above? Aren't they all a part of intelligence?

When you step back you realize these are important parts of intelligence and further, it is these varied aspects of intelligence, not academic IQ, that usually determine success and happiness in life. Before you sell yourself short, think about these things and about all of your skills and aptitudes and how much you really have going for you.

Plan for the World of Tomorrow

The world is going to be very different ten years from today. The greatest catalyst for change is that the creation of new technology is now doubling every two years. Its impact on your life will be nothing short of explosive. As you plan you need to be aware of, and factor in, the enormous changes that are underway.

To give you some idea of what I am talking about, here are just a couple of examples of the changes happening now, most of which come from the research of Karl Fisch, Scott McLeod, and Jeff Brennan as explained in their amazing video *Did You Know?* Some of these things may have little or no impact on you directly, but others will. Change isn't always easy to deal with, but it will serve you well to stay aware of what is going on and to be positive and flexible in your approach.

- The top ten in-demand jobs for 2010 did not even exist in 2004.

- For students that are freshmen in college, half of what they learn in school will be outdated by their junior year. One in five will hold jobs that didn't exist in their freshmen years.

- Within the next ten to fifteen years, most office jobs will no longer be in the office but done from home or whatever other location from which employees choose to work. Every year, more and more people will be given the opportunity to live where they wish, not where they work.

- The relationship between employers and employees is undergoing huge fundamental change. Many people's job relationships will shift toward one of customer (former employer) to sub-contractor (former employee). Fringe benefits such as health care coverage, paid vacation time, and retirement benefits will be the responsibility of the "employee/sub-contractor" with the money to fund those things becoming part of the package negotiated with the "employer/customer."

- More and more the internet will be completely mobile and with you wherever you are during the day. Your real-life world, who your friends are, and how you spend your time will start with, and be driven by, the internet. It will become your primary medium of education, surpassing the traditional educational institutions you have relied on to this point.

- In less than ten years people will be replacing their diseased or injured body parts such as their arms, legs, and even their hearts, with brand new parts grown from their body's own cells. (This is not science fiction. The first regenerative medicine transplants have already been done.)
- By 2013 it is expected a super-computer will be produced that will exceed the computational capabilities of the human brain. Predictions are that by the year 2049, a $1,000 computer will exceed the computational capabilities of the entire human species.

On my website I maintain an updated posting of links, articles, and other references on this subject with discussion of how these changes might affect our lives. I strongly suggest you continue to follow this unfolding story and adjust your plans as needed. Be sure to focus on the things that are actually happening, not on what anyone thinks *will* happen. You will find the latter to be quite misleading, as the track record is clear that nobody can reliably predict what will happen in the future except in the most general of terms.

In the meantime, it is imperative that you sit down and carefully decide what you want out of your life. Until and unless you do, it is highly unlikely that you will achieve the life you wish to live. (You can find more about choosing and achieving your goals and dreams on my website.)

PART TWO

LEARNING THE FUNDAMENTALS

CHAPTER THREE

THE 9 RULES OF MONEY

There are nine rules to the game of money. They are absolutely critical to your success when it comes to money and its role in your life. Follow them and you will quickly begin to see a terrific positive momentum, building you a winning hand when it comes to money and its role in your life. Break them often enough and you will almost certainly insure that money ends up subtracting from your happiness rather than adding to it.

Money Rule #1: Have a Positive Attitude

I first saw the following quote about thirty years ago. I keep this one in my "paper pile," which I go through about once a month. That means I've looked at it about three hundred times or so in the last thirty years. Every time I do, I react to it, because it's true, and I always appreciate being reminded of this truth. The world is full of educated derelicts; rich, miserable people; and brilliant losers. Just look around you. In life it isn't about what happens. It's about how you choose to react to what happens. It's all about your attitude.

Attitude

> The longer I live, the more I realize the impact of attitude on life. Attitude, to me, is more important than facts. It is more important than the past, than education, than money, than circumstances, than failures, than successes, than what other people think or say or do. It is more important than appearance, giftedness or skill. It will make or break a company . . . a church . . . a home. The remarkable thing is we have a choice every day regarding the attitude we will embrace for that day. We cannot change our past . . . we cannot change the fact that people will act in a certain way. We cannot change the inevitable. The only thing we can do is play on the one string we have, and that is our attitude. I am convinced that life is 10 percent what happens to me and 90 percent how I react to it. And so it is with you . . . we are in charge of our attitudes.

> —Msgr. Dunne, Catholic Diocese of New York

When it comes to money and also to your life as a whole, the key to your success or failure will be whether or not you possess, or adopt, a positive attitude. It will not be your intelligence, how you look, the amount of money you did or didn't inherit, the education you did or didn't get, your skills, your job, or a lucky break. If you buy into that kind of thinking, you're done. You'll learn a lot reading this book, but if you don't have a positive attitude you'll only achieve a fraction of what you could have otherwise.

If, on the other hand, you do possess, or adopt, a positive outlook, you're in for some wonderful surprises. Many wise people have talked about this down through the ages. Recently, it was covered in a book called *The Secret*. Prior to that, Dr. Wayne Dwyer had a bestseller called *The Power of Intention*. Sixty years ago it was Dr. Norman Vincent Peale's *The Power of Positive Thinking*. All present the same message: What you expect, you get. If you really want all that life can offer, you must have a positive attitude.

Money Rule #2: Be Disciplined

Discipline simply means being committed to doing what you need to do to get the things you said you wanted. To be successful with money and to be successful in life, you need to be disciplined. If you are not, you are unlikely to achieve anything like the life you wish.

With a positive attitude (Money Rule #1) and good discipline your chances for success with money and in life are very good. You will find that these first two money rules have an especially large impact on your chances for success.

Money Rule #3: It Isn't How Much You Make, But What You Do with It That Counts

There are two roads to success regarding money. The first is to make more money; the second is to spend more wisely. Most people focus on the first road while downplaying or outright ignoring the importance of spending wisely. However, study after study shows that for most people the overwhelming majority of financial success in their lives comes from being smart about how they spend their money.

I am not suggesting that you don't try to make more money or that you live like a pauper. I'm just asking you to recognize which spending will really end up adding to your happiness in the long run, and which will not. I'm asking you to be smart and reflective about your spending choices. If you do that and spend your money wisely, it will pretty much insure you will end up being financially successful. If you make a lot more money in the future, that's great, but the second road, spending wisely, is pretty much a sure thing if you work at it. Do not pass it up.

Money Rule #4: Have a Written Plan and Follow It

You must have a written plan that identifies what you want and how you're going to get it. If you do not, you will have created a very high probability that you will never reach the kind of financial freedom you would like.

You already developed the first part of your plan in chapter two, where you identified your major life goals and the steps and timetables required to get them. The second part of creating your written plan is to map out how you will spend and save your money. In chapter six, "Creating Your Spending and Saving Plan," I will guide you through this process in detail.

Once you have created your Spending and Saving Plan it is imperative that you compare your actual spending to your plan each month and adjust it as you see fit. Over the years through talking and working with a lot of people regarding their personal money management, I have been stunned that most people do not really know where their money goes. Plus, half of the people who believe they live within their means do not. They just don't know it. If you do nothing else, you absolutely must know how you actually spend your money and its impact on your life.

When it comes to making a plan, changing your spending habits, and really beginning to build your financial success, a common pitfall is to want to do it "later." *Do not put it off.* Your most powerful ally regarding money, and potentially your most powerful enemy, is time. Every day you delay can grow into months and years, and then you lose. Every day you spend wisely, you win.

A simple example will illustrate the true impact of procrastination. In this example (and throughout the book) I will use a 40% tax rate on the final or highest dollars earned. (If the rate on your last/highest tax dollar is significantly different you may need to adjust my numbers accordingly.)

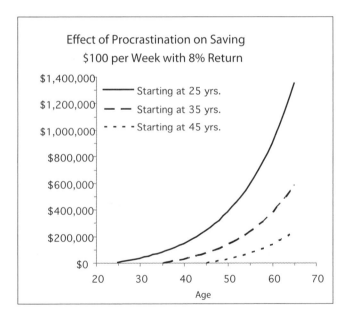

If you save $60 a week, that's $100 a week before taxes, provided the money is saved in a tax-deferred account. If you start at age twenty-five and get a return of 8%, at sixty-five you'll have $1,346,000. (For now I will assume that invested money, in general, will have a return of about 8% per year. In chapter nine, "Planning for Your Future," I discuss this subject in detail.) Starting at age thirty-five, the result is $588,000; at forty-five, it's $238,000. Look at the difference! Time and **compounding** (making money on your money) are such amazing allies. You will find that the rewards from not procrastinating will absolutely blow away any minor pleasures you give up today. Procrastination has the potential to be your single biggest mistake in this process. If you continue to procrastinate, it may well end up as one of your life's biggest regrets.

Personally, I struggle with procrastination. Fortunately, I have found a solution that works for me. I just make myself go do whatever it is I'm procrastinating doing for just fifteen minutes, and promise myself that I can stop after that and do more at another time. Almost without exception, those first fifteen minutes solves the problem. Once I start, I find that whatever the fear was that kept me from starting was greatly exaggerated or even baseless, and I continue on and get the job done. It was the fear I had created that was the uncomfortable thing, not the task itself. Think of times when you have experienced this in your own life. It's true, isn't it? So try the fifteen-minute commitment.

By the way, often the reason people procrastinate about saving is because they feel they don't know what to do or won't be able to do it. A lot of this relates back to not having learned about money. In reading this book you are solving that part of the problem.

Money Rule #5: No Debt

Fifty years ago people didn't buy something unless they had first saved the money. Then the world of business discovered they could make a lot more money if they could change that kind of thinking. Now debt is considered normal and "not a problem," especially when you're "just starting out." The minute someone enters college he or she is inundated with free credit card offers. By the time they graduate, the majority of students are already substantially in credit card debt. What happens is really quite simple. The banks know the odds are good that the students will run up debt they won't pay off each month and they will end up being locked into years of interest payments. They are charged a rate high enough so that the responsible people who pay their bills end up paying for those that default. Most importantly, the next generation of customers has now been created, conditioned from the start that it's okay to be in debt and to continue to spend their money before they've earned it.

As the years unfold, the game continues. To show their appreciation, the banks increase the credit limits of these "good" customers, rewarding them with a higher balance due and greater interest payments. Over time, increasing debt payments gradually, but constantly, cuts into the person's free money. The inevitable result, at some point, is a declining standard of living. Very few are lucky enough to escape this dead end, as nobody gets to live beyond their means indefinitely.

It is tempting to believe that your income will grow faster than your spending, but that is very seldom the case. Even those that end up making more are, by then, usually well conditioned to just keep spending more. All you have to do is look around you.

Unfortunately, debt has become the norm and getting rid of it is the first big step many people need to take. It may feel overwhelming, but it almost always can be accomplished. Yes it's hard, and it might take eighteen to twenty-four months or so of really "doing without." But it will turn out to be one of the best things you have ever done in your life. Seventy-five percent of Forbes' richest people in the world say the best way to build wealth is to become debt free.

Is any debt good? Yes. Taking on a reasonable level of mortgage debt is usually a good thing, as the financial and quality-of-life benefits from owning a home are usually worth the trade-off in debt. Education debt is another, provided you've done all you can to minimize it and still need to take on some debt to pay for an education. Properly done, the payback from taking on education-related debt is likely to come out in your favor over the long run. Lastly, if you are hit with a true emergency and haven't the funds to handle it, then the debt you take on resolving the emergency is good debt, provided again that you pay it off and don't add to it. Each of these is an acceptable debt to take on, but that's about it.

When you carry a lot of debt, the impact is probably a lot greater than you realize. Take a look at what percentage of your income is available for your use after you pay for the basics of life like rent, food, health care, gas, etc. How much is free for large purchases such as a car, a new TV, vacation, college education, or for saving toward financial freedom? It's not a very large percent, is it? After you've made the minimum payments on your debts, what's left? Do not judge the impact of your debt payment by comparing it to your income. Compare it to your free (discretionary) money because that is the money that matters when you talk about all your future options. For example, to have debt payments (excluding mortgage) of 10% of your take-home pay may not sound bad. But, if your discretionary money is 20% of your pay those payments are taking away half your free money and your future options have been greatly reduced.

If you make only minimum required payments, your debt will never go away. Nothing will ever change. If, on the other hand, you aggressively start paying things off, you will find a terrific momentum developing. More free money each month attacks less debt each month and the process begins to accelerate dramatically. Once the debt is finally gone, all of that money, including all the interest you were paying to others, is now yours.

What a positive impact this money will have on your life from that moment on!

Let's compare two couples in their mid-thirties that earn about the same amount. Couple-A does not save any money and averages $15,000 in credit card debt at 15% interest. The interest on their debt costs them $2,250 each year. If their tax rate is about the same as the average family, it takes about $3,750 of their income each year to get the $2,250 they need after taxes to make their minimum payments.

Couple-B has no credit card debt and saves that same $3,750 in a **tax-deferred investment account** with an average return of 8% a year. The next chart shows the result for each couple over time. As the years go by, the gap between the couples becomes pretty amazing, doesn't it? The power of no debt, especially when tied to the power of compounding, or making money on your money, is just huge.

If you have a debt problem, you are probably sitting there nodding in agreement that you need to get rid of your debt. Unfortunately, that's not enough. What's necessary is for you to truly decide to change both your spending habits and your attitude regarding debt—and to do it *right now!* In chapter seven, "Getting Out of Debt," we explain the actions you need to take.

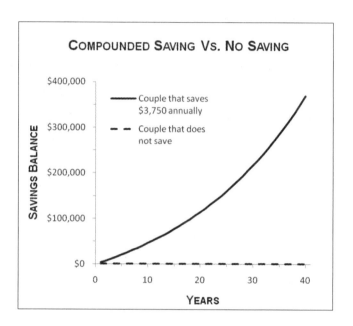

Money Rule #6: Live Below Your Means

In 1968, at twenty-eight years of age, I left International Paper and went to work for Johnson & Johnson. I went from making $12,000 a year to $14,400. It was a big raise. Up to then, every time I got a raise we spent it. That day my wife and I decided we should start saving the extra money instead of continuing to increase our standard of living. We realized that the benefits from living "better yet" were a lot less than the benefits of greater financial flexibility, less financial pressure, and the opportunity to be financially free sooner. It was one of the best decisions we ever made. Within five years we had saved enough to make our first investment in land, a 13-acre sub-dividable parcel in Hope, New Jersey. That investment, in turn, ended up allowing me to leave the corporate world four years after that and go to work for myself.

Do you spend every raise you get? Are you living at or above your means right now, spending more than you make? If you are, you're not alone. In the United States, about half of all families live at or above their means. Look at what living below my means did for my life. Do you think for one moment it's not the best thing for you, too?

Let's pretend you just got a letter in the mail from the company you work for. It is an announcement that they are laying off 20% of their employees, but not you. The letter assures you that you are a "valued employee and have a bright future with the company. But, for now, for all remaining employees, there will be a 15% pay cut." What do you do? What can you do? You are forced to spend less, and guess what? It's really not that big a deal.

Okay, back to reality. You still have all your money coming in. Stop for a moment and think about the upside of not spending that last 15% and of living beneath your means. The difference in your finances can be dramatic, especially if you are currently in debt. As you proceed, you will start to feel very good about what you are doing. As financial pressures decrease, you will experience a growing sense of accomplishment, a sense of being in control of your life, and a huge increase in your options. There will be an increase in possibilities for job and career changes, and for living where and how you'd really like to live.

Live below your means. Almost every financially successful person does.

Money Rule #7: Do Not Let Other People Decide How You Spend Your Money

Unless you have unlimited money, you need to insure that your spending is based on *your* priorities, not somebody else's. The world of business does not like that idea. Most sales and marketing programs are created to sell to you, regardless of what your priorities might be. They want you to choose their priorities and are absolutely relentless in trying to convince you to do that. They want you to spend your limited money where you already decided you didn't want to.

Do not let them control you. Should you find yourself wanting to make a purchase that is not one of your priorities consider it to be a red flag. Identify what you're trading away in order to get it and then *sleep on it*. Ever notice how powerful the effect is of sleeping on any decision? It's enormous! The human mind is pretty amazing and it loves to sort things out while you're sleeping. Personally, I do it with almost every significant decision, not just spending decisions. I can't tell you how many times that less than twenty-four-hour delay has saved me.

What about all those great sales? 30% off! One day only! It's only smart to save all that money isn't it? Well, is it one of your current priorities? No? Then don't do it. If you do, they just got you. You just spent your money on their priorities, not yours. Remember, salespeople are always trying to sell you something. It's their job. By the way, you didn't really save 30%, because the 70% you paid was money you hadn't intended to spend. And you don't really think that's the "last" sale, do you?

Here's yet another way of looking at all this. These days the typical millionaire does not spend his money based on what other people think. He lives in a modestly-sized home, drives a two-year-old or older car without a loan and wears jeans a lot. I think that says something, don't you?

Money Rule #8: Do Not Trade Away What Matters Most for Money

What matters most to you? Is it financial achievement? Accumulating the right possessions? A happy life seldom comes from material wealth. Good health, meaningful relationships, and spending your days in an enjoyable and satisfying way are what really matter most in life. I don't think that anyone, at the end of their life, wishes they made more money. If you make the mistake of trading away the things that matter most for money I believe it will end up among your life's greatest regrets.

J. Paul Getty was at one time the richest man in the world, but I believe that nobody in their right mind would want to have traded places with him. Alone in his seventy-two-room castle for the last seventeen years of his life, even his children, it is said, avoided talking to him. He was the richest man in the world, but what good was it with no one to share his life with?

Just like money, the pursuit of fame at all costs fares no better. I once met a man who used to be one of the kingmakers in the world of pop music in the 1980s and 1990s. He said he knew of very few music stars whose lives weren't a disaster from drugs, alcohol, or mental problems.

I vividly remember the moment I personally learned this lesson. All my life I had always been very focused on getting rich and being (and looking) successful. By 1987, I had accomplished my goal, culminating in receiving a check made out to me for nearly a million dollars. I was ecstatic. But over the months to come the ecstasy faded, replaced by what can only be described as a very hollow feeling. What mountains were left to climb? Why didn't I feel any different or happier?

I began to think of all I'd sacrificed to get where I was. It was a bitter realization. Why hadn't I spent more time with my kids when they were little? Why didn't I enjoy each day more instead of always being so focused on working? It was one of the biggest wakeup calls I have ever had. From that day on I began to change. Slowly at first, then more and more, as I realized what actually made me happy. Guess what? It wasn't money or status or power. It was really enjoying what I was doing and who I was traveling through life with. It was things like good health, a really great meal, a hearty laugh, or a new and interesting experience or challenge. It is something for which I say thanks every single day.

You do not have to be among the rich and famous to be guilty of breaking this rule. Millions of people are doing so every day of their lives. Do not be one of them. Do not make the mistake of trading away the things that matter most for money.

Money Rule #9: Give Back (And Do It Now)

Give back. Help others. When you do, something rather amazing happens. When you give, you get back all that you gave and more. You will find it to be a law of the universe. Try it, and see for yourself. Many very wise people have learned this truth down though the ages and written about it. There are many popular books on this subject that you can read, or you can just try it for yourself and see the result.

Do, however, be cautious in your giving to insure you really are making a difference. Don't give money in response to a telephone solicitation. You are almost always talking to a solicitation company employee and not someone who works for the charity. It is quite common for over 50% of your donation to go to the solicitation company as their fee.

A February 22, 2009, *Sacramento Bee* article titled "Donations Increasingly go to Charities' Telemarketers in California" reported:

If you give to a charity over the phone, there's a growing likelihood that most of your donation will go to the telemarketer instead, according to a *Bee* analysis of state records. More than a third of California charity telemarketing campaigns sent less than 20 cents on the dollar to the charities during 2007, the most recent year on record. Those campaigns and a smaller number of charity auctions and concerts raised $93 million for commercial fundraisers, and just $3 million for the charities. In 76 of those campaigns, California charities got no money at all.

Further, you only want to give to organizations where your money really will do good, rather than just perpetuate the organization involved. Before you give money to any organization, large or small, spend a little time finding out what they do with it. They will all tell you most of the money goes to help others and show you the pictures of the people they are helping. Unfortunately, what they claim is frequently untrue. Most of the people associated with them are usually quite sincere, just badly misinformed. Don't be fooled by prestigious names as, in many cases, they can be among the very worst offenders.

Most importantly, do not limit yourself to third parties. Try helping someone you know directly. Start with a couple of hours of your time a month or even just a gift of twenty bucks. Maybe you could drive an old neighbor to the store to go shopping, or help a kid with a school project. See for yourself how great that feels and how you are rewarded many times over. Make it a regular occurrence and watch how the world gives back to you.

The Rules' Role in Your Life

If you follow these nine rules, they will change your life for the better. They are the *what* in what you have to do to gain financial freedom.

The rest of this book is about *how* to do it.

As you continue reading, I want to be very clear. *Money Smart* is really all about these rules. Follow them and you will succeed. The *how* of it is actually much less important. Even if you don't do every last thing perfectly, you will still succeed, as long as you do not break these rules.

MONEY $MART Money Rules

---

1. Have a Positive Attitude

2. Be Disciplined

3. It Isn't How Much You Make,
    But What You Do With It That Counts

4. Have a Written Plan and Follow It

5. No Debt

6. Live Below Your Means

7. Do Not Let Other People Decide
    How You Spend Your Money

8. Do Not Trade Away What
    Matters Most for Money

9. Give Back (And Do It Now)

CHAPTER FOUR

The 10 Rules of Spending Wisely

If you want to do well financially, there is a sure-fire way to do it. Spend your money wisely. Money Rule #3 says it all: It really *isn't* about how much you make, but what you do with it that counts.

Here is how to get the most from the money you spend.

Spending Rule #1: Do Not Break the Rules of Money

Wise spending starts with this most fundamental rule. Be constantly aware of the money rules and consider them with every spending decision you make.

Spending Rule #2: Know Your Priorities and Stick to Them

You've already covered your larger priorities in chapter two, under "goals and dreams." Now take a couple of minutes and make a simple list of every immediate smaller purchase you want or need to make. I'm talking everything except normal weekly food purchases. New underwear, dishwashing liquid, toothpaste—you name it. Add to this list any larger purchases that are now at the top of your priority list (a new couch, TV, etc). Then just keep changing this little list whenever there's something to add or delete and whenever your priority sequence has changed.

I do this on my computer. (The way the world is changing, I'll probably end up doing it on a Blackberry or iPad.) Every day I print out a single updated page containing five little lists: The appointments of the day, the things and people I'm waiting on, what I'm looking to buy, an immediate "do" list, and a lower priority "do" list. Doing this, I almost never have to make a special trip because I ran out of something. And I know what I want and what my priorities are when I walk into any store. Here is a sample of the list I use.

Apptmts: 1:00 PM—Berkeley group, 4:30PM—conf. call w/NYC
Waiting: Marc/Cmk, planogram, PenSys/proposal, USAA/$ wired
Buy: Printer ink, shampoo, wedding card, blank CDs, laptop

Do list:

Re-edit Chapter VI	Bangkok dentist aptmt
Send invmt email	Payroll in
Final display pricing	Desk pprs org'd
Move Capital 1 acct	Read 2 articles
Do 3 new banks	Back up files
Kat's green cd	Dmv.ca.gov

Lower priority: Cc old pix, learn camera, add to diary—Mr. X/Kabonger, find Johnny D, printer to Charter school

When you are out shopping and see something you want to buy other than normal food or household supplies, and it's not on your list, don't buy it. You especially need to avoid such impulse purchases when the item is more than $25. It's the red flag discussed in Money Rule #7: Do Not Let Other People Decide How You Spend Your Money. If you still want it after you've left the store, sleep on it. If you still want to buy it when you wake up, and it involves a significant amount of money, look at your priority list and decide what you're willing to trade to get it. If you like the trade, then fine, go buy it.

Now that you have your little list, you know what you are about to buy and what you will be purchasing fairly soon. When you're out shopping and feel like it, take a look at the various offerings for your next purchase(s). Think about the exact item you'll buy when the time comes. I have come to love what this pre-shopping does for me. I end up buying so much smarter and being so much happier with my purchases. This simple strategy also greatly reduces buying again too soon because I bought what I really wanted. It is also the most important spending rule of all, because it insures that you don't break Money Rule #7.

I am not anti-business. Quite the opposite is true. Free market capitalism is the most successful economic system on this planet, and business has every right to pursue your money. When what they're offering is one of your current priorities, great. When it's not, tune them out.

Spending Rule #3: Understand Today's Sales Game

Thanks to computers, the internet, and today's marketing databases, the game of selling has changed quite a bit in recent years. That's why you need to understand today's sales game. If you don't, you will be at high risk of spending far too much of your hard-earned money where you really didn't intend to—and even being played for a sucker at times.

Let's say you want to buy a car. You go to a dealer and take a test drive. The salesperson makes a copy of your license, as required in case you take off with the car. While you're driving, he keys your license number, and the license number of the car you just drove in with, into his computer. By the time you get back he knows a lot about you, like your credit history, car ownership profile, financing history, and more. If you've already visited another dealer the chances are good he now knows what happened there, like how much you were offered for your trade-in and the reason why they didn't close the sale. Don't think he's just trying to sell you a car. He's after a lot more. On the financing alone he doubles his commission. And the same goes for the trade-in. Then there are the warranties, maintenance contracts, VIN etching, fabric protection: The list goes on and on.

If you decided to do some research online before getting out and shopping, your local car dealerships will usually have immediate access to much of your online exploration as well. Some of the consumer-oriented websites you will encounter are anything but what they appear. They are owned and operated by the auto industry to identify you as a sales prospect, feed you the information they want you to know, and to block or discredit the information that might hurt their sales. You can forget about all those jokes about used-car salespeople. Today's auto industry is on the cutting edge when it comes to sales techniques. Learn to handle auto salespeople and you can handle almost other any type of salespeople.

Both to protect yourself and to become a smarter consumer, I strongly suggest you read the book *Don't Get Taken Every Time* by Remar Sutton.

This is a terrific book about buying or selling a car, and is a must-read before you buy your next car. When you read it, however, think beyond cars to everything you buy, as the sales techniques Sutton explains apply everywhere. I believe you will find this book to be an excellent consumer crash course for understanding today's game of selling and marketing a heck of a lot better than you probably do now. While I'm at it, I will recommend one more book of tremendous value for your consideration—"*Give Me A Break*" by John Stossel. This award-winning journalist (19 Emmys) is in a class by himself in exposing the games and illusions fed to us almost daily by the media, business, and government.

Spending Rule #4: Never Respond to Service Advertising or Infomercials

Another key element of spending wisely is to avoid responding to service advertising or infomercials. Do not call, send an e-mail, or stop in. It is highly unlikely that what is being advertised is your best choice. When it comes to services, some of the worst choices advertise the most. Most good business people will tell you that thriving businesses get the majority of their sales from repeat business and referrals. That is how the good ones prosper and usually do so without much advertising. The inferior businesses don't have that going for them and must resort very heavily on advertising to constantly pull in new customers.

When you have need for a service, reach out and learn about the choices yourself from whatever sources you feel will be of help. Get referrals from people you know and surf the internet. Even the sites that are dominated by advertising can often provide useful information—and those sites are sources you choose, not one that is trying to choose you.

As for infomercials, I recommend you never buy anything from one. If you ever did, ask yourself how many times it was worth the money in the past. Ask your friends. Yeah, I know, there is something hot, a special buy that's not available in stores, or it's some great new secret thing. "Secret" is a very reliable red flag telling you not to buy. Not available in stores? Why not? Almost all good products are there, aren't they? In the history of infomercials, I can't personally remember seeing anything advertised that was worth buying.

Spending Rule #5: Use the Internet

Make it a habit to check prices and options on the internet for everything you plan to buy that costs over, say $100, or even less if it's something you buy regularly. Go online to check prices at your local stores, shop for your cars on the internet, and reserve airfare and hotels as well. You will find that online purchasing has become cheaper than store buying for quite a few of your spending categories. Even when you don't buy online, you'll still end up buying smarter. There is also the added benefit that spending less time in stores reduces both impulse buying and your exposure to the influence of advertising.

Spending Rule #6: Shop at Costco, Sam's Club, or BJ's

These companies do the buying homework for you, the quality is consistently very good, and the price is usually a lot below what you pay elsewhere. Some people look at the large quantities frequently involved and feel it makes buying an impractical thing. If you're single, or don't really use that much of any one item, it may just seem like overkill. Still, I challenge you to examine if that's really true. I was single for a lot of years and always shopped at Costco without any problem. For the things you don't buy there, or for those of you without access to these stores, your next step is another low-price source such as Walmart. Just remember to stick to your list and use the sleep-on-it rule when you shop at these places. They're also really good at getting you to buy, so you have to stick to the rules.

Spending Rule #7: Always Look at the Annual Cost

To understand the real impact of your spending choices, always look at the cost spread out over a year, not just at the cost today. Let's say you spend $4.50 for a fancy coffee, or $10 to eat lunch out five days a week. Those seem like small expenses, but the annual costs are $1,125 and $2,500, respectively. That's $1,875 and $4,165 before taxes; $212,000 and $471,000 in thirty years at an 8% investment return. This is what you are actually trading away with those small purchases. Remember to also look at how much sooner you can stop working or spend time at something you'd enjoy more. This doesn't necessarily mean you shouldn't spend that money. It's your life and your choices. Just be sure you fully understand the true size of the trade involved.

Spending Rule #8: Buy Quality

When you buy quality items you almost always win. You are far more likely to be happy with what you bought and it won't need to be replaced as often as inferior products will. How often are you re-buying the same thing because it didn't hold up or didn't satisfy you? The examples are quite endless—clothes, shoes, tires, vacuums, sheets and towels, furniture. For most purchasing, quality wins. Even though the initial purchase costs more, it will still cost less in the long run.

Spending Rule #9: Negotiate Wherever Appropriate

Negotiate whenever there's a possibility it might work and a decent amount of money is involved. If you make $20 an hour after taxes ($33 before taxes), every $20 you don't spend saves you an hour's work. If it's not someplace you're absolutely sure negotiating is a waste of time, always ask for a better price.

You'll be surprised how often it works and not just on product purchases, but on services as well. Try negotiating on cell phone plans, bank account fees, credit card interest rates, and even doctor bills.

Think I'm kidding? According to a November 2007 survey by the Consumer Reports National Research Center, among those who have tried to negotiate medical bills, 93 percent were successful at least once. As for things such as furniture, electronics, and appliances, etc., their study found that over 90% that asked for a better price were successful. Are you surprised? Don't be. Most things are negotiable, even though the businesses or people involved will usually do their best to get you to think otherwise.

Negotiating becomes especially valuable when you make your biggest decisions such as homes, cars, business investments, and pay raises.

Here is a specific suggestion on how to make a *lot* of money in just a couple of hours. Call every single company you deal with and ask for a lower rate or fee. That includes every credit card, bank account, and loan (including your mortgage). If they won't give you a better deal, tell them you wish to close your account. That will usually get you transferred to someone with more leeway to negotiate. In the worst case, should that fail, wait a week or two then call back and talk to another party.

Chapter fourteen, "How to Negotiate," provides a quick crash course on the subject. Unless you're already a highly experienced negotiator, I strongly recommend that you take the time to read and literally memorize that chapter. It's very short, and by knowing the basics, you're almost certain to save a lot of money at some point.

Spending Rule #10: Simplify Your Life

If you are like most people, you probably can benefit greatly from simplifying your life. If and when you do, you will surely find that the financial rewards can amount to some pretty terrific numbers over time. Even better yet will be the improvement in quality of life you'll likely experience. I promise, once you get into it, simplicity will amaze you. Time and again you will find that less is actually more, and the rewards of simplicity outweigh the rewards from whatever you were doing or owning before.

Each thing you do takes time and energy. This is also true for the things you own. There is an ancient Asian belief that every possession you own takes some of your energy. Think about the last time you cleaned out your closets or garage and gave away a bunch of stuff. Didn't you literally feel a small weight lift off your shoulders?

Take a few minutes to think about who you are and what you have been doing. How complicated has your life become over the years? How many things do you do every day, week, and month that you'd rather not do? Look at the things you do out of habit and the things you've been convinced to do by others. How many things do you own that you don't use? Do you really need such a big residence? Do you live far from your job and commute hours each day, leaving you tired and with too little time for your family or for yourself? Is each thing you do, each thing you own, really worth it? Be honest with yourself about whether each of these things actually adds to the quality of your life.

Simplifying your life doesn't necessarily mean doing without, but rather is about living with less stress and more balance. I first learned this truth back in the late 1980s when I was forced to live out of a suitcase for over a year after I lost everything. What a wonderful surprise that turned out to be, as it opened my eyes to so many things I no longer wanted to own and introduced me to a truly more enjoyable lifestyle. Once I started to see the benefits, my eyes were opened to more ways to simplify, especially when it came to how I spent my time.

(Should you like more information on how to go about simplifying your life, my website will point you to some resources on the subject.)

MONEY $MART Spending Rules

1. Do Not Break the Rules of Money

2. Know Your Priorities and Stick to Them

3. Understand Today's Sales Game

4. Never Respond to Service Advertising or Infomercials

5. Use the Internet

6. Shop at Costco, Sam's Club, or BJ's

7. Always Look at the Annual Cost

8. Buy Quality

9. Negotiate Wherever Appropriate

10. Simplify Your Life

CHAPTER FIVE

The 10 Rules of Investing Successfully

Just as there are overall rules for money and rules for how to spend it, there are also rules for investment. If you—like millions of others—rely on the advice of others to choose your investments, the time has come to take charge personally. These people—in investment houses, as well as in media and in print—make investing seem very complicated. It's in their best interest to do so because that is how they earn their money. It is not, however, in your best interest. There are ten rules regarding investing that will help liberate you from dependency on professionals and guide you in making the best choices for your investments. These rules apply to all investments and all investment markets.

Investing Rule #1: Make Your Own Investment Decisions

Decisions you make on your own behalf are likely to yield results far superior to anything the experts will recommend. The rules provided here, and the specific guidance in the following chapters on investing and getting out of debt, should fully equip you to both dig out of any debt, and to obtain and evaluate the information you need to make smart, sensible investment decisions on your own behalf. It is very tempting to let a financial professional make or greatly influence your investment decisions. Financial professionals are very good at convincing you to trust them. They are selected, trained, and rewarded for their sales performance, not for whether they are right or wrong regarding their investment advice. Very few rise above the training and reward structure they work under; very few develop a real-world track record of investing successfully. You *cannot* trust the advice of people who make money from giving that advice.

I tell you these things from personal experience. When it comes to the world of stock market investment, I went though stockbroker training when I was fifty, with a room full of people primarily in their early- to mid-twenties. I saw the impact of that training firsthand and then watched it all put into practice for years to come. Similarly, in the world of real estate, my partner and I selected, trained, and managed more than one hundred real estate agents over a period of ten years. We did train them to do what was best for the customer, but they did so maybe half the time. These were not bad people; for the most part they were nice and honest. Their behavior was just a reality of the circumstances and pressures to sell and earn a living that almost all commissioned salespeople are faced with.

What about professionals who work for set fees that do not change, regardless of the advice they give or the amount you invest? Is it okay to follow their advice? Maybe, but usually not for choosing your investments. (In chapter nine, "Planning for Your Future," this subject will be discussed in greater detail in the section, Guidelines for Hiring Financial Professionals, on page 179).

Lastly, do not pay full commissions when purchasing or selling your stock or fixed-income investments. Always use a discount broker whenever possible, where the commission is only a couple of dollars per trade. The impact of a full or even half commission is a lot more harmful than you may realize once inflation and taxes are taken into account.

Investing Rule #2: Do Not Invest in Anything You Don't Clearly Understand

Many times you will have a chance to invest in something you don't fully understand. When that happens to me, I simply don't invest. At one time I didn't use this strategy, but experience has taught me a painful lesson that to do otherwise is usually a bad move.

Perhaps the worst pitfall in such investments is that it is difficult to be truly confident in your decision. It's common for even the best of investments to drop in price before they turn into winners. When the drop occurs, if you are not confident and well informed, you will often end up selling when you shouldn't. In this case, the investment was destined to be a loser for you, regardless of what it did for others.

Whenever you find yourself unsure, the best action is to do nothing. There have been times when I've kept my money in cash for as long as a year or two before making my move. When I did, I did so with confidence and, looking back, usually ended up very happy that I waited. You will have a lot of opportunities to invest. Be patient and stick to the options you understand.

Also, don't put yourself down or feel you are at a disadvantage when you don't understand something well enough. I've been investing for almost fifty years and there are still an awful lot of things I don't understand. Warren Buffet is arguably the most successful stock investor in history. Time and again you will see him quoted as saying he has passed by loads of investments for only one reason: He felt he didn't understand them well enough. What's good enough for Warren sure as heck is good enough for you and me. So don't sweat it. Nobody knows it all, or even close to it all.

This principal applies to all investments, not just the stock market. That includes buying or starting a business, investing in real estate, or taking out a CD at a bank. Never invest in anything you don't clearly and thoroughly understand.

Investing Rule #3: If It Seems Too Good to Be True, Then It's Too Good to Be True

The world is full of people who want to "help" you get rich. Translation: They want to get their hands on your money. Fortunately, they usually telegraph who they really are by using certain words and phrases. Here are some of the most common "magic words" to look out for when used to describe an investment opportunity: *free, secret, sure-fire, anyone can do it, always, no risk, foolproof, insider, confidential, the smart money, nothing down, easy money, magic, not a get-rich-quick scheme, become a millionaire, just a few hours of your spare time, almost nothing to do,* and *makes-you-money-while-you-sleep.* Every one of these is a huge red flag. If you hear more than one, run the other way!

Nothing is free. You don't get high rewards at low risks or for little effort, and there are no secrets. In the stock market, by the time a stockbroker calls to tell you the "smart money" is buying something, what do you think is probably happening? You're either too late or they're *selling to you.* Investment infomercials are usually loaded with the "magic words." You need hear nothing further to tell you to turn the channel.

There is no end to the investment traps you can fall into should you not follow this rule. On my website, www.MoneySmartOnline.com, under the "just-in-time" subject of Investment Traps and Scams, I do my best to provide information on this subject, plus links to sites and sources that can provide further details. The range of these scams is very wide, from disastrous investment "opportunities" and phony "save your home" scams, to an endless list of devious setups where your money is gone the minute you turn it over and you don't even know it. Should you ever have any doubt on something being offered to you, please be sure to check with my website. These situations are quite common, so do not let your guard down!

Investing Rule #4: Only Listen to People with a Track Record of Success

Only follow the financial advice of people who have been successful at doing whatever it is they are advising you to do. Never follow those without a track record of success. Unfortunately, the trap of bad and usually self-serving advice is almost always there waiting for you. In the world of money, the majority of the "financial advisers" are really just salespeople, selected for their ability to convince others to purchase their financial products. They're very good at it and are trained and motivated to represent their interests and those of the firm, over yours.

Take the stockbrokerage industry. Many professionals in that industry are not called Stockbrokers. Instead, they opt for more respected titles such as Investment Advisor, Financial Advisor, even Vice President. Stockbrokers usually become Vice Presidents based on their sales production. They might be twenty-something college graduates with a gift for gab and without any track record of knowing how to invest successfully but hey, they did convince a bunch of people to buy the latest offerings. Impressive titles, designer-suits, genuinely likeable personalities, fancy offices, and glossy marketing literature don't mean a thing. If Warren Buffet is telling you what to invest in, you listen because he has a track record that documents that he knows how to invest successfully. You do not want to take the investment advice of someone who hasn't successfully made good money through good times and bad times.

There may be times, however, when you wish to be helped making certain decisions and there are reliable people out there who have successfully done it and can help you. You just have to be extremely careful you have found one as they are, unfortunately, quite rare. In the chapters to come we'll talk more about who to trust and when.

Investing Rule #5: Tune Out All Investment Advertising

Every day you are likely to be hit with investment advertising. You see people so happy that they turned over their retirement future to company X, wonderful tips available for free from company Y, a free evaluation from company Z. Tune it out. All of it! *Never* contact anyone because of an ad. Don't stop to talk to an "expert" at your local bank or wherever else you might run into one. Whenever you need to select someone to work with, go to the internet and do some research. After you've done that, get recommendations and advice from people you know who believe they've found someone competent. Good businesses get most of their business from repeat customers and referrals, the bad ones get theirs from advertising and marketing.

While you're at it, beware of free investment seminars. The free seminar is a popular sales tactic where a face-to-face approach is used to try to win trust and then push people to "act now." Doing so eliminates any chance to research and evaluate the decision involved. You don't ever want to make important decisions that way. Whenever you are given the opportunity to attend such a presentation, pass on it, especially if they're using one or more of those "magic" words listed earlier.

Investing Rule #6: Put as Much as Possible in Tax-protected Accounts

The impact of avoiding or deferring taxes on the money you invest is nothing short of amazing over time. In chapter ten, "When to Invest— A Critical Key to Success" (page 207), this impact is explained in detail. The bottom line is always to tax protect every dollar you possibly can.

Investing Rule #7: Do Not Borrow Money to Invest

Stick to investing the money that you have saved. Personal loans, first or second mortgages, margin loans on stock, and borrowing from a 401(k) plan are not the place to find investment money. Do not take loans of this nature for the purpose of investing. If you do you will reduce the backup resources you may very well need in order to succeed. You must also consider this: Any return you make must exceed the interest you are paying on the loaned money, which substantially reduces your chance of success. Worst of all, you will have greatly increased the pressure on yourself to succeed. Such pressure you do not want, as it both damages your quality of life and increases your chances for failure.

Investing Rule #8: Do Not Make Decisions Based on Emotion

When making an investment decision, stop and ask yourself how much greed or fear is influencing your decision. Step back and do your best to clear your brain and be objective. Pretend it's someone else's money and you are just advising that person. If necessary, talk to someone you respect and ask for his or her help. Decisions made that were driven by emotion are usually bad ones.

The damage of emotional investing can be broader and deeper than you might think. When the stock market was going so well in the 1990s, emotion became a dominating factor in the investment decision making of millions. People who hadn't saved enough for retirement convinced themselves that the market could solve their problems if they just invested aggressively enough. For many, investment had now become little more than gambling. You know how that turned out.

Avoid tracking daily and weekly stock fluctuations because they are almost always meaningless, but can wear on the nerves. Even tracking investments quarterly or annually can create a sense of pressure and lead to bad investment moves based on emotion. The only exception is if you invest in individual stocks, which less than 10% of people should do.

Investing Rule #9: Understand and Act on Market Cycles

All investment markets go through periods where it's hard to lose and when it is very unlikely to win. It is absolutely critical that you understand and act on market cycles. Here are some things I saw and lived though during the last ten years that really underscore this point.

One day, in the fall of 1999, I was eating lunch next to three young professionals, two men and a woman. One of the men was trying to convince the woman, a financially conservative person, to invest heavily in tech stocks. He was telling her she couldn't miss and was being foolish to pass up making all that money. "You buy it at sixty, it'll be ninety in less than twelve months," he stated. The culminating moment was when she asked, "But what if the prices go down?" That "wise" young man looked at her like she had two heads. He shook his head sadly and said, "Man, you just don't understand, do you?" Six months later the tech-laden NASDAQ index started its historic drop from the grossly overpriced level of 5,100 to 1,236.

At that time, I could see that the entire stock market was in a terrible bubble. I sold my stock investment business and about 70% of my stocks (unfortunately only 70%) in January 2000. I told my clients the U.S. stock market was unlikely to be any higher for many years to come and to shift to investing extremely conservatively, primarily in fixed-income investments. At the time, the DOW Industrial Average was around 11,000. As I write this (October 2009) the DOW is about 10,700, the NASDAQ, a little under 2,200—ten years later! When you factor in inflation, that's a loss of 29%! It was such a no-brainer, yet where was the advice to sell from the financial experts and the financial media?

Was this some kind of brilliant deduction? No, it was just common sense. All markets have a fundamental value. For the stock market, that value over the last one hundred years had been approximately sixteen times **trailing earnings**. (Trailing earnings are the profit per stock share earned by a company, or, in this case, all of the companies in the market during the previous twelve months.) By the fall of 1999, the market was selling at over thirty times trailing earnings. I didn't know exactly when it would drop, but drop it must, and a lot! It turned out the market would rise for only another few months. In retrospect, I cut it way too close.

After I sold my stocks I invested some of that money in the fixed-income market. I also put quite a bit of it into an expensive house. The values in the real estate market had become very favorable, thanks in no small part to everyone over-investing in the stock market.

By the end of 2004, the median price of a home in the U.S. was more than $275,000, well beyond what the average American family could afford. By then, most prospective homebuyers were caught up in the emotion of the real estate upcycle, just like the young investors eating lunch with the woman. Almost all the real estate professionals thought that prices would soar and they would make a lot of money, too. The reality behind that old Wall Street adage about confusing "brains with a bull (upward) market" was now in full flower.

In the fall of 2005, I told our family and friends that the housing market, especially on the coasts, was in a bubble and would inevitably drop. I estimated it would peak in the spring/summer of 2006 and bottom in 2008 with an average drop of about 30–35%, especially on the coasts. The coastal markets peaked in the summer of 2006 and will likely bottom at least a couple of years later than I thought. At that time (the end of 2005) I put my expensive house on the market and sold it for 92% more than I paid. For the millions of hardworking people who did not understand and act on the cycle going on, this time period was a disaster. Millions lost their homes and most, if not all, of the money they had saved during their lives.

In 2006 when we sold that home, my wife and I wanted to buy another house. There was no way we would do it however, given the terribly overvalued level of the real estate market nationwide. Our choice was clear. We decided to rent for as many years as it would take until purchasing another home made good investment sense. Had we bought the house we wanted in 2006, we would have already lost almost 30%.

These stories underscore two key points. First, they demonstrate that you always have other markets to choose from at any given moment in time, including the U.S. and non-U.S. stock markets, the fixed-income market, the real estate market, the commodities market, and the market of individual small businesses. Most importantly, they underscore how critically important it is to understand market cycles and to use that information to guide your investment decisions. As for my "brilliant" performance during that time period, remember that I went bankrupt when the real estate cycle broke in the late 1980s. Brilliance had nothing to do with it. It was like getting punched in the face and being willing to learn why it happened.

In chapter ten, "When to Invest," I will go deeper into the subject of understanding and acting on market cycles. My website will also keep you informed about where we are in the cycles of these markets at any given point in time.

Investing Rule #10: Diversify Your Investments

I recently read a book in which the author tells a story about how he went from being a real estate multi-millionaire to becoming bankrupt in the mid- to late-1980s when the real estate cycle turned nasty. I went from real estate multi-millionaire to bankrupt at that same moment, in the same business! Then he talked about the unforgettable moment when he was filling his soon-to-be repossessed Jaguar with gas, holding his breath and hoping that the station wouldn't find out that his credit card was no good before he got the gas. Boy did I smile, because I did exactly the same thing! There I was, filling my soon-to-be repossessed Porsche, holding my breath and hoping that *my* card wouldn't be checked before I got enough gas.

What's the point? Well he's a pretty smart guy and by that point he knew quite a bit about money and investing. So did I. And look what we two fools did. We broke a key rule: We put all our eggs in one basket.

The moral is clear. Always diversify your investments as no single investment decision will ever be a certainty. We all like to feel certain when we invest, but the reality is that it's a game of probability. Diversifying into a series of high probability investments is the best we can do, and is also usually enough. This doesn't mean that you should over-diversify by investing in loads of different things. That, too, is a bad idea, as there is no way you can successfully understand and keep your finger on too many different investments at once.

Asset diversification is a two-step process. The first step is to decide what percent to put in each **asset type**, i.e. your home, the stock market, fixed-income markets, real estate, a business, etc. The second step is to decide how much to put into each individual investment, that is, each stock, each piece of real estate, and so forth. (At the end of chapter eleven, "Evaluating Your Investment Alternatives," I discuss asset allocation in further detail, starting on page 265.)

Finally, I caution you when it comes to investing in the U.S. stock market. The success of the 1990s and of all of the brainwashing that says you will "always win in the long run" has badly twisted the views of most people regarding the role the stock market should play in their plans. Investing in the stock market should likely be a significant *component* of your long-range financial plan. It must never be the *whole* plan. Many things must make up your plan, including no debt whatsoever, owning your home free and clear, maxing your tax-deferred saving, fixed-income investments, U.S. stock market investment, investment in the markets of other countries, and perhaps investments in commodities such as grain and oil, in real estate and small businesses. True diversification is accomplished when you do a number of these things and never rely on just one of them.

MONEY SMART Investing Rules

1. Make Your Own Investment Decisions

2. Do Not Invest in Anything
   You Don't Clearly Understand

3. If It Seems Too Good to Be True,
   Then It's Too Good to Be True

4. Only Listen to People with
   a Track Record of Success

5. Tune Out All Investment Advertising

6. Put as Much as Possible in
   Tax-protected Accounts

7. Do Not Borrow Money to Invest

8. Do Not Make Decisions
   Based on Emotion

9. Understand and Act on Market Cycles

10. Diversify Your Investments

Self-assessment

On the next page is a list of all twenty-nine rules—the nine money rules, the ten for spending wisely, and the ten for investing. Consider each rule and put a check next to the ones you have been doing well with up to now; put a star next to the ones that could use some improvement; and put two stars next to those where you have not done well. This will reveal a clear picture of the strengths and weaknesses in your money management approach to date. More importantly, you will have identified the changes you need to make going forward in your attitudes, and your actions, regarding money. These are the key changes to focus on, and will most help you get all you want from your life.

Put this list where everyone in the family can see it all the time, like on the refrigerator door. It doesn't hurt to be reminded daily of both the rules and of the changes that need to be made. At a minimum, be sure to come back and do this self-assessment every few months as you proceed, as it will help you to understand and track the progress you're making.

For those of you who find yourselves putting one or two stars next to almost everything, do not be discouraged. What you are seeing reflects big opportunities for growth and shows your willingness to change your attitudes and become more disciplined. This is a very doable process. Decide that you truly want what you said you wanted from your life in the goals and dreams chapter. You will find that you can make everything unfold from there.

The 9 Rules of Money

____ Have a Positive Attitude

____ Be Disciplined

____ It Isn't How Much You Make, But What
You Do with It That Counts

____ Have a Written Plan and Follow It

____ No Debt

____ Live Below Your Means

____ Do Not Let Other People Decide
How You Spend Your Money

____ Do Not Trade Away What Matters Most for Money

____ Give Back (And Do It Now)

The 10 Rules of Spending Wisely

____ Do Not Break the Rules of Money

____ Know Your Priorities and Stick to Them

____ Understand Today's Sales Game

____ Never Respond to Service Advertising or Infomercials

____ Use the Internet

____ Shop at Costco, Sam's Club, or BJ's (if you can)

____ Always Look at the Annual Costs

____ Buy Quality

____ Negotiate Wherever Appropriate

____ Simplify Your Life

The 10 Rules of Investing Successfully

_____ Make Your Own Investment Decisions

_____ Do Not Invest in Anything You Don't Clearly Understand

_____ If It Seems Too Good to Be True,

        Then It's Too Good to Be True

_____ Only Listen to People with a Track Record of Success

_____ Tune Out All Investment Advertising

_____ Put as Much as Possible in Tax-protected Accounts

_____ Do Not Borrow Money to Invest

_____ Do Not Make Decisions Based on Emotion

_____ Understand and Act on Market Cycles

_____ Diversify Your Investments

3

THE ACTION PLAN

CHAPTER SIX

Creating Your Spending and Saving Plan

Setting up a Spending and Saving Plan is not difficult. In this chapter I provide you with the information you need to create your plan, including specific input and recommendations for each spending and saving category. Creating a Spending and Saving Plan is both more flexible and effective than creating a traditional budget and is a critical step toward achieving your goals. Here is what you need to do:

Step 1—Read and follow the advice provided in this chapter for each of your spending categories.

Step 2—Write down every single expenditure for the next thirty days. Well before the thirty days are up you will know the truth about where your money is going.

Step 3—Do all spending on a credit or debit card wherever possible to make it easy to track your spending. Save your receipts, especially whenever a purchase of multiple items is involved. For those items that need to be in cash, take a set amount of money from the bank every week or two. Sticking to a set amount should give you pretty good control over the spending you do in cash. If you haven't already done so, arrange to get access to all your accounts online, as it greatly simplifies the process.

Step 4—Create your plan by taking your available net (after tax) monthly income and allocate it in whatever way you choose. If your income varies quite a bit from month to month use 1/12th of your estimated annual income for your monthly figure.

Step 5—Once a month, compare what you actually spent with your plan. Learn from what happened and adjust whatever you wish. For tracking your goals and spending, you can use a software package, the worksheets I provide, or, if you prefer, a simple list. Should you prefer to use a software package to track your spending and savings, see my website for resources and information on that subject.

Setting up your plan and checking it each month is extremely educational. You will see how you are actually spending your money and you can decide whether you wish to continue spending the same way. You are in charge. This process insures that you are 100% aware of the choices you are making.

As you proceed, please be realistic. Unrealistic plans don't work and will just discourage you from continuing with this critical process. It is likely that some big changes will be needed—and big changes are never easy. Never doubt you can do it. Just decide, right here and now, that it's worth it, because it is. At times you will find it will take several small changes to free up, say, $100 a month. That's fine, as $100 a month is $1,200 a year or $136,000 in thirty years at an annual 8% return. As you can see, even modest savings end up creating a big impact over time. So every time you free up $100 toward debt reduction or savings, take a moment to smile because you're on your way.

On page 93 is a sample plan that shows the spending and saving categories we will be using. At the end of this chapter there are some blank forms for you to copy. All of the forms in this book are also available on my website, www.MoneySmartOnline.com.

Also at the end of this chapter is a page for you to list your assets and liabilities and calculate your net worth. Assets are the value of what you own and liabilities the amounts of money you owe. The difference, or net worth, is how much money you really have. Think of it as your scorecard. Every three or four months take a few minutes and update it to see how your net worth is growing.

You will also need to keep track of how much you have saved in each savings category, as well as for the expenses that do not occur every month. At the end of the chapter is a simple form you can use for that purpose. Be sure you do this reliably, as about half of all your spending and saving categories involve this situation.

Each of the spending categories will be covered one at a time. Please finish reading this chapter before you begin developing your plan. When you are ready to start, pull together your spending records, your written checks, credit card and debit statements, receipts, and the like. You may wish to refer again to the discussion of certain categories before filling in your numbers for those items. Do the best you can initially and know that you will go back in a month, after you have been tracking everything, to update your plan.

The spending categories should capture all of your spending, so do your best to fit your expenses into one of the categories or add another as needed. At times you may find that it is hard to estimate what you spend on a particular item. In this case, make your best guess and then adjust your plan the following month when you know the actual cost. After you're done, add it all up and adjust the numbers as you wish. Your spending and saving should equal your monthly income. Make adjustments, if necessary, until everything matches. After three months or so you will find that your plan has become finely tuned.

Month Sample Plan

Net income ($)

Estimated 5,155

Actual 5,038

Difference −117

Non-Rollover Spending	Estimated	Actual	Over-spent −	Under-spent +
Regular Monthly Expenses ($)				
1. Home Payment, Taxes, Rent	1370	1370		
2. Utilities, Association Fees	165	173	−8	
3. Telephone, Internet, TV	185	203	−18	
4. Car Payment(s)	334	334		
5. Health Care Insurance	486	486		
6. Debt Payments/Debt Reduction	150	50		+100
7. Other Required Payments				
8. Gas	173	145		+28
9. Public Transportation				
10. Food & Supermarket Spending	700	798	−98	
11. General Shopping	350	298		+52
12. Out-of-Pocket Spending	250	280	−30	
13. Other Spending				
14. Recreation & Entertainment	75	90	−15	

Rollover Spending and Saving	Estimated	Actual	Subtract from Fund −	Add to Fund +
Periodic Expenses ($)				
15. Medical, Dental, Pharmacy	50	0		+50
16. Car Maintenance, Repair, DMV	50	334	−284	
17. Education Expenses, Lessons				
18. Property Maintenance	85	127	−42	
19. Insurance	57	0		+57
20. Unexpected Events	100	0		+100
21. Giving	25	0		+25
22. Gifts and the Holidays	50	0		+50
23. Vacations	150	0		+150
Saving ($)				
24. Saving for Emergency Fund	100	100		+100
25. Saving for Your Next Car				
26. Saving for Large Purchases				
27. Saving for Financial Freedom	250	250		+250
28. Saving for Education				

Totals   5,155   5,038

Regular Monthly Expenses

1. *Home Payment and Taxes or Rent*

For now your payment is what it is, so just fill it in. If you own a home, include your property taxes and homeowner's insurance, but not any second mortgage or home equity payments, which you should include in the Debt Payments category. If you rent, include renter's insurance, if paid monthly, in addition to the rent. For homeowner's or renter's insurance, use what you are currently paying. (Chapter thirteen, "Choosing Insurance," will get into all of your insurance needs and options in detail.)

Be extremely careful about taking on any kind of home equity loan. They are a very aggressively marketed product and are very good things for the banks, but generally not for homeowners. Use these loans only for major home improvements. Do not set one up for emergencies. It opens the door to temptations that could, in the end, cost you your home. If you think you might want to use a portion of your mortgage equity to invest, think again, as this is also highly likely to be a losing move.

If your home equity is over 20%, be sure you are not paying for Private Mortgage Insurance (PMI). Banks, when granting a mortgage that is 80% or more of the home value, require PMI. When your mortgage becomes less than this, be sure to get the bank to eliminate the PMI charge. Do not purchase mortgage life insurance and, if you have it, kill it as soon as you can. If you feel you need life insurance, buy a term-life policy. It's a lot cheaper. (Chapter thirteen, "Choosing Insurance," covers the subject in detail.)

As a rule of thumb, look into refinancing your mortgage only if you can get a rate that is at least 1% or more below what you are paying and don't expect to move in the next four or five years. Calculate how many months it will take you to break even by dividing the monthly interest savings into the one-time costs involved in refinancing. If you do choose to refinance, do not increase either your balance owed or the number of years left to pay. Your goal should be a smaller payment, and paying off your house is not something you should shift farther into the future.

Here are several things to consider regarding this spending category.

- If you don't currently own your own home, should you buy one? If so, when should you do so, and how should you go about it? In chapter twelve, "Buying and Selling a Home," these issues will be covered in detail.

- Would you be happier and live a better life, overall, living in a smaller home or possibly in an apartment? How about living in an area that costs less or that shortens your commute? Do not dismiss these questions without thinking them through. Your home is one of the biggest financial and quality-of-life decisions you are ever going to make.

- When I grew up, the size of the house we lived in was an awful lot smaller than today's dwellings. The average family was a lot bigger, with more kids and, often, grandparents living in the same household with their children. Also, there were fewer divorced couples. The average house in 1950 was 1,100 sq. ft. and 1,400 sq. ft. in 1970. By 2004, it was 2,340 sq. ft. even though there were now fewer people in the average household. Was the house you grew up in too small? Was it really? If you feel your house should be larger than the house you grew up in, then by how much? Four hundred sq. ft.? Eight hundred sq. ft.? How much of your income are you willing to trade to have the extra space that you want, but probably don't need?

- A lot of people choose to make a long daily commute so they can live in a bigger or better house. They end up tired by the time they get home and are unable to spend quality time with their family and do the things they like. For most, this is likely a very bad life trade. If you happen to be one of these people, I again suggest you stop and take a hard look, with an open mind, at what you are doing.

2. *Utilities, Association Fees*

Association fees are what they are, and your utility bills are very heavily tied to the size of your residence. Beyond that, here are a couple of worthwhile things you can do to reduce your expenses:

- Make sure your house is insulated properly and your appliances are reasonably energy efficient. If not, fix the problem. Many electronic appliances, such as computers, continue to drain energy even when they are turned off. To fix this problem get a "smart" power strip that kills the electricity draw when those devices are turned off.
- In cold weather, lower the nighttime temperature to 65°–66°. In hot weather, keep it between 77° and 79°. Your body will adjust, and keeping the temperatures a little closer to outside temperatures is probably healthier for you. To make you feel better, you might want to know that air conditioned air at 78°, with its lower humidity, is equivalent to an average outdoor temperature of 72°.

- Close the air vents in unused rooms.
- Use energy-efficient light bulbs.
- Do your laundry with cold water and set your dryer to shut off based on moisture content.
- Use low-flow shower heads and lower the temperature of your hot water to 120°.
- Do you do laundry more than once a week? Wear things only once? Use new towels every day or two? Change your bedding more frequently than weekly? It's not necessary to do any of these things. Not only are these opportunities to save energy, you will have freed up a little of your time, too.

These things may seem small, but collectively can add up to some significant money over time.

3.   Telephone, Internet, TV

For most people, this trio has grown to be a sizeable annual expenditure and there are a number of possible changes that may reduce the costs involved. For each of these changes you should, of course, weigh the personal benefit to you versus the cost involved. For a lot of people these can be really good moves, as small dollars will become big dollars over time.

Consider combining your cell, internet, home phone service, and even your TV service under one provider and killing your extras such as caller ID, call waiting, and internet on your cell(s). Consider using one of the ultra low- to no-priced services on the internet for long distance and overseas calls. How about a webcam? It's not only dirt cheap or possibly free calling, it's video too! Perhaps you can eliminate your home phone altogether. Over 18% of U.S. households have done just that.

Get rid of your mega-channel package, go back to basic cable/DTV, and rent the movies, documentaries, and the TV shows you like to make up the difference. Many television shows are also available for free on the internet. Increasingly, there are options for connecting your television to the internet to retrieve this content. It's worth a little research into this quickly expanding alternative. You can also improve the quality of your life by watching less TV and doing more reading, using your body, and spending more quality time with family and friends.

4.   Car Payment(s)

According to the Department of Labor's Bureau of Statistics, "car owner-ship costs are the second largest household expense in the U.S. In fact, the average household spends almost as much on their cars (17%) as they do on food and health care combined for their entire family." Cars are not just a huge expense. For most people they are a huge waste of money. This means they can also be one heck of an opportunity for saving.

Let's start from the beginning, which is the moment you began to consider purchasing your car. Think about most of the new car com-mercials. Have you noticed there is a sameness to their underlying message? It goes something like, "Hey you! Yeah, you! Get behind the wheel of the new 555i. Man, you will own the road. The power, the freedom, the luxury! You're really gonna be somebody. Boy are you gonna be happy!" So what happens? You buy the new car and it really does make you happy for the next few weeks. After that you're pretty much back to where you started, except now you're out a lot of money.

They won. You lost. Ain't advertising grand? So how do you win when it comes to purchasing or leasing a car?

First you need to fully understand the car-buying process. In chapter four, "The 10 Rules of Spending Wisely," I recommended that you buy, read, and follow the advice in Remar Sutton's book *Don't Get Taken Every Time*. You should never buy or lease another car without doing that! I don't know this guy, but I sure know his book is worthwhile. Spend fifteen bucks for one of the best consumer-buying courses you'll ever find.

Next comes the most important step of all. Unless you are rolling in dough, or can't handle buying a used car and are *absolutely* committed to keeping the car for a long time, like seven or eight years or more, do *not* buy a new car! To quote Remar Sutton, "Unless you plan to keep a vehicle for a long time, a *new* car is probably one of the worst investments in the world." Ask yourself, what is the real difference between a new car and a three-year-old car? Do you notice the difference when it drives by? Most people do not. Is there a noticeable discrepancy in safety? Sometimes, yes, but such a situation is not the norm. Would it be more comfortable? Not really that much of a difference, is there? How about having less miles left on the car? When it comes to mileage, the well-made brands these days are usually good for 150,000 miles or more. As to the warranty, any saving will be blown away by the difference in the cost of purchasing the car. Nicer looking? You just like it better? Are you talking status? If so, you will break Money Rule #7 again by letting others decide how you spend your money.

So what *is* the real difference between a new and a three-year-old car? It's money, baby, one *heck* of a lot of money.

According to SafeCarGuide.com:

> New vehicles lose an average of 20% of their value the instant they are driven away from the dealership. When coupled to the average yearly depreciation of 7% to 12%, your first year's loss is anywhere from 25% to 35%. That translates to a first year $6,000 to $8,000 loss on a $22,500 new vehicle, or a $10,000 to $15,000 loss on a $40,000 one. And that's for a vehicle only driven the average 13,500 miles. If you drive more than that, your depreciation will be greater (35% to 50% for the first year). Don't forget to factor in your financing, which will add another $1,000 to $3,000."

To say that this is a big loss is quite an understatement. For the average person or family it is a *lot* more than that. As you are about to see, your approach to cars alone can truly alter your life by changing how soon and how much you can be free to do whatever you wish with your time. In its study of 2003 vehicle costs, the AAA found that:

> Motorists pay an average of 64.2 cents a mile, or $6,420 a year for 10,000 miles of motoring . . . . Based on the size of your vehicle, it will cost you more or less: 55.3 cents a mile for a compact car, 62.1 cents for a midsize car and 75.2 cents a mile for a full-size car. Costs take into account gas, oil, maintenance and tires, as well as insurance, depreciation, financing charges, license, title and registration."

Should you wish to calculate your own actual costs, go to www.edmunds.com and click on the "True Cost to Own" link.

The following table compares the approximate annual cost of purchasing a $30,000 car new, driving it 15,000 miles/year and keeping it for five years versus buying it when it's three-years-old. What it shows is a savings of $2,200 a year, or $3,650 before taxes, by buying the three-year-old car over the new one (assuming a tax rate of 40% on final or highest dollars earned). If you also save $1,100 a year before taxes on gas by driving a more economical car, you are now looking at a total pre-tax saving of $5,500 per year from changing your car buying habits.

Think about what this means. If you earn $45,000 a year, you, my friend, are working one and a half months each year for the sole purpose of paying for your "nicer" car. Is it worth it? Alternatively, say you invested that money at a return of 8%. The amount involved, $5,500 a year, adds up to $149,000 in fifteen years and an amazing $622,000 in thirty years. Think of how that much money can change your life and how many years sooner you can be free to do what you wish, all from one simple decision.

Annual Cost Comparison

Cost Factors	$30K New Car	$17K Used Car
Depreciation	$3,300	$1,700
Interest Paid @7%	$2,100	$1,260
Maintenance, Repairs	$550	$800
Annual Totals:	$5,950	$3,760

The bottom line is to keep driving your current car and pay off the loan, so long as it's not a gas guzzler with a lot of years left on the loan. Once the loan is paid off, keep making that car payment, but put it into savings for the purchase of your next car (see Item 25, Saving for Your

Next Car). When you're ready, go out and buy a two- to four-year-old car and keep it for at least four or five years. Should you still need to get a car loan, it should be shorter—three years max. After that, you should have succeeded in eliminating car loans altogether and your car payment becomes the cost of an average depreciation, or about $200 a month. Everything over that will be money you used to hand to others. So don't buy any new cars, and, as soon as possible, don't take out any car loans. You'll even get a bonus. You will have beaten the banks and the car dealers at their own game.

Here are some other things everyone can and should do:

- When buying a car, don't purchase an unnecessarily expensive car for its image. For example, if you compare an Accord or a Camry to the cars costing a lot more, you will usually find them to be almost as safe and reliable as the more expensive models. As to comfort and handling, you will find there is not that much of a difference. The same goes for that "ultimate" truck or RV. Why would you pay more unless you have more money than you need for the rest of your life? If you do pay more, you almost certainly bought into the advertiser's brainwashing. You also broke Money Rule #7 by letting other people decide how you spend your money. Whatever you get is unlikely to be worth the price you paid for it.

- Don't buy a gas guzzler. If you already own one consider getting rid of it in favor of a reasonably fuel-efficient model.

- When it comes to car leasing, an experienced salesperson can usually "prove" you win if you lease, even though you may not. They often stand to make a bigger commission if you lease, and the games here can get pretty confusing. The bottom line is, listen to Remar. That means no car leasing unless what you read in Remar's book convinces you, for sure, that you can win by doing so and are going about it the right way.

- Consider selling your second car and using public transportation or carpooling. Depending on where you live and work maybe you don't even need to own a car. If so, rent a car when you need one. If you live and work in Manhattan, San Francisco, Washington, D.C., or another big city with good public transportation, this is likely your best bet. You'll free up a lot of money and simplify your life.

- The internet has greatly improved the process of buying and selling a used car. About half of all used-car buyers now use the internet as part of their car buying and selling research. Remember to turn off your **cookies** first (see the glossary for an explanation on this). If you're very uncomfortable with the process of buying a car, get a friend to help you or, if necessary, hire one of the online services that will do the buying for you for a fee.

- When buying a used car, it is worthwhile to look at the inventory at your nearest CarMax. This will give you a pretty good idea of the market situation for the car you're looking for. Further, if you are uncomfortable negotiating your price or are worried about being stuck with a car with hidden problems, CarMax may be a good place to buy. You may end up paying somewhat more there, but are likely to be satisfied with the quality of the car.

- Check out www.ConsumerReports.org and www.JDPower.com for reviews and owner input about the reliability and owner satisfaction of the particular make, model, and year you are considering buying.

- Arrange your financing and know the value of your current car before you start to buy. *Never* finance through the dealer. It'll almost always cost you thousands more.

- Once you find a car you want, tell the salesperson you need to think about it. Make no offer whatsoever. No matter what price he offers you to get you to buy, leave the dealership. Call him back several hours later or perhaps the next day and do all of your negotiating over the phone, not in person. The salesperson will try very hard to get you to come in because it gives him more control of the situation. If you don't give in, most will cave and deal with you over the phone or the internet. Focus on the price you will pay because that is *not* where the dealer wants you to focus. He wants you focused on the car, the options, the size of your payment—anything but the price. Always negotiate the price (see chapter fourteen, "How to Negotiate," for a crash course on negotiating). Don't buy unnecessary extras like rust-proofing, extended warrantees, fabric and paint protection, VIN etching, etc. All are either unnecessary or way overpriced.

- Do not give a deposit without first getting the manager's approval or you are subject to the game not being over. Always make the deal on a used car subject to getting *your own* diagnostic service report, a VIN-number-check (you do this online; it costs about $35 for a detailed history on the car), and on getting the name and contact information of the previous owner and calling the person.

- You must read *everything* you sign very carefully. Be on the lookout for add-ons you didn't agree to. It is common for car dealers to add-on something "standard" you never asked for and do not need or want.

- Be wary of car dealers who try to work you by having a series of people take over talking to you for the purpose of wearing you down. Do not become a prisoner by handing over the keys to your existing car before a manager has agreed to your deal. If they want to drive your car to appraise it before you have the manager's agreement, go with them. The bottom line here is that it must be you that controls the sequence of events, not them. If you can't get this to happen, leave.

- Lastly, and most importantly, be sure to read Remar Sutton's book before you even start this process. Listen to him, and follow what he tells you.

5. *Health Care Insurance*

The purchasing of health care insurance will be covered in chapter thirteen, "Choosing Insurance." For now, enter whatever you pay in total for medical, dental, and pharmaceutical insurance.

The other advice you already know. Take good care of your body. If you don't, I'm sure you know what that is costing you. Consider this: The majority of all U.S. bankruptcies (at least up until the recent real estate meltdown) occurred as the result of medical bills, even though 75% of those families had health insurance when they first became sick.

6. Debt Payments/Debt Reduction

For now, please enter whatever you feel you can do here. If you are significantly in debt, what to do about it is covered in the next chapter.

7. Other Required Payments

Use this category for things like childcare, child support, spousal support, miscellaneous monthly dues, and so forth. Fill in what you currently pay.

As for the future, you need to be aware that the cost to raise a child is currently about $13,000 a year and $221,000 to age seventeen. Your house, your car, and the cost of each child are the biggest financial responsibilities you will probably ever take on. I love children, and I'm sure you do, too. For most of us, children turn out to be among life's greatest blessings. When planning to expand your family, however, it's wise to take into consideration the true costs involved in that decision. (There is more information on my website on planning for a child.)

8. Gas

You should own a reasonably economical car. A lot of cars will get twenty-eight to thirty miles or more per gallon (mpg), whereas a big pickup or SUV is more likely to get sixteen to eighteen mpg, or worse. If you drive 15,000 miles a year at $3 per gallon for gas, the difference is $1,100 a year, or $1,600 before taxes. This doesn't even count the probable higher purchase price involved for the big truck or SUV. How many weeks do you have to work each year for that money? Is it really worth the trade?

Only use regular gas, unless your car requires a higher octane. If your car allows it, and most cars do, why would you do otherwise? If your car manual says to use a higher octane for improved or best performance, remember that's not the same as required, and the performance improvement is very minimal. Any small savings from better engine wear are generally insignificant.

Keep your tires properly inflated to maximize both your mileage and especially your safety and watch your driving habits. According to *Consumer Reports*, every five mph over sixty uses 10% more gas!

Another great way to save on gas and also on car expenses is to drive no more than necessary. Do multiple things on the same trip whenever possible. A reasonable assumption is that every mile you drive is costing you at least 40¢ between gas and wear and tear on your car. If you drive an extra forty miles a week, that's $800 a year or $1,330 before taxes. To do this effectively, use your little list of the things you want to buy and the things you plan to do. When you're running low on something, add it to the list. Doing this frees up your time, saves on gas and car costs, and reduces impulse spending.

9. Public Transportation

Fill in what you pay and smile; you're no doubt saving some nice money.

10. Food & Supermarket Spending

Here are some things to do to make the most of your money:

- Consume fewer prepared foods and do more cooking from scratch.

- Eliminate most processed snacks and drinks. Do not discard this suggestion without really thinking about it. You can save serious money, eat better, and be healthier by making these changes.

- Avoid spending money in convenience stores. The prices are usually much higher than those in supermarkets.

- Try the store brands. They've gotten a lot better. Also, get a discount card for the stores you frequent to take advantage of sales and special "member" prices.

- Minimize food shopping when you're hungry.

- At times you'll have to do some fill-in purchasing of food and supermarket items between your Costco, or other discount store, visits. Assuming you are eating less prepared food, you will want to shop once or twice a week for fresh food items at a local market. Just be sure to limit your buying to just that, fresh food items. Also, the less often you go the better. Every time you shop, you open the door to impulse buying. Spending $20 extra twice a week on an impulse buy is $1,000 a year! Be fully aware of it whenever you want to buy something not on your list.

11. General Shopping

This category includes any and all routine shopping like clothes, shoes, cosmetics, and household items that are not covered by any of the other categories. For this spending here are a few suggestions to consider:

- Think twice about paying through the nose for an "image" brand name. In most cases you can buy equivalent quality and look without the name. For example, high-quality sunglass knockoffs are available in a lot of places these days. The quality, including the lenses, is often very good. They look just like the originals and cost 80%–90% less than the brand-name equivalent.

- Never buy extended warranty coverage on anything. The odds greatly favor that the cost of the insurance will far outweigh any costs you might otherwise incur.

- Stop wearing clothes that have to be dry-cleaned, except for special occasions.

- Don't buy any home exercise equipment unless you are sure you will use it. An awful lot of such equipment ends up going unused. Want to prove you're the exception? Do any form of exercise three to four times a week, for the next thirty days. If you can do that, then go buy a piece of used equipment. It'll be like new and probably half the price. When it comes to fitness club memberships, don't sign up for an annual or multi-year membership for the first three months, regardless of the "get this great deal or lose it" pitch you will usually get. Pay month to month if at all possible. The great sale will almost always be there in some form. Despite good intentions, about 30% of new gym-goers are gone in less than ninety days.

- For the purchase of items such as bikes, toys, cribs, books, exercise equipment, etc., garage sales can be a great source at dirt-cheap prices.

- How about diamonds? Now there's a tough one. The brainwashing here is so incredible that I have to walk on eggshells. Everyone who knows me will tell you I am a very romantic person, yet you know what I'm going to say. I direct this primarily at women, as no guy can give you an imitation diamond unless it's what you want. Here's the thing: Nobody can tell the difference, especially if you keep the size believable. Ask yourself what the money or lack of debt will mean to the both of you, then make your decision. Does my wife have any diamonds? No. Fortunately, I am married to a woman with terrific values.

12. Out-of-Pocket Spending

For one week, honestly add up everything you spend every day. Then multiply the number by fifty-two weeks. This can be a huge eye opener and often an answer to much of this question: Where does all the money go? Still, out-of-pocket spending is the home of some deceptively good saving opportunities. Eating out every day; daily purchases of coffee, cigarettes, snacks, energy drinks, soda, lottery tickets— all are bigger opportunities for saving than you might think. Here are a few examples:

- Bring your own coffee and lunch to work four days a week. If it saves you $25 a week, that money, pre-tax (about $2,000) and invested, becomes about $227,000 in thirty years assuming an 8% return. It may also allow you to stop working a year earlier, if you wish.
- Consider replacing your soda, juice, diet drinks, and even coffee with water. It'll save you money and it's a lot better for you. Also, should you need to lose a few pounds, drinking water exclusively should knock off a pound, or maybe more, a week. It's quite common to feel hungry when in

actuality you're dehydrated. Most public water is good to drink right from the tap, or you can filter it. Using a reusable water bottle is cost effective and will also greatly reduce the amount of waste you generate.

- If you do drink something other than water, stop buying it during the day and bring it from home. Make your purchases at Costco or Sam's Club or somewhere with a good price. You can spend 25¢ to 35¢ each versus $1 to $1.50. At $2 saved a day, that's $500 a year after taxes, $800 before.

13. Other Spending

This line item is included to capture anything not included in the other categories, such as personal grooming, pets, etc.

On pets, if it's mostly pet food and an occasional vet checkup, cover these expenditures under things like Item 10, Food and Supermarket Spending, etc. If, on the other hand, you frequently spend more than that on grooming, boarding, and toys, then enter those pet expenses here. Pets are one of those sensitive categories, as they are a joy, and they cost money. The average dog costs about $1,600/year, or $2,660 before taxes, and $900/year for the average cat. Over thirty years, $2,660 saved per year at 8% will become $300,000. Once again, you want to make a conscious decision about your choices and trades before making a commitment to a new pet. For the pets you already have, keeping them on a leash and not letting them get fat are good steps to take to reduce costs, optimize their health, and insure they live longer.

When it comes to personal grooming expenditures such as hair appointments and products, skin care, and manicures, take a moment to calculate the total annual cost involved. You might be surprised at how much money is actually being spent. Ask yourself whether the trade is worth it and what alternative approaches you might take to save some money in this category.

14. Recreation & Entertainment

This is your fun money, the place where you reward yourself by eating out, going to the movies, attending sporting events, etc. Here are a number of things to consider for making your dollars go farther:

- Eat out less, especially at expensive restaurants. Save the more pricey places for special occasions only. When eating out at the less-expensive places, consider sharing a main course if it's bigger than you need (or taking half home for a future meal), drinking water only, and skipping dessert. Admittedly, these are personal decisions, but I suggest you at least take them into consideration, as they are good for both most people's health and can also save some nice money over time.

- Don't buy movies unless it's one you or your children will watch many times. You can rent for a fraction of the price of buying. There will be less to store, and you won't have to throw them out when the next improved format (like blu-ray) arrives. While you're at it, consider getting your movies from an internet source such as Netflix to save time and money and to simplify your life. If you just don't rent that often, consider using a local DVD kiosk such as Redbox ($1 a day rentals at over 15,000 locations).

- Kill your magazine and newspaper subscriptions unless there is something you really love to get. I believe most magazines and newspapers are soon to be dead media anyway, blown away by the superiority of the internet. Making the switch will simplify life a little more, too. There are also some great online reading resources, like Google Reader, that help organize the news or topical sites you are interested in following.

- Do not buy a boat, unless it's a small one for fishing, canoeing, kayaking, etc. The old expression is true that "A boat is a hole in the water into which you pour money." If you've got the money and have the urge, go rent something nice for those few days a year you'll actually want to get out on the water, and save the rest of your money and a lot of annoyance. If you already own a boat, ask yourself how often you use it. Is it worth the time and money involved?

- Do you own an RV, a trailer or motor home, or are you thinking of buying one? Sit down and do an honest cost analysis. Examine how often you really plan to use it versus the true cost of ownership. RVs are a lot like boats, the primary difference being that the hole is sitting in your driveway or in an off-site lot where you're paying rent. They are all pretty much awful as investments, as their value tends to drop like a rock.

- Do you gamble? There are only three situations where it makes sense to do so. The first is if you enjoy doing it just for fun; have saved for the losses under the entertainment category of your budget; and strictly limit yourself to a pre-set, acceptable loss amount that counts as your entertainment cost. If you go to a casino a couple of times a year and spend $50 to $100 for the fun of it, no problem. The second acceptable situation is if you like to go frequently, but just play the 25¢ slots, again with a very strict spending limit, which fits within your budget. The third is if you are extremely good at something like poker or video games and you can reliably win money from others, not the house, doing it. No one beats the house. Other than these three modest exceptions, gambling is just a very destructive thing to do. As for buying lottery tickets, it's the same losing proposition with the odds set to insure that you lose. As for winning the jackpot, according to the Powerball's own site the odds are one in 195,000,000; you are twenty-five times more likely to be struck by lightning. If you buy a lottery ticket once or twice a year for the fun of it, no problem. If you do it as a regular thing, you're just throwing your money away.

Rollover Spending and Saving

The following Periodic Expenses and Saving items are not paid monthly. To keep track of how much money is available for each category, it is best to track each one as a separate fund using the Rollover Saving-Funds Worksheet provided in this chapter, as well as on my website. Money saved in each category is added to the fund balance which rolls-over (is carried over) each month. Whenever you spend more for a given category than the monthly amount you have allowed for, subtract the excess amount spent from its fund. Setting aside money each month for these items may mean making a transfer into another savings, money market, or other account where the fund's money is saved, or it may only be a matter of tracking the fund's balance with the Rollover Saving-Funds Worksheet, depending on where you choose to save for that particular fund.

Periodic Expenses

For the following periodic expenses, estimate the annual cost, and then divide the annual cost by twelve to get the amount that should be saved each month. Each month, enter this amount on your Spending and Saving Plan Worksheet, and add that amount to its fund balance. When a periodic expense does hit it will usually be greater than the normal monthly amount being saved, and the shortfall is then covered by subtracting the additional spending from the rollover savings fund for that item.

15. Medical, Dental, Pharmacy

For this category, fill in the spending, co-pays, pharmacy costs, etc. not covered by your monthly health care insurance premiums. Use generic drugs as much as possible and buy from a discount source. Ninety-day supplies through the mail are available under many plans at substantial savings. The sources on the internet, as always, should be explored.

Medicines and operations often have side effects and can damage the body in some manner as well as helping fix what's wrong. When you do truly need an operation or a medicine, kiss the ground that the medicine or operation is there. They may well save your life. However, do not accept all medicine and medical procedures lightly. Discuss the pros and cons with your doctor. Ask whether you definitely need the medicine involved, and, if so, to what degree you can limit the amount you take. Always go on the internet and read about the downside of the medicine you take or are considering taking.

If it's an operation you need, always get at least two independent opinions, maybe even three. Go on the internet and read up on every medical procedure you are considering. Studies have concluded that over half of all operations performed each year should never have been done. There are few people I respect more than those in the medical profession. Good doctors, nurses, and emergency medical technicians are among our society's greatest treasures. Try as they might, though, they won't always be right. Just like with your money, you must take personal control of, and final responsibility for, your own health.

People spend a lot of money on dietary supplements and quite frankly most of that money is wasted. Sometimes, however, it can be money very well spent. As you age, shifts in your body's chemistry and functioning are unavoidable. If you can find that uncommon person who really understands the use of natural supplements to adjust the body's chemistry, they may be able to help you find supplements that can have amazing results. I have personally benefited enormously from such help. Sometimes natural supplements can accomplish the same thing as medications, but without the harmful side effects. Sometimes they can even help where medicine cannot. Be careful to get the best advice, however, as supplements can sometimes also be quite harmful.

If you have or encounter a health problem, I recommend you Google the problem and read everything that comes up. If it appears there may be an answer using supplements, be cautious and do not just buy whatever is being suggested. Find that knowledgeable person to help you out. It may be an effort to do so, but it will be worth it. Talk to people you know, and go to a number of health food or supplement stores and ask to speak to their most experienced person. Ask how long the person has been doing the job. For the good ones, it will be many years. If that doesn't work, I would make an appointment with two different medical specialists knowledgeable about supplements. If you do choose to buy supplements, be sure to look at prices on the internet as they are usually dramatically cheaper than other sources.

16. *Car Maintenance, Repair, and DMV Fees*

Be sure the average monthly amount you enter to cover oil changes, tires, brakes, and minor repairs is realistic. Lowballing just interferes with your planning. If you need some help to make this estimate, see my website for a helpful link or two. Do not, however, cover major repairs here. Include that money as part of Item 20, Unexpected Events. Here are a few things you should do to get your money's worth on this expenditure:

- Buy your tires at Costco or Sam's Club or a similar genuine discount source. Buy high-quality tires. Yes, they cost more, but, as I've said, always buy quality. You'll do less re-buying, get more satisfaction, and you'll be a lot safer, too. Also, know that a lot of the new tires sold each year have been sitting around, new, for a lot of years. Once a tire is over five- or six-years-old it should no longer be considered safe, as the adhesive may now be too dry and could be hazardous if it doesn't hold. On the tire is a number that tells you the month and the year the tire was made: i.e. 459 is the 45th week of 1999, 1302 is the 13th week of 2002. Now that you know, insist on seeing the date and buy nothing over a couple of years old. And while you're at it, you can say thank you to John Stossel, a true friend of consumers, for bringing this information to the attention of the public in his ABC special on July 24, 2008.

- Go to a car dealer for repairs that only they can do. Get your oil changes, brake jobs, and other maintenance somewhere cheaper. The problem with using a dealer is that they will far too frequently "up-sell" you by tacking on other charges for checkups and adjustments that you usually don't need. Watch out for this tendency to add on unnecessary services wherever you go. Also, always insure that no routine maintenance items that don't yet need to be done get added in error. Errors of this nature are surprisingly common.

- The service frequency recommended by the car manufacturers can sometimes be too conservative unless your car is subject to brutal conditions. Things like oil changes, radiator flushes, transmission fluid replacement, belt replacement, etc. can perhaps be done somewhat less frequently. I suggest you take a couple of minutes and go on the internet and read up on this regarding the vehicles you own.

- If you're modestly handy, learning how to change your own oil, air and oil filters, and keeping your fluid levels up can be worth your time. You can buy the materials you need for a fraction of what you will otherwise be charged.

17. Education Expenses, Lessons

Use this category for any and all education expenses including music lessons, summer camp, and the like. If you are paying for any form of private education including a private pre-school, elementary, high school, or post-high school education, please be sure to read chapter eight, "Paying for an Education," to help you fine-tune your spending for those expenses.

18. Property Maintenance

Home maintenance costs, like utilities, are greatly influenced by the size of your residence. Beyond that, here are a couple of other things to consider:

- Buy a good "do-it-yourself" book for routine household repairs. A lot of things are fairly easy to do yourself rather than having to hire a professional.

- Replace as much of the grass in your yard as you can with river gravel, ground cover, or native plants that require little water. These things take little or no maintenance and, when done right, look just as good. Think about what it costs to maintain a lawn. The average cost of cutting and trimming is about $40 to $50/week these days. Then there's the cost of fertilizer, weeding, mowers, weed whackers, spreaders, etc. It all adds up. Simplify your life a little and save money—it's a two-fer.

19. Insurance

This category should cover your payments for auto, homeowner's (unless already covered under Item #1, Home Payment and Taxes or Rent), renter's, umbrella, life, disability, and long-term care insurance policies. Use the amount of what you are currently paying now. Add them all up and divide by twelve to know the monthly cost. This is what you must put aside each month so that you are prepared. In chapter thirteen, "Choosing Insurance," all of your insurance needs and options will be covered in detail.

20. *Unexpected Events*

It's important to allow a decent amount of money in your budget for unexpected events, as unplanned-for spending *will* happen. If at all possible, I'd start with no less than $100 to $150 per month.

21. *Giving*

Don't forget Money Rule #9: Give Back (And Do It Now). Budget some money for this, even if it's only $20 a month to start. Be a little creative when you think about how to give back. You'll be surprised at the amount of good you can do with just a little of your time and $20. I truly believe that you'll love how it makes you feel and you will discover for yourself that when you give, you get back all you gave and more.

22. *Gifts and the Holidays*

It's important to save for gifts, and especially the holidays, so that you are prepared to cover the expenses when the time comes. Consider the gifts and expenses for each present-giving event in your year, add them up, and divide by twelve to know the monthly cost. This is what you must put aside each month so that you are prepared.

Also consider not buying Christmas and birthday presents for most adults. No, I'm not a Scrooge, just practical. Take a look at the benefits versus the drawbacks. If you stop exchanging these gifts you will simplify your life and save a nice chunk of change, too. Talk to the people you're exchanging gifts with and see if they might prefer to stop as well. I think you will find that most will be happy to end the obligation or perhaps agree to a gift limit of $10 or so. After all, what percent of the gifts you've ever gotten have you actually wanted and used? I think presents are for children, for your mother and father, grandmother and grandfather, wife or husband, and that you can stop there. Are you still sending Christmas cards? If you take the time to write a personal message to each person, that's great. But if you're like most people and just fire them out, it's not very personal, is it? Simplify your life and save the money. Instead, send an e-card, if you like, for free, and do it for birthdays, too.

23. Vacations

Vacations are great, but you need to vacation within your means. By saving money each month you can take a trip without acquiring debt. This may mean being a little creative, and it may mean waiting or taking a road trip. Depending on where you're going, you might want to take a look at sites like www.vrbo.com and consider renting a condo or cottage from a private owner. When it comes to vacationing, there are lots of interesting options out there.

Saving

For the following saving categories, it's important that you reliably save a set amount each month. Enter this amount on your Spending and Saving Plan Worksheet, and add that amount to its fund balance on the Rollover Saving-Funds Worksheet. When you need to spend money from a given saving fund, subtract the spending from the rollover savings for that item.

24. Saving for Emergency Fund

You absolutely must have an emergency fund for events involving a lot more than the routine money you will budget under the Unexpected Events category. If your family has one income I recommend saving six months' salary; for two incomes, four months' is adequate. *This is so important that even if you are in debt, you must first save enough emergency money to cover at least one month's living expenses, before paying down a penny of your debt.* I say this because the unexpected *will* happen. Car repairs, appliance repairs or replacements, medical bills, the loss of a job—you name it. When it happens, you will be in a very bad situation if you have nothing to fall back on. Do not go there. If you are already in debt this is even more important, as you will otherwise just keep adding to your debt for every single thing that comes up that you didn't plan for.

A good trick to keep you honest, and also make you some money, is to put those dollars in a six- to twelve-month CD. That way you're less tempted to use it when you shouldn't, as withdrawing it early will cost a penalty of about three months' interest.

One last piece of advice: Many people assume that their unused credit card or home equity lines can serve as emergency money. Do not do that! Banks can and do reduce credit lines and home values can fall and these things have a way of happening exactly when you will need these resources the most.

25. Saving for Your Next Car

As explained in Item 4 (Car Payment[s]), after you pay off your car loan, keep driving that car and continue making your car payment but saving it for the purchase of your next car. When you're ready, go out and buy a two- to four-year-old car and keep it for at least four or five years. Should you still need to get a car loan it should be for a shorter time—three years max. After that, you should have succeeded in eliminating car loans altogether and your "car payment" becomes savings in this category. For most people that amount should be about the same as the rate of depreciation of your car. Everything over that amount will be money you used to hand to others as interest on a loan.

26. Saving for Large Purchases

Your wish list is up to you. Whether, when, and where you buy, however, should be governed by all that has been covered to this point. When you are ready to buy, do not put any of your large purchases on credit. Save what you can for this category and wait to make a purchase until you've saved enough. (Note: Saving towards your next car should be listed under Item 25.)

27. Saving for Financial Freedom

First and foremost, always have the money you save for your financial freedom taken directly out of your paycheck via direct deposit. Save first, and then live on the rest until the next paycheck. What you don't get you can't spend. Start with no less than 7% or 8% of your pay and look to increase this percentage as soon as you can to at least 15% (preferably 20%) of your after-tax income. This may sound like a lot, but it is doable. In the long run you will be very glad you did. If necessary, pretend your pay was cut. Also, be sure to save all raises beyond the amount needed to cover the impact of inflation on your living expenses. There is seldom a good reason not to.

28. Saving for Education

Should you be considering saving anything for this category, please be sure to read the information provided in chapter eight, "Paying for an Education."

Prioritize Your Savings

One of the key decisions you will have to make will be to prioritize your saving and debt-reduction efforts. Unless you have a very good reason not to, I recommend that you adhere to the following priority sequence. It provides guidelines for setting priorities when it comes to saving for the various needs described in this chapter and balancing that against debt reduction.

1. Save for an emergency fund starting with at least one month's expenses.

2. If your employer matches what you save in your 401(k), save the amount necessary to get the full matching dollars.

3. Allocate 50% of all you are able to save to your emergency fund, and 50% to debt reduction until you have four to six months' of living expenses in your emergency fund. (Four months for a two-income family, and six months if there is only one income.)

4. Eliminate all debt except that which involves your home and your car.

5. Maximize the tax-deferred savings allowed to you by IRS guidelines. Once you reach this point and are saving as much as you can pre-tax, throw a party and reward yourself with something very special. You've earned it!

6. Pay off your car and start saving $250 a month in a car fund.

7. Increase your saving to at least 15% of your pre-tax income. If you don't own a home, accumulate the money needed to buy one. If you already do, accelerate your payoff until you own it free and clear. Also, during times when fixed-interest rates such as CDs have fallen below 3.5%, be aware that making extra payments on your house will give you a better after-tax return on your money.

8. If you have children you might want to start a specific education fund. (Please read "Paying for an Education" in chapter eight to see if this is something you should do.)

Other Money-saving Ideas

As I'm sure you know, the information on money-saving tips and ideas is never ending. Every day you'll see new stories, columns, net postings, etc. on ways to save and spend your money better. This information is, for the most part, highly repetitive. I believe you won't save that much more than is covered in this book by doing whatever is recommended.

Provided below are a few additional ideas and suggestions that didn't fit into any of the categories above.

- Cash advances, payday loans, renting to own anything, pawning things, or doing business with "tote the note" car lots are all terrible ideas. The interest rates associated with these products are awful, and you will risk digging a financial hole you may never climb out of.

- Pay your bills online. This saves stamps and envelopes, avoids late fees, is quicker, and simplifies bill paying. Many of your bills can be sent to you electronically or deducted directly from your bank or credit card account. E-bills also reduce paper clutter and put everything right at your fingertips.

- Do not withdraw money from ATMs, other than your set weekly or bi-weekly cash amounts. To do otherwise destroys your system for monitoring your cash spending. Should you hit an occasional exception where pulling extra cash is necessary, write down the amount in your records as soon as you get home.

- Get your free credit reports every year from the three credit agencies at www.annualcreditreport.com and fix any errors. Mistakes are very common and they may hurt your credit if you don't correct them. You might also choose to get one free report every four months to keep a closer eye on identity theft. Identity theft has become a serious problem, so be sure to follow the key steps to avoid having it happen to you. Check your account activity online once a week, shred or tear to pieces any documents containing personal information, and never give out personal information to someone you don't know who has called or e-mailed you. Provide this information only to those you call. It is the only way you can be sure that the person you are talking to works for the company they say they do.

- If you get a sizeable tax refund each year, increase your deductibles and use the extra money in your paycheck for immediate debt reduction or saving. The money will do a lot more good in your hands than sitting with the government.
- Lastly, please take some time and teach your kids about money. If you have children, I encourage you to go to my website where I provide advice on teaching your children about money, and links to other good resources.

Making It Happen

Creating your Spending and Saving Plan is truly a critical step, but you will only benefit from it if you use it. Every month, take about an hour or so to compare how you actually spent your money with your plan's target numbers and then make whatever adjustments you choose as you go into the next month. There may be months where you fall off the wagon a little. Don't let it derail you; just get back to your plan. Success is never hurt by temporary setbacks unless you choose to quit. By creating and following a written plan, and not breaking the rules of money, you are very likely to be on your way to a life of financial success and the happiness and peace of mind it can bring.

For those of you who are working on your plan and are sitting there frustrated by your inability to save and pay off debt, here is what I have to say to you: You need to go back and do a better job because you've probably broken the rules of money and have not been honest with yourself. I say this because most spending is *optional*. Here are some examples:

- Move to a smaller, cheaper place. I understand you don't want to, but you can if you have to. You can even go farther and live in a shared living arrangement. Tens of millions of people do just that.
- Sell your car and buy a cheaper one. If you have two cars you can often sell the second one and find a way to get by with one vehicle by using public transportation, carpooling, and the occasional car rental.
- Eliminate eating out and buying prepared foods. Cook all your meals from basic natural ingredients. It's surprising how little you can spend on food and still eat very well.
- Avoid buying anything new except needed shoes, socks, and underwear. Wear what you have.

I'm not suggesting that these are the specific things you should do; it's up to you to cut your spending. Barring a job loss or big medical expenses, most people can significantly reduce their debts each month and/or save money if they really want to. Once again, it's your life and your choices. I'm just giving you the tools to help you choose a winning path.

If you are dealing with a major problem such as job loss or overwhelming medical bills, you can find more on these "just-in-time" subjects on my website. If you are simply finding it a struggle to execute an effective Spending and Saving Plan that meets your needs and desires, you can also find more advice, support and resources on my website.

How to Use the Worksheets

Please note that all of the worksheets in this book are also available on my website.

Spending and Saving Plan Worksheet

This worksheet is the foundation of your Spending and Saving Plan. Do a new worksheet for each month and save them for reference as you go forward. Fill in the estimated amounts for your income and for each of the spending and saving categories. When you add up your numbers you will probably find your first estimate of spending plus saving does not match your income. Go back and adjust as you see fit to get the numbers to match. After the month is over, post your actual numbers to the worksheet. Tracking your spending at the end of the month will not be difficult if you follow my advice under Step 3 at the beginning of this chapter. (Found on page 90.)

Think about what happened and then create the next month's worksheet using what you learned to further fine-tune the numbers. Do not fall into the trap of thinking this is too much work. It's only an hour or two a month, and if you do not do it you will have broken Money Rule #4: Have a Written Plan and Follow It, and are at a disadvantage in managing your money.

Rollover Saving-Funds Worksheet

A number of the categories on your Spending and Saving Plan involve saving a monthly amount for expenses that occur on an "as-needed" basis. The Rollover Saving-Funds Worksheet will help you track the money you have saved and made available for each of those "non-monthly" categories. Be sure to reliably save the money required and use this form—a lot of your spending and saving categories involve this situation.

Each category for which you are putting away money should be considered its own savings fund. The Rollover Saving-Funds Worksheet gives you a place to track these funds. For the first month you start, decide how much of your current savings to use as a starting balance for each of the saving categories on the worksheet. Write these amounts down on a separate sheet of paper.

At the end of each month, transfer the amounts to be added to or subtracted from your Spending and Saving Plan Worksheet to the Rollover Saving-Funds Worksheet. Be sure to enter these numbers with either a plus (+) or minus (-) symbol. Then add or subtract these amounts from the previous month's fund balance which will give you a new balance to enter into the Fund Balance column. There is also a column for you to identify which of your financial accounts each fund is in. For each of your financial accounts, there is an area for recording transfers and rollover balances.

Net Worth Worksheet

Your net worth is the difference between what you own and what you owe. Filling in all of your accounts on this form every three or four months will give you a clear picture of your financial progress.

Month _Sample Plan_

Net income ($)

Estimated **5,155**

Actual **5,038**

Difference **-117**

Non-Rollover Spending	Estimated	Actual	Over-spent −	Under-spent +

Regular Monthly Expenses ($)

	Estimated	Actual	Over-spent −	Under-spent +
1. Home Payment, Taxes, Rent	1370	1370		
2. Utilities, Association Fees	165	173	-8	
3. Telephone, Internet, TV	185	203	-18	
4. Car Payment(s)	334	334		
5. Health Care Insurance	486	486		
6. Debt Payments/Debt Reduction	150	50		+100
7. Other Required Payments				
8. Gas	173	145		+28
9. Public Transportation				
10. Food & Supermarket Spending	700	798	-98	
11. General Shopping	350	298		+52
12. Out-of-Pocket Spending	250	280	-30	
13. Other Spending				
14. Recreation & Entertainment	75	90	-15	

Rollover Spending and Saving	Estimated	Actual	Subtract from Fund −	Add to Fund +
Periodic Expenses ($)				
15. Medical, Dental, Pharmacy	50	0		+50
16. Car Maintenance, Repair, DMV	50	334	−284	
17. Education Expenses, Lessons				
18. Property Maintenance	85	127	−42	
19. Insurance	57	0		+57
20. Unexpected Events	100	0		+100
21. Giving	25	0		+25
22. Gifts and the Holidays	50	0		+50
23. Vacations	150	0		+150
Saving ($)				
24. Saving for Emergency Fund	100	100		+100
25. Saving for Your Next Car				
26. Saving for Large Purchases				
27. Saving for Financial Freedom	250	250		+250
28. Saving for Education				
Totals	5,155	5,038		

133

MONEY $MART Rollover Saving-Funds Worksheet

Month <u>Sample Plan</u>

Spending and Saving	Additions/ Subtractions	Fund Balance	Account
15. Medical, Dental, Pharmacy	+50	218	Savings
16. Car Maintenance, Repair, DMV	-284	485	"
17. Education Expenses, Lessons			"
18. Property Maintenance	-42	255	"
19. Insurance	+57	348	"
20. Unexpected Events	+100	495	"
21. Giving	+25	70	"
22. Gifts and the Holidays	+50	250	"
23. Vacations	+150	600	
24. Saving for Emergency Fund	+100	8,700	CDs & Money Market
25. Saving for Your Next Car			
26. Saving for Large Purchases		850	Money Market
27. Saving for Financial Freedom	+250	24,174	401(k)
28. Saving for Education			

Account:	Amount Transferred	Rollover Balance
Savings	$ 106	$ 2,721
Money Market	$ 100	$ 2,050
CDs	$	$ 7,500
401(k)	$ 250	$ 24,174

MONEY SMART — Rollover Saving-Funds Worksheet

Month _____

Spending and Saving	Additions/ Subtractions	Fund Balance	Account
15. Medical, Dental, Pharmacy	_____	_____	_____
16. Car Maintenance, Repair, DMV	_____	_____	_____
17. Education Expenses, Lessons	_____	_____	_____
18. Property Maintenance	_____	_____	_____
19. Insurance	_____	_____	_____
20. Unexpected Events	_____	_____	_____
21. Giving	_____	_____	_____
22. Gifts and the Holidays	_____	_____	_____
23. Vacations	_____	_____	_____
24. Saving for Emergency Fund	_____	_____	_____
25. Saving for Your Next Car	_____	_____	_____
26. Saving for Large Purchases	_____	_____	_____
27. Saving for Financial Freedom	_____	_____	_____
28. Saving for Education	_____	_____	_____

Account:	Amount Transferred	Rollover Balance
_____	$_____	$_____
_____	$_____	$_____
_____	$_____	$_____
_____	$_____	$_____

Spending and Saving Plan Worksheet

Month _____

Net income ($)

Estimated   _____

Actual   _____

Difference   _____

Non-Rollover Spending	Estimated	Actual	Over-spent −	Under-spent +
Regular Monthly Expenses ($)				
1. Home Payment, Taxes, Rent	_____	_____	_____	_____
2. Utilities, Association Fees	_____	_____	_____	_____
3. Telephone, Internet, TV	_____	_____	_____	_____
4. Car Payment(s)	_____	_____	_____	_____
5. Health Care Insurance	_____	_____	_____	_____
6. Debt Payments/Debt Reduction	_____	_____	_____	_____
7. Other Required Payments	_____	_____	_____	_____
8. Gas	_____	_____	_____	_____
9. Public Transportation	_____	_____	_____	_____
10. Food & Supermarket Spending	_____	_____	_____	_____
11. General Shopping	_____	_____	_____	_____
12. Out-of-Pocket Spending	_____	_____	_____	_____
13. Other Spending	_____	_____	_____	_____
14. Recreation & Entertainment	_____	_____	_____	_____

Rollover Spending and Saving	Estimated	Actual	Subtract from Fund −	Add to Fund +
Periodic Expenses ($)				
15. Medical, Dental, Pharmacy				
16. Car Maintenance, Repair, DMV				
17. Education Expenses, Lessons				
18. Property Maintenance				
19. Insurance				
20. Unexpected Events				
21. Giving				
22. Gifts and the Holidays				
23. Vacations				
Saving ($)				
24. Saving for Emergency Fund				
25. Saving for Your Next Car				
26. Saving for Large Purchases				
27. Saving for Financial Freedom				
28. Saving for Education				

Totals _____ _____

Net Worth Worksheet

Assets ($)

1. **Primary residence** – Market value, less 8-9% selling costs* _____

2. **Retirement accounts** – 401(k)s, IRAs, SEP's, etc. _____

3. **Other stock market assets** _____

4. **Cash** – Checking & savings accts, CDs, Money Markets _____

5. **Insurance** – Cash value, including annuities _____

6. **Other real estate** – Market value, less 7-10% selling costs* _____

7. **Automobiles and RVs** – Market value, less selling costs _____

8. **Personal possessions** – Value, less selling costs _____

9. **Other assets** – Market value, less selling costs _____

includes commission, closing costs and cost to prepare property for sale

Total Assets _____

Liabilities ($)

1. **Residential first mortgage** _____

2. **2nd mortgage, home equity loans** _____

3. **Credit card balances** _____

4. **All other loans or liabilities** _____

Total Liabilities _____

Net Worth (total assets – total liabilities) _____

CHAPTER SEVEN

Getting Out of Debt

For over fifty years the relentless message that debt is "normal" and even "good" has brainwashed the American public. This is the machinery of business and commerce doing its job of going after its interests, and you're not going to stop that. But here is what you need to know: Except for mortgage and education debt, debt is *not* good. Debt problems can damage the quality of your life. If you are one of those people and do not address this situation, the damage will only continue to grow.

You may owe a lot and feel like the debt can't be eliminated. Do not let your current situation discourage you. I assure you that if and when you are genuinely ready to do so, you *can* eliminate your debt. Over a million people do it every year. It's hard, and it might take as much as eighteen to twenty-four months, sometimes more, of really doing without. Nonetheless, it will turn out to be one of the best things you have ever done in your life.

Adopt the Right Attitude

Are you willing to make the commitment needed to eliminate debt? Are you ready to pay the price involved? Until you are, your debt is not going to go away. If you are ready, the first step is to adopt the right attitude:

- There are one or more undermining attitudes that are the root cause of your debt situation. You need to find and work on what it is. Until you do, it will be very difficult to permanently end your debt. On my website I provide information on this subject, plus links to sites, articles and books that can help you in this area.

- Immediately stop breaking the rules of money, especially rules #1 and #2, which tell you to maintain a positive attitude and exercise the discipline to do what you said you'd do in order to get what you want. Once you do, you will begin to see the many situations where spending money will end up making you less happy, and where the small immediate pleasure of spending is wiped out by the negative results that follow.

- Understand that you almost certainly already make enough money. Becoming money smart is seldom about how much you make. The only valid exceptions to this are things like loss of your job, being hit with huge medical bills, or having a large family depending on you, and you are the only breadwinner. If you are dealing with these challenging "just-in-time" subjects, you may find helpful information on my website.

Take Action

With your positive attitude intact and some understanding of the root problem(s) involved, here are the specific steps you need to take:

- Talk openly with your family about the situation. Every member of the household must agree to reduce spending until your family has solved this problem for good.
- Do an honest, realistic, and thorough job on your Spending and Saving Plan.
- Stop all borrowing! Do not borrow any more money for *any* reason other than for a true emergency, such as a job loss or large unexpected medical bills.
- Write down every single expenditure, every day for thirty days. The few minutes a day you dedicate to this exercise will have amazing results. Well before the month is up, your mistakes, problems, as well as the solutions should start becoming clear.
- Cut up every credit card and every department store charge card. No exceptions. Use only a debit Visa or MasterCard tied to your checking account for your non-cash purchases. Keep a separate debit card for each adult so that there is complete accountability and no confusion about how much money is available. It's better not to close any credit card accounts you are no longer using for a while, even if the balance is zero, as it could hurt your credit score a little if you do so.
- Make no new purchases of significance until your debt is eliminated.
- Always pay each bill when you receive it rather than waiting until just before it is due. If you are going to have a problem

being timely, always call your creditors beforehand and tell them when you will be making the payment.

- For every account you have, call and request an interest rate reduction. That includes car loan(s), mortgage, home equity loan(s), all of your credit cards—everything. Tell them you're going to be killing your account and switching to a better deal even if you probably can't. It's likely that you will get a lower rate right over the telephone.

- If you make only the minimum payments on credit card debt, things will slowly but surely get worse. In this situation, the awesome power of compounding, of charging interest on your interest, will work *against* you. If, on the other hand, you start paying things off, you will find it develops an enormous positive momentum. More available money each month will attack the debt and the process will begin to accelerate dramatically.

- Although you might want to take advantage of low- or no-interest balance transfer offers, be careful. If you are just doing this to delay paying off your debts it is not the way to go. Every time you transfer a balance it shows up on your credit report as a signal that you are not interested in paying off your debt. There can also be significant hidden penalties in the fine print. For example, there may be a one-time transfer fee of 3% with a 0% interest period of four months. Under these terms, the 3% actually translates to an annual interest rate of 9%, not 0%. There may also be clauses that cause you to lose the 0% and jump to a high rate if you make late payments. Also, remember Spending Rule #5:

Never Respond to Service Advertising or Infomercials. That includes any and all offers you get through the mail. Throw them out and select your best options on your own.

- If you can use money from a lower interest home equity line to pay off your debts, consider doing so.

- Always have the money you save for both debt reduction and savings taken directly out of your paycheck via direct deposit.

- If you have money in a 401(k) account you can probably take out a loan against it, but be sure you know the rules. I don't recommend doing this unless the situation is really bad. If you change jobs or get laid off, you must repay the loan immediately or it will be treated as a distribution and subject to taxes and penalties.

Continue Until You're Debt-free

- Save at least one month's worth of living expenses as emergency money if you haven't already done so.

- Unless you are absolutely confident you are and will remain extremely motivated, forget about which card has the highest interest rate. List your debts in sequence from the smallest amount owed to the largest. Focus on paying off the smallest one first by making only minimum payments on all the others. When you eliminate a debt you will get a very strong positive reinforcement. You want and need that reinforcement and will start to develop a very positive and addictive momentum. Each account you eliminate will give you more money to put toward paying off the next one.

- Take half of what you save from eliminating an account and add it to your emergency fund until you have four- to six-months' worth of expenses saved. With the rest of your free money, move to attacking the next smallest debt, and so on.

- If you carry a lot of debt, consider taking a temporary part-time second job and use 100% of that money for debt reduction. If there are any non-working adult members in the family, they should also consider working full- or part-time unless the cost of childcare exceeds the amount they can earn. Adding to your income, even temporarily, can be a very powerful thing when it comes to debt elimination, as it accelerates the process dramatically.

- If you have one or more car loans with a lot of payments left, sell the car and replace it with a less-expensive model that gets good gas mileage.

- If you're trying to reduce debt but not making the progress you would like, stop using your debit card. Make an envelope for each spending category. On payday, put the amount of cash needed for each category into its envelope and then do all spending using that cash. Spending cash almost always hits home and should cut your spending quite a bit.

- Get your free credit reports and fix any errors. If you're unsure of how to do that, go to my website for some links to information sources that can help you.

- If you need to repair your credit and feel you cannot work things out on your own, contact the National Foundation for Credit Counseling (NFCC) at www.nfcc.org. They will refer you to a local non-profit member organization that will properly advise you and do what they can to help you. The charges involved will be very modest and fair and they will work with you regardless of the level of debt involved.

- Whatever you do, *absolutely* tune out every advertisement for reducing or eliminating debt, including bill consolidation services and, especially, credit repair clinics—even if they say they're nonprofit. These are almost all parasites and you will lose if you call them. There are no "secrets" and the odds are terribly high you will pay a lot more than you think. By the time you're done you will be in a worse position than when you started. If you have any doubts on this advice, Google the companies in particular and the subject in general. Fees or percent of asset charges that are over $100 or so, or requirements that you have more than a certain level of debt, are red flags telling you to avoid such sources of help.

- If you feel you need to renegotiate your mortgage, do *not* contact an attorney or group or company that offers help! Contact your local NFCC organization for assistance and advice.

- If the size of your debt is just overwhelming, filing bankruptcy should be considered, but it is an option of last resort. I provide information about bankruptcy on my website. After learning more, if you feel you are or may be at that point, first sit down with your local NFCC organization. They will help you, without a vested interest, to make the right decision.

In Conclusion

Eliminating a sizeable amount of debt takes time and discipline, but whatever temporary sacrifices you make will be well worth it for a better tomorrow. As you proceed, watch how the momentum and the feeling of success build as your debts get eliminated. Not only will you end up free of debt; all that money you were paying out will be yours to keep. What a positive change that will bring to your life going forward. (For references to additional information on getting out of debt and rebuilding your credit, please visit my website.)

CHAPTER EIGHT

Paying for an Education

Education can be very expensive. Although this chapter concentrates on the subject of post-high-school education—technical schooling and/or a college education—we will first take a quick look at some of the issues involved in paying for a primary or high school education.

For those of you who are already, or are considering, paying for a private elementary or high school education, you may well be doing a good thing. In many communities, our government-run schooling system has become nothing short of a disaster for today's children. Choosing to send your children to a private school because of serious deficiencies in your local public schools, if you can afford to do so, is probably a good thing. If, however, your local schools are indeed good, and academic and/or peer superiority is your motive, you may be doing both yourself and your children a disservice. You may end up paying an awful lot of money for a slightly better academic education, but quite possibly a worse education when it comes to life experience.

I lived through such a situation when we moved to a rich community while our children were still in high school. We found the education to be no better than that in the middle-class community we had moved from. The bigger surprise was when we discovered that the values of their new peers were in no way what we wanted for our children. The dominant values promoted the idea that life is all about "me" with an unhealthy overemphasis on status and materialism and a social life centered heavily on drinking and partying. Looking back on that situation and others like it that I have seen over the years, I now realize that the children of the well-to-do are frequently not a happy bunch of campers. Obviously, this is not always true and the right educational choice will depend on the specific circumstances involved. I'm just cautioning you to be sure to consider the whole picture.

Also, remember what an important role you play in your kids' education. Do not rely solely on the schools to educate your kids. Add to that education yourself. Start with talking to your kids and teaching them things they need to know that aren't likely to be covered in school. If you can afford it, pay for some extra private tutoring for subjects your kids are interested in.

I married for a second time and now have a fifteen-year-old daughter. I told her I thought she should consider taking martial arts, as it's such a discipline and character-builder. She really liked the idea and has been going for over six months now. Then she introduced a second idea to my wife and me. She's really good with computers and bugged us to give her the opportunity to learn more. We were fortunate to find a young cutting-edge techie who is now teaching her how to diagnose and fix hardware and software problems. Maybe she'll use those skills to make $40 an hour in her spare time in college. Regardless, what a great skill set to have. It sure makes her a stronger candidate for most jobs, too.

Look at the Whole Picture

It is certainly possible that a four-year academic education (henceforth referred to as a "college education") can offer a better life through superior jobs, more money, and a life-enriching experience. But is it necessary? Is it worth the crippling debt-loads parents and students must often take on these days in order to get it? Most importantly, is it the best route to a successful and happy life for your kid? Many parents automatically assume that their children should go to college. Yet college dropout rates in this country are nothing short of disastrous, and that doesn't begin to count all of the students who end up graduating even though they should never have gone in the first place.

According to a *New York Times* article on September 8, 2009:

> At its top levels, the American system of higher education may be the best in the world. Yet in terms of its core mission—turning teenagers into educated college graduates—much of the system is simply failing. Only 33 percent of the freshmen who enter the University of Massachusetts, Boston, graduate within six years. Less than 41 percent graduate from the University of Montana, and 44 percent from the University of New Mexico.

To me this is just a part of a bigger set of signs that times have changed. A college education is no longer the end-all-be-all of education, nor is it a guarantee of success. There is no end to the number of careers and self-employment opportunities that do not require such an education and that can provide both a very good income and a very satisfying life. Obviously some fields require the standard academic route. If you want to be a doctor, lawyer, scientist, engineer, teacher, or architect, for example, it's the only way to go. However, in my experience, many employers now value the skill set more than the proven ability to be taught. They no longer have the time or the money to invest in teaching the skills they need. They want people who will be productive the minute they walk through the door.

These skills can be acquired in more places than in a four-year academic institution. It may mean a two-year degree, an online degree, trade or technical schooling, real-world work experience, or any combination of these. These alternatives may end up costing a lot less than a regular four-year college education and also provide a better entrance to the work force. Maybe the best path for your kid is to start his or her own small business. After all, small business is historically one of the most successful routes to both financial and personal success.

It so happens that the subject of whether or not to send a child to college is one I faced personally. My youngest son, Dan, is extremely bright and was designing video games in high school thirty years ago, back when they essentially didn't even exist yet. His mother and I thought that he should go to college. Well Dan didn't exactly see it that way. His college experience lasted a grand total of about two weeks, after which he pretty much cut every class, flunked out royally, and never went back. After all, it was his life and he was the one in control of it.

Don't feel sorry for Dan. He went on to become one of what the techies call the "Masters of the Universe," the "Architect" of a cutting-edge software firm. Every time you use the internet, or even your cell phone, Dan has probably been there somewhere. For Dan, the noncollege route was his path to a very successful career. Best of all, he loves what he does.

In telling you this story I am by no means suggesting that your kid follow Dan's path. Each person is unique, as should be his or her path in life.

As you make this truly critical life decision, however, think about this: The national high school graduation rate is about 70%, with 42% of those graduates then entering a four-year college program. As covered above, roughly half of that 42% will end up graduating with a degree, which is just 21% of the students that graduated high school on time.

Remember in chapter two, "Your Goals and Dreams" (page 23) that studies fail to link academic IQ and success in life? It is other factors that are more significant. Please keep this in mind as you help your child choose a path that will lead to success and happiness.

So when considering with your child if college is the best step after high school, keep an open mind. Also consider that for the many young people who start college but ultimately drop out, college was a loss of money and time that could likely have been better spent. As with all important decisions, the choice is yours and only you can make the best selection for your family. The bottom line is clear. Attending a four-year academic institution is a good idea for many, but for others it is not. Your decision here is a very critical one. Which group is your child in?

Making It Happen

Assuming you have decided that a post-high-school education is the way for your children to go, and assuming you do not already have the money you need, there are basically four ways to pay for an education: save money for that purpose; work one's way through school; take out education loans; and/or qualify for scholarships, grants and/or work study programs. Let's start with the option of saving money.

There are currently many different education saving programs to choose from. For the most part, their purpose is to offer significant tax advantages for money saved and used for education. Listed below are the most common choices at the time I am writing this.

- State 529 College Savings Plans that vary by state
- Independent 529 College Savings Plans sponsored by groups of colleges
- Coverdell Education Savings Account
- UGMA—Uniform Gifts to Minors
- UTMA—Uniform Transfer to Minors
- Your tax-deferred account(s)—Funds used if and when you wish
- A Roth Account—Funds used if and when you wish
- A Hope Scholarship
- A Lifetime Learning Credit

Don't let this list confuse you, as I will sort it out and tell you how to get help, if and when you need it. If you have no debt except a house and are saving the maximum tax-deferred amount allowed by law, you qualify as a "strong saver." If you're not yet a "strong saver," your decision as to whether and how to save for advanced education is very simple. You don't.

You should not be saving anything in an education-specific account, nor should you personally take out any loans for that purpose. Your first priority is to yourself for your future needs and financial freedom. Only after you have done all you can in that regard should you consider saving for anyone's education. This may sound very selfish, but it is not. The bottom line is to do nothing until you have no debt and have maxed out your tax-deferred retirement contributions.

The only one taking care of your future is probably you. You can't count on anyone else being willing or able to do it. It is unfair and, frankly, unwise for you to risk your future quality of life to save for someone's education. How do you know if a child will end up going to college or technical school or that they should attend either one? If they do, what is wrong with a mixture of them working their way through school, applying for grants and/or work-study programs and, if necessary, accepting education loans. The real-life experience and the confidence gained will probably prove invaluable when they venture forth into the world. Should you happen to be a grandparent, this same advice applies to you, too. Do not risk your future quality of life for someone's education.

My message is simple: First things first. Concentrate on becoming that strong saver and on insuring your own future. After you have done so, you will be in a position to save toward your children's education, and you should.

Now, for you strong savers: first, I congratulate you. You should be very proud of your achievement. Having taken the right steps for your own future, you are now in a position to save some additional money for your children's potential educational expenses. However, choosing from among the various government programs available for saving for an education can be confusing. Most of those programs turn out to be a bad idea and the rules and the program choices change quite frequently.

At the moment, the best plan for most people is probably a College Savings Plan based on Section 529 of the Internal Revenue Code.

You can't count on that still being true into the future, so do your homework and, if necessary, consider getting some professional help for this decision. (See page 179 for Guidelines for Hiring Financial Professionals.)

Always keep all education money in your name and not in your child's name. There are good reasons to do this. Consider that at eighteen a child can take the money and spend it on whatever he wishes. You may have more children or grandchildren come along than you expect, or you may find that you want to help some more than others and don't want to divide the money equally. You may not like or approve of that little kid's choices after he or she grows up. And finally, how can you guarantee you might not need the money yourself some day?

The solution to this problem is an **IRA**. The current tax laws allow you to withdraw as much as you like from a Roth or regular IRA at any time for educational purposes without prepayment penalty. If it's a Roth, the taxes have already been paid. For a regular IRA you will have to pay the taxes. Using an IRA allows you to save for the education of your children or grandchildren without restricting in any way how much or for whom the money gets used. You are also free to change your mind if you end up needing that money for yourself.

Even for you strong savers, the amount of money required to pay for an advanced education can be scary. A very common reaction is to feel overwhelmed by the impossibility of coming up with such large sums and choosing to do nothing. That is a bad decision. Save what you can, as it all really adds up. A parent's contribution, along with a student's part-time work, possible grants, and, perhaps, a modest amount of student loans, can all work together very well. Maintain a positive attitude that you and your children will find a way to make it all happen, and you will.

As you lay out your plan of attack, here are some things to do or consider:

- While your child should actively participate in the selection of his or her college, the final decision must be yours when it comes to the amount of money to be invested. This is a huge financial decision affecting both your future and that of your child, and you are almost certainly far more qualified than a teenager is to make such a decision. On the other hand, I believe it is a bad idea for you to be pressuring or dictating which institution he or she "should" attend or even which educational path they should pursue. You certainly want your child to participate actively in those decisions.

- So how do you go about balancing both of these objectives and arriving at the best answer? To me, it starts by recognizing that this is a key opportunity to teach your child about money. If you haven't already done so, explain the family's financial situation, as well as your plans and needs for the future. Your child needs to understand what it takes to make the money necessary for the family, as well as to see the ways in which that money can be used for the benefit of each family member. Once that has been done, I believe you will be in a position to have a productive discussion on the issues and alternatives involved. (I provide more information on teaching your children about money on my website, www.MoneySmartOnline.com.)

- Do not choose a "name" school you cannot afford. Studies have proven over and over that success in life is seldom related to either the cost or prestige of the school one attends, or to a person's academic performance. For most students, the return on investment of a more expensive name is usually not there. There are, admittedly, a few fields of work and a few schools that are exceptions to this, but not many. Most employers don't care where a degree is from, just that it's there. For these reasons, seriously consider selecting an in-state college or a public college, as they are usually a lot cheaper. Another option worth serious consideration is having the student live at home and attend a local community college for the first two years. The earned degree will carry only the name of the final college.

The table below of annual college costs shows the huge difference college selection can make in the cost involved. Notice the impact different costs can have on the lives of those paying them. Best of all, observe that a college education is seldom out of reach.

Annual College Costs			
College Type	Tuition & Fees	Room & Board	Total Costs*
Public Two–year:	$2,544	–	–
Public Four–year:			
Resident:	$7,020	$8,193	$15,213
Out of state:	$18,548	$8,193	$26,741
Private Four–year:	$26,273	$9,363	$35,636
Source- College Board, 2009-2010 Trends in College Pricing			

- Working a part-time job can go a long way to help a student cover expenses while going to college. There is also the possibility of participating in a co-op or internship program. There's lots of room to be creative. For example, the people who deliver pizzas at night can make some pretty darn good money from the tips. The benefits can often be a lot more than just the money. Regardless of the job chosen, exposure to the real world of work is also likely to turn out to be some of the best education a person can get. It has also been shown that students who work ten to twelve hours a week are actually more efficient in their studies and tend to increase their grade point average while working.

- When needed, a moderate amount of debt for the student to pay off may not be such a bad thing. The key word here is *moderate*. It is so very easy to depend on borrowing rather than doing things like saving money or working through college. The pressures and problems from too much graduation debt are not a good thing. If your child takes this route, do everything you can to keep the amount borrowed as low as possible.

- As discussed, technical schooling is the way to go for many young people. Should you choose that route, however, be careful to select a school with good credentials, relevant curriculum, and a solid track record for job placement in the intended field. Unfortunately, there is a significant number of technical schools that are more interested in their profits than in the success of their students.

- An option that is often overlooked is the U.S. Armed Forces and Armed Forces Reserves, including their ROTC (Reserve Officers Training Corp) options. Every year they turn out to be an excellent path for about 200,000 young people. For the right person, the benefits can be impressive. First, there's the money provided for education. Next, it doesn't hurt to have both some job training and additional life experience under your belt before going to college or getting military training during college. The combination of the discipline gained, job training, and real-life experience involved can be quite powerful. The result is often that the student gets more out of the college experience, performs better, and ends up both landing a better job after graduation and being more successful in life. Considering the years of service required after college, this route is not for everyone, but for some it is very worthwhile.

- Another option is for the student to take time off from schooling to work, rather than going non-stop for four straight years. The potential benefits are pretty much the same as those just discussed under the Armed Forces option. And, of course, there is no obligation to serve after college is completed.

If you are among those who feel that you've let your kids down by not having saved enough, take heart. According to The College Board, about 65% of college students currently pay less than $10,000 a year for tuition and fees, and more than 40% pay less than $6,000. This doesn't mean that you should do nothing, as every bit helps.

Grants, Scholarships, Work-study Programs, Education Loans

An enormous amount of scholarship and grant money is given out each year. These are gifts of money that usually do not have to be repaid. I must caution you, however, not to depend on grants or scholarships as part of your planning. In response to being stunned by the numbers involved in a college education, many parents convince themselves that their children are the exception and will earn sizeable scholarships or non-repayable aid packages. You need to be realistic, even conservative, about whether this might happen, since there is tremendous competition for the limited resources available.

That said, you should certainly put in the effort to apply to every grant or scholarship for which you or your child may be eligible. Most high schools and all colleges have financial aid offices or personnel, and they can be an excellent source of help on this subject.

The sooner you apply, the better. Always put in your application the very first week you are allowed to do so, as it increases your chance of success. Also, understand that there is no grace period for submitting any financial aid application late.

Grants

Grants are essentially gifts of money that do not usually need to be paid back unless the student drops out of school very early in the term. They are issued mostly by the federal government, although some grant money is also available at the state level. Federal grants are renewable so long as the student maintains eligibility, whereas state grants may or may not be. Most grants are given to families with very low income, although there are some limited situations where academic performance is the primary determining factor. Many private name brand educational institutions have a substantial amount of endowment money that is awarded to students they want who can't afford the costs involved, so be sure to look into those sources if the circumstances might apply to you.

Scholarships

Scholarships are awarded by a wide variety of sources including families, individuals, educational institutions, corporations, service organizations, and religious organizations. The federal government also provides some scholarship money that is awarded through the state. Many high schools will also have a number of locally sponsored scholarships available. Many scholarships are not renewable, requiring the student to re-apply again each year, and few cover more than a portion of school costs. There are several sites that can assist in your scholarship search including finaid.org, scholarships.com, fastweb.com, and collegeboard .com. For example, fastweb.com maintains a database of about 180,000 scholarships to consider and allows you to enter search criteria to find those that apply to you.

When you do your searches, do not fail to answer all the questions or the lists you get back will include a lot of scholarships for which you are not eligible. Do not skip over the ones with the small dollar amounts as it all adds up. Should someone offer to do these searches for you for a fee, I'd suggest saving your money and doing it yourself for free as it's really a pretty straightforward process.

Work-study Programs

Work-study programs are a good deal for students. They work ten to twelve hours a week, receive regular pay checks, gain experience working, and do not have to pay back the money. Many of the jobs are on the campus, in the library, the cafeterias, and/or at the information booths. Answering telephones or working in the various offices, grounds, and landscaping are other possibilities. If the students change jobs periodically, they will have several experiences and sets of references to use when they are looking for full-time jobs in the future.

The jobs will be listed in the financial aid office on campus and students can pretty much rest assured their work hours can usually be changed to fit their school hours, including during finals week. This is a big advantage over working just any job they may have found, where it can sometimes be difficult to keep both the job and the school schedule. The minimum pay for work-study jobs is the federal minimum, but many will pay more depending on the duties required. The largest of these programs is the federal work-study program. This is "first come-first served" money so the student must complete an application in the first week or two of January for the school year that begins the following August/September.

Education Loans

Most education loans come from the U.S. Department of Education. These loans usually offer a more favorable rate than other alternatives. The Department of Education's website, www.federalstudentaid.ed.gov, provides information on federal student-aid programs. The first step to getting any federal money, and most state money, for college is to complete the Free Application for Federal Student Aid, or FAFSA. Apply at www.fafsa.ed.gov. Your state's Department of Education website should also be visited to see what is offered. Some financial aid provided by your state or college may require you to submit additional information or applications.

CHAPTER NINE

Planning for Your Future

At this point you've identified your goals and dreams and have a written plan for how you will spend and save your money each month. If you are in debt, you now know what you must do to solve that problem. In this chapter I will explain how to go about planning for your retirement and/or financial freedom. First, the subject of understanding the numbers will be covered—the impact of inflation, taxes, compounding, and the **rate of return** on your investments. After that you'll see how to create your own personal plan. Finally, several additional topics that should prove to be of value at some point will be discussed, including:

- Guidelines for Hiring Financial Professionals
- Selecting Tax-deferred Accounts
- Taxes: Return Preparation, Tax Advice
- Estate Planning
- Legal Matters

Understanding the Numbers

To make good investment and long-term financial-planning decisions, you first need to understand several very powerful real-world influences on the money you save and invest. The money you save today will grow over time. The value or buying power of that money, however, will shrink over time. Anticipating how much it will grow, and how much it will buy in the future, is essential to making a solid plan. To reasonably predict what today's savings and investments will do for you tomorrow, you need to consider the impacts of taxes, inflation, compounding, and the rate of return you get on your investments.

Taxes

When it comes to your decisions regarding investing, spending, and saving, your overall tax rate isn't what matters. What matters is the tax rate you pay on the very last dollars you earn in a year, because that is the rate which determines the amount of taxes you are saving or deferring with your decisions. For the average family, the combined tax rate on their last dollars earned, both federal and state, is about 40%. This means that deferring those taxes will give this average family all of that additional money to invest for years and years to come. The higher your tax rate, the higher the amount involved.

Deferring taxes is almost always in your favor. The primary way to do that is to contribute to tax-protected accounts. If your company matches your contributions to such an account, like a 401(k) account, it's an even bigger "wow." Matching money is nothing less than a tax-deferred cash bonus—free extra money—so do not turn it down by failing to make the contribution that will draw the maximum match.

In addition to tax-protected accounts, there are several other ways to save on your taxes. The interest on your home mortgage is usually tax deductible and the investment return on your primary residence is either tax-deferred or tax-free, depending on what the tax laws allow if and when you sell. Owning your own business and investing in real estate can also offer significant tax advantages. Are these things you should do? Maybe. You'll know better after we discuss those subjects.

For now, I will leave you with one surefire strategy: Put every penny you can up to the legal limits in tax-protected accounts. There is no other investment that will give you anything like the instant, guaranteed return you're going to get by deferring tax payments.

They say a picture is worth a thousand words, so here is a picture for you. The chart below assumes an investment of $500 a month at an annual return of 8%. The solid line shows what happens when the taxes are deferred. The dashed line shows the result when 40% of the profit each year is lost to taxes. As you can see, the impact from delaying taxes can create a pretty amazing difference over time.

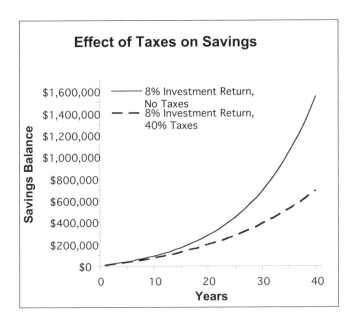

Inflation

Inflation is the rise in the prices of goods and services. Over time, it causes the value of a dollar to fall as you no longer can purchase as much with that dollar as you previously could. For instance, what once cost $1 in years past now costs $3, and in the future that same item will cost a lot more. Today it may cost you $40,000 a year to support your lifestyle. In twenty years it will cost a lot more to support the same lifestyle because prices will go up.

The average annual inflation rate in the U.S. has been 3.3% over the last ninety years and 4.87% since 1972. Based on this data I recommend using an inflation rate of 4% in your financial planning. At an inflation rate of 4% per year, a $40,000 cost of living will cost $41,600 next year, or $1,600 more. That may seem pretty harmless, but it adds up quickly. In five years you'll need $48,800 for that same lifestyle; in ten years it will be $59,600. In twenty years you'll need a little more than double, or $88,900, because the buying power of the dollar will be cut in half by inflation. A reasonable assumption is that the real value of a dollar in twenty years, in terms of what it will buy, will be 50¢. This means that an annual inflation rate of 4.0% will double your cost of living in twenty years.

As long as you're working, inflation is not a big deal, as your pay will usually rise to track the rise in inflation. The difficulty arises when you are looking to your savings to cover all or most of your living costs. If you make a return of 4% after taxes on those savings, you actually are making nothing when inflation is taken into account. You are breaking even. I do not tell you this to upset you. I just want to be sure you factor in the impact of inflation into your plans and decisions, as it is a fact of life. Inflation can be a difficult thing to compensate for. Provided you have enough assets, income, and/or years left to work, it will probably not be a problem. This speaks volumes about the importance of having a well-thought-out plan for your life and not procrastinating with it. Also, it speaks to the necessity to spend, save, and invest your money wisely.

Compounding

Here's some good news. Unlike taxes and inflation, compounding is a friend that can solve the problem of inflation and a lot more. Compounding is the effect of getting interest on your interest and profit on your profit. Compounding occurs when the money you earn on your investments is reinvested and then that larger balance earns even more money. The effects are exponential as the money grows faster and faster because of the additional money you make on the new money added.

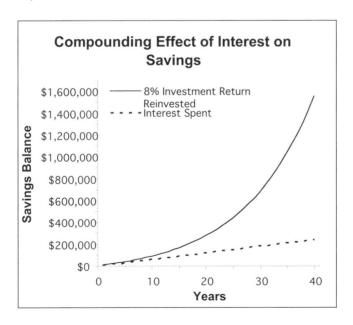

The chart assumes an investment of $500 a month at an annual return of 8%. The solid line shows what happens when the money earned each year is reinvested. The dashed line assumes that the 8% made each year is spent and, therefore, no compounding is taking place. Just look at the difference! Provided you give it enough time, the impact of compounding can be nothing short of amazing.

Rate of Return

The rate of return you get on your investments is determined in large part by the level of risk versus reward involved. Over the long haul, if you take no risk you'll slowly lose, as your money is eroded by inflation. As discussed, you should expect this to be the case for most fixed investments such as CDs, money markets, Treasury Bonds, etc. If there is modest risk, you're likely to be in the 8%–10% return range. This is a good return to shoot for, especially for the money invested in the stock market.

When the rate of return is over 10%, the risk begins to rise. Go for too much more and the risk of losing becomes higher than the odds of winning, unless it's a business arena you know really well. If you shoot for too much you will also find that greed and fear begin to warp otherwise sound investment decision making. It's all common sense, really. No risk, no reward; modest risk, modest reward; high risk, high reward potential. High risk is something you should not take on unless it is an investment arena you are extremely familiar with. For an investment area you do not know well, higher risk can often mean just that, higher risk, and *without* the increased likelihood of higher reward.

The investment return for fixed-income investments over the last one hundred years has averaged about 5%. As for the stock market, the average return for the S&P 500 from 1950–2008 has been 10.8% and consisted of 2.4% real earnings growth, 3.8% inflation, 3.6% dividends, and 1% multiple expansion (valuing stocks at a higher multiple of the earnings of the companies involved). As our country is more mature, economically, at this point, its growth is likely to be somewhat slower in the years ahead. We have also recently come through a period that has created unrealistic expectations and there are always "experts" who will lead you to believe you can do a lot better. Given all of the above, I believe it's wise to plan on getting no more than 8% on your investments over the long haul.

This leads to another key piece of information. A 5% tax-deferred return provides only 1% after inflation. At 8%, you end up with 4% after inflation. The 8% rate of return is *four* times the return that was made at 5%. The impact of every 1% is huge. While a cost difference on an investment of 1% or 2% seems small, the impact is dramatic over the long haul. In fact, 2% can cost you almost half your total return. (In the section on investing in stocks and mutual funds, starting on page 231, I will discuss this again in relation to commissions and fees.)

A very commonly pitched approach by the financial community these days is to recommend having a "**wrap account**." The pitch is that there are no commissions, just a set annual fee of a small percentage of the assets being managed. This way, their interests are your interests: that is, to grow your money. The problem is that the fees plus other costs involved are likely to run about 2% or so and, once again, 2% will, on average, cost you about half your real average return. The bottom line is that it's a good deal for them, but bad for you.

Whenever you wish to calculate the impact of these factors—taxes, inflation, compounding, and rate of return—go to my website where

I provide a basic multi-year calculator and also a retirement planning calculator.

Planning for Retirement/Financial Freedom

In chapter two, "Your Goals and Dreams," you established your goals for your retirement and/or financial freedom. This section will help to insure that you have a comprehensive and executable plan for achieving those goals.

I originally assumed that I would just recommend the best existing online retirement calculator for you to use, but was surprised that I couldn't find one that did a really good job. So, I've created one for you that is comprehensive and easy to use. The worksheet on page 172 lists the input you will need to create your plan, and following is an explanation of how to assemble this information. Use this worksheet as a guide to help you gather your information, then go to my website and enter your data to see how your plans will unfold over time. A printable version of the worksheet is also available on my website. Additionally, you will find a simple spending and savings calculator, which you can use to project individual sets of numbers into the future.

Gathering the Worksheet Information

The following is the input you will need for your plan. For simplicity's sake I have used the word *retirement* rather than *retirement/financial freedom* in my explanations. Do not let that mislead you. As explained in chapter two, "Your Goals and Dreams," financial freedom, not retirement, should be the goal for most people.

1. Identify your employee retirement benefits, if any.

If your employer or ex-employer offers any retirement benefits, find out the amount you are likely to receive and enter the monthly sum expected. Most employers will provide a projected benefit statement on request. If you are married and your spouse will also be receiving retirement benefits at some point, enter his or her monthly payment separately. If you are divorced, find out if you are entitled to any benefits from your ex-spouse's plan.

2. Estimate your Social Security benefits.

For the average retiree, Social Security has been providing about 35%–40% of their pre-retirement earnings. Provided you've been working for enough years, you can go to www.ssa.gov/estimator to get an estimate of your benefits. If not, call the Social Security Administration at 1-800-772-1213 to see if they can provide a free statement of your estimated benefits, and then learn the rules involved by going to www.socialsecurity.gov.

If you are married, enter the information for each of you separately. If you are divorced or your spouse is deceased, and you were married for enough years, you may have a choice between your own benefits or 50% of your ex-spouse's benefits, which may be higher. If you have any questions on this, call the Social Security Administration and ask for help in determining whether this might apply and what to do.

Fill in the amount(s) per month expected at retirement. If the amount comes from www.ssa.gov/estimator, their estimates are given in today's dollars. If you get your estimate from any other source, be sure to enter it in today's dollars as the retirement calculator will adjust for inflation.

Name:_____   Age:_____   Age of spouse:_____

1. **Estimated employer benefits:**

   You: $_____ /Mo.   Age start benefits: _____   Inflation adjusted: ☐ Yes ☐ No

   Spouse: $_____ /Mo.   Age start benefits: _____   Inflation adjusted: ☐ Yes ☐ No

2. **Estimated Social Security benefits:**

   You: $_____ /Mo.   Age start benefits: _____

   Spouse: $_____ /Mo.   Age start benefits: _____

3. **Current retirement savings balance:** $_____

   Contribution: $_____ /Mo.

   Rate of return until retirement: _____ %   After retirement: _____ %

4. **Other assets, current value:** $_____

   Rate of return until retirement: _____ %   After retirement: _____ %

5. **Estimated earned income in retirement:**

   You: $_____ /Mo.   Years expect to work in retirement: _____

   Spouse: $_____ /Mo.   Years expect to work in retirement: _____

6. **Other income in retirement:** $_____ /Mo.   Inflation adjusted: ☐ Yes ☐ No

7. **Estimated cost of living in retirement:** $_____ /Mo.

8. **Years left before retirement:** _____

   Estimated rate of inflation: _____ %

   Estimated tax rate in retirement for non-earned income: _____ %

As to when you expect to begin drawing Social Security, I would, for now, use the age at which you are entitled to full benefits. As you approach the date at which you can choose to take partial benefits early, you can make your final decision whether to start collecting then, to wait for full eligibility, or even to delay past that date. Most people will find that starting on the date of full eligibility is probably the best way to go.

Lastly, I repeat my caution that you should expect Social Security benefits to be tied to (indexed to) your income in the not-too-distant future. If you expect to have a substantial retirement income, I would depend on little-to-no money from Social Security. If you're unsure what number to use, consider entering half the amount that you are currently expecting to get.

3. *Identify your current retirement savings.*

List the current total of all of your retirement savings and the amount you plan to save/invest each month from this point on, including any company matching dollars. The retirement calculator will assume that you will increase the amount saved annually at the rate of inflation. If you expect to substantially increase the amount you are now saving to a much higher number within the next couple of years, use that higher number. The error introduced by doing so is likely to be quite small, so I wouldn't worry about it. As for the expected rate of return, I will again recommend using 8% for your expected rate of return from the stock market and 5% for fixed income. If you have a mix of stocks and fixed income, calculate the average rate of growth expected. For example, if you have 50% of your assets at an expected return of 8%, and 50% at 5%, your expected growth rate would be 6.5% percent. If some of your savings are not tax-deferred, be sure to subtract the percent of the return lost to taxes to get an after-tax rate of return for this portion of your savings. As for your rate of return after retirement, it should be a more conservative number, probably no more than 6%.

4. *Other assets.*

If you have any additional assets or investments (such as a business or other real estate) that you plan to retain or sell, enter that amount in *today's* dollars. The retirement calculator will adjust your number for inflation. As for the equity in your home, if you plan to downsize, include in your calculations the amount expected to be freed up. Here's how: If your house is worth $275,000 if sold today, and you expect to have it paid in full by the time you retire, and you plan to downsize to what is today a $200,000 condo, the difference of $75,000 (in today's dollars) becomes your "other asset." As residential real estate historically appreciates at the rate of inflation, I suggest using that rate, about 4%, as your expected rate of return for this example. If you do not plan to downsize or become a renter at some point, I recommend excluding your home equity in your calculations and letting it serve as a source of last resort emergency backup money.

Do not underestimate the value of owning your own home free and clear. We have seen such an emphasis in recent decades on the stock market as the "end all" financial salvation that it has blurred the benefits of owning a home. For most people, owning a home will prove to be the cornerstone of the saving they do. It provides a good hedge against inflation (provided you have a fixed mortgage), increases financial flexibility, adds to a sense of security, and, as mentioned, provides further financial security if needed. Additionally, a home is the one asset you can enjoy using every day.

One option that is likely to present itself at some point during retirement is getting a reverse mortgage. A reverse mortgage is a type of loan that allows you to borrow against the equity in your home without repaying for as long as you still live in it. It can be an attractive option, but it also has its downsides. The upfront costs are usually quite significant and you can end up paying a terribly high rate of interest if you end up drawing only a small amount or borrowing for a short time. Worse yet, the FTC (Federal Trade Commission) claims that reverse mortgages have the highest incidence of fraud in the mortgage business. As you can guess, I am not a fan of reverse mortgages. Depending on your situation, you might be a lot better off getting a home equity line of credit or selling and downsizing.

5. *Estimated earned income in retirement.*

Decide whether either you or your spouse will continue working in retirement on a full- or part-time basis, for how many years you expect to do so, and the amount you expect to make per month. Enter that information in today's *after tax* dollars; the retirement calculator will automatically adjust that number for inflation. As you look at this option, don't limit your thinking to working only for others. Take some time to look around you. You will find the world is full of opportunities to make money on your own. Understand that things have changed when it comes to retirement. The old pattern of go to school, work, and retire is disappearing for most people. The new pattern is more likely to be go to school, work, and change jobs (maybe a lot), go back to school, work, retire, go back to work, and then maybe retire again.

As I said in chapter two, "Your Goals and Dreams," this very often turns out to be a better quality of life.

6. Other income in retirement.

Should you have income from any other source not covered above, enter the current amount per month and indicate whether or not that amount is adjusted for inflation.

7. Estimate your cost of living in retirement.

Most people should plan on needing about 70%–80% of their current spending level after they stop working. Again, enter the amount per month in today's dollars; the retirement calculator will automatically adjust that number for inflation. To assist you in the estimation of your future cost of living, refer to the Spending and Saving Plan Worksheet on page 136 and consider how each of the items in your current budget will change in retirement.

Be especially careful when estimating the cost of your health care insurance. To estimate your future health insurance costs you need to understand the benefits you are likely to get from Medicare and the costs involved. Go to www.medicare.gov, which will give you a pretty good rundown. You should expect Medicare costs to rise far faster than inflation over the years to come. I would use at least 40%–50% more than the premium amounts people are currently paying under Medicare as your input ("today") cost. The same holds true for private health insurance.

Also be sure to account for the issue of long-term care in your plans, with either a policy or a family circumstance you are confident you can count on at some point in the future. Most people should be purchasing long-term health care insurance at some point in their fifties. In chapter thirteen, "Choosing Insurance," this subject is covered in more detail. (See page 309.)

8. Enter the remaining input information.

Fill in the number of years left before retirement or until your target date for financial freedom. Should you also wish to have a rough estimate of your expected life span and that of your spouse, you can find links to life-expectancy calculators on my website.

I recommend using an inflation rate of 4% in your financial planning. The average annual inflation rate in the U.S. has been 3.3% over the last ninety years, and 4.87% since 1972. The most commonly used inflation factor these days is 3.5%; however, based on the average since 1972 I feel it is more prudent to use a higher number.

For your retirement tax rate for your non-earned income (income from other than working), hopefully you will not have to pay anything in the way of Social Security and Medicare taxes on that income. I do believe, however, that regular income taxes will be somewhat higher in the future. Federal rates are at their lowest level in decades and the now-massive federal deficit points to no choice but having to pay higher taxes in the future. For these reasons, I would calculate your non-earned income retirement tax rate as follows: Say you expect to need $60,000 per year to live on, and you need to make $78,000 today to net that amount after taxes. Assuming that your current Social Security/Medicare taxes are about $6,000, the remaining $12,000 is your income tax. That's an overall income tax rate of 15.4%. To be safe, I'd add at least 5% to cover the strong possibility of higher rates in the future. For this example, you would get an assumed rate of 20% on any non-earned income you may have after retirement, including the money you draw from your tax-deferred accounts. Also, if you plan on working after retirement, be sure to check the rules regarding how much you can make, before you will be required to pay additional Social Security/Medicare taxes.

Once you've gotten your report, if you are happy with your projected results, I congratulate you. If you are like most people, you are somewhere between unhappy with them and quite worried by your first results. Do not let that discourage you. What you need to do in this instance is take a hard, new look at all of your plans. Examine the factors and approaches that can or may change those results. Pay particular attention to how you can reduce your cost of living in retirement and on how you can save more now. Making small adjustments in both of those areas can make a big difference in the outcome of your plan.

A shortage of time to save is the most difficult obstacle you may encounter. To address this, the first option is to live a lot more frugally now to save a lot more. The second is to pare back your lifestyle and spending expectations for retirement. I remind you again that most spending is optional, so look for the right balance between your spending of today and your needs of tomorrow, including whether you can and should downsize your retirement plans a little. As you consider this balance, I recommend you go to my website and take a look at the advice and links provided there.

The third option is to delay your retirement. Use the retirement calculator again and see what happens if you delay your retirement for three or four years more. Such a move can often go a long way toward solving any shortfalls, as it both preserves and adds to your assets. Are you planning to retire just because you're sixty-five, or because you hate your job? It's far better to base your decision on waiting until you've made the money you need to retire comfortably. You may also find that a decision to continue working, either on a full-time or part-time basis, may not be such a bad thing. Many people end up getting a better overall quality of life than they would have had being totally "free," by following that path.

Guidelines for Hiring Financial Professionals

First, I trust you now clearly understand that you must make your own investment decisions and that you can usually do so better than the experts, regardless of the titles or credentials they might have. In chapters ten and eleven I will show you how to go about doing so and that there are ways to keep this task from becoming too complicated. If you've absorbed all that I have said in this book and still feel you need help on your investment decisions, your next step should be to turn to someone you know and trust to help you. Turning to an expert for input needed to make an investment decision should be your next-to-last resort; having them make the decision for you should be your very last resort.

I must caution you that selecting a good financial professional is truly a difficult thing. Despite your best effort you may end up choosing the wrong person. Once you have selected and begun working with someone, I urge you not to just accept his or her recommendations without first learning a decent amount on your own to double-check them. The recommendation they make may not be the right choice for you and who you thought was a good professional may turn out not to be so good after all. You may be thinking that's why you're hiring the professional, that it's his or her job to do the homework, not yours. Unfortunately, it's not that simple. The only way you can both protect yourself and get the results you seek is to invest the time to learn a decent bit on your own on the subject involved.

I say these things because, for any given job, an awful lot of the people doing it are not that good at what they do. Worse yet, how can you know for sure if a financial professional is right? How can the people who referred them know? Yes, I understand they trust them, have known them, and have used them for years, but I still ask you, How do they know they're good? If you get a referral for a plumber, a cook, a carpenter, or an auto mechanic, the person referring them has hard real-world proof that the person is good. How do you do that with an estate planning expert, a tax expert, and so on? How do you measure their performance? So they made you or saved you money, but maybe it was a lot less than they should have.

Here is an example. In telling you this story I will end up embarrassing myself but, hey, it won't be the first time. I am especially embarrassed because it took place just recently. After all my decades in business I knew better. I just got lazy.

Over the last ten years I built a small wholesale company and turned its operation over to a terrific general manager. I wanted to find out what might be the best tax-deferral program to set up for the company, a 401(k) or whatever, and my general manager asked if we could use the guy she had used for years to manage her investments to advise us. She knew and trusted him and he had, coincidentally, spent the majority of his career as a CPA/tax accountant. The guy's background couldn't have been better so we decided to use him. He, in turn, had a working relationship with a decent-sized area firm that specialized in setting up such company plans. I also had an accountant doing our company and personal tax returns. I told him about the recommended plan and he seemed comfortable with the selection. So we held a company meeting where the two experts explained the recommended plan to all. Everyone was happy and the new plan was installed. Sounds good, huh? It's hard to go wrong when you had not one but *three* different tax experts involved, each from a different company.

Are you ready? The decision cost me a *lot* of money out of pocket that next year and my general manager was also financially hurt. Our people lost too, as we would've given them more money. The experts didn't do their homework properly and recommended the *wrong* plan! Three experts were involved! So whose fault was it? It was *mine*, that's whose! Why didn't I do just a little homework instead of just trusting the experts?

The moral of the story is clear. Do enough homework to optimize the odds you're getting what's best for you. I wish it could be simpler, that we didn't have to do any work and could let the pros do it all. Unfortunately, that's not the smart thing to do. I recommend that every four or five years or so you should go out and interview other professionals and not just comfortably continue on forever with the same people. I now tell them that no offense is intended; it's company policy. If you're a couple, just blame the other party.

One of the rules of spending wisely is to never respond to service advertising or infomercials. This rule also applies here. Good businesses and professionals get the majority of their business from repeat business and referrals, and the bad ones get most of their business from advertising. Do not contact any financial professional as a result of advertising. All candidates should be selected by referral from people you know and respect or by homework you do personally.

Always find and interview at least three candidates before making your selection. If you're not satisfied you've found someone you feel is good, do not settle. Find and interview more candidates. The modest amount of time involved is likely to be very well worth it.

Think through and write down a list of the questions you want to ask them before you start your interviews. Don't start with your questions. Let the candidate go first. Pay *a lot* of attention to the questions asked to learn about you and your financial circumstances and needs. By the kinds of questions they ask—and don't ask—you can often learn a lot between the lines. Also, if they aren't very thorough, it's a bad sign.

Do not be influenced by titles and credentials. Most of the candidates will have these things. The list of potential credentials and certifications is endless and, in the final analysis, are pretty much meaningless when it comes to choosing who to go with. What will be a lot more valuable will be them having been recommended, your personal reaction to them, and the information they give you.

Ask them for a complete list of their services, a breakdown of their charges, and how they are paid. Get an estimate of what their total charges are likely to be. Avoid services tied to commissions of any kind. Whenever possible, you want to get a set fee for the job. Do not back off to a fee per hour unless you've first sweated them out by telling them you prefer to deal with a set fee but that you'll think about it. Even if they give you a set fee, always leave and think about it. Read and absorb the crash course on negotiating in chapter fourteen (see page 335), and use that information. Consider everything to be negotiable because it often is.

Lastly, there will sometimes be instances where you can obtain the input and recommendations of more than one professional in the same field, and do so for little or no cost. This may well be a good thing to do as it may give you a better set of input than just using one source. Be careful, however, to remain fully independent and in control of all decisions.

Selecting Tax-protected Accounts

In chapter six, "Creating Your Spending and Saving Plan," I provided a priority sequence for the money you allocate to debt reduction and saving. Please be sure to follow that priority sequence. Once you hit the point where you can and should be putting money in a tax-protected account, you are then faced with the process of selecting the right type of account or accounts. As the choices and the rules are constantly changing I will only provide a very brief introduction to this subject based on IRS rules as of 2010.

Basically there are three types of tax-protected accounts. They are deductible accounts, non-deductible accounts, and Roth IRA accounts.

With a deductible account you get to deduct the money you put into the account from your tax bill. This means you pay no taxes today on the money you put into such an account, but you will pay full taxes on every dollar that comes out at some point in the future. The advantage is that you get to make money on the largest possible amount, as it includes the money you would have otherwise lost to taxes. The disadvantage is that you will end up paying a full tax on every penny you take out someday, including any and all profit made from that account. If you have a company-sponsored plan where you work, it will almost always be a deductible account.

With a non-deductible account you are fully taxed on the money before you put it in. The money in the account then grows, untaxed, until you take money out. Once you do, you are taxed on all of the gains but not on the original dollars. For most people a non-deductible account is usually not a good choice. If you think you might be an exception or wish to learn more, go to my website for sources that will explain the pros and cons based on the latest rules in place.

The third type of account, a Roth IRA, works quite differently. All of the money that goes into a Roth account is fully taxed before it goes in. In return for paying the taxes up front, all of the money that comes out someday is tax free. If you have a fairly long-term horizon, this is a very big advantage. Another particularly valuable advantage is the flexibility to withdraw your contributions, but not any earnings on that money after five years, for any reason, without paying tax or penalties. Sometimes you are even allowed to withdraw the earnings, such as paying for someone's education, certain medical problems, and such. You never know when you might unexpectedly need that money someday so it's nice to have the option. It's also nice to know exactly where you stand; 100% of the money is yours.

If your employer offers a plan that matches a portion of what you save, always match every dollar until you reach the maximum amount of the match. It's free money with an immediate 100% tax-free return on your money. For every $1,000 you invest, look at what happens if you take the match versus if you don't. Don't take the matching money, and you have $600 to spend after taxes. Take it, and you have $2,000 that then also gets to grow, tax-deferred. Beyond that, you can put additional money up to the maximum amount allowed by the plan and the IRS limits in your company's plan, if you have one. Or, you can probably open your own Roth IRA and/or Traditional (tax-deductible) IRA.

For most people your first choice, after matching dollars, should probably be to open a Roth IRA, provided you meet the eligibility requirements and have a ways to go until you retire. Some company plans now offer a Roth option as part of the plan so be sure to ask your company if they have this.

For the self-employed, there are truly a lot of options and combinations to choose from. If the most you can save for now is less than $15,000 a year, you are probably best off having a SEP IRA or Simple IRA. If you can save more than $15,000 a year but less than $49,000 (the current IRS limit), a simply constructed 401(k) account may be your choice. If you are using a CPA to do your taxes, be sure to ask for advice. If that's not the case, many sources, such as Costco online, can do a good job of assisting you at no charge in understanding what is involved in setting up the account of your choice. Any legal business entity can establish these plans (sole proprietorship, S-Corp, partnership, LLCs, etc.), and spouses can often be added to the payroll to increase contributions.

If you can contribute over $49,000 on an ongoing basis and you are roughly over age forty-five, then a Defined Benefit Plan should be considered. Depending on your age and income, your tax-deferred contribution can run up to as much as $200,000-plus. If you feel this situation might apply, your best bet is to seek professional advice.

Although many types of professionals may offer to help, I believe you are best off using a firm that specializes in setting up and administering such programs for the self-employed and for small- to mid-sized companies. Such firms, usually called Pension Plan Administrators or Third Party Administrators (TPAs), will provide you with their proposals at no charge. Should you decide to use them there will be a setup charge of at least $1,500 or more and an annual fee based primarily on the number of employees. Given the tax savings involved, these fees are worth it.

In interviewing and selecting the firm(s) to deal with, be sure to follow the advice at the start of this section on hiring professionals. I would also ask your tax accountant to offer his or her thoughts on the alternatives proposed by those companies.

That's about as far as I can go here, given the ever-changing picture regarding tax-free account rules and choices. I track significant changes to the tax law on my website at www.MoneySmartOnline.com.

Taxes: Return Preparation, Tax Advice

If, like most people, your tax return is very simple—you don't itemize your tax deductions, make less than the current cut-offs of $1,500 a year in interest income, and $100,000 in total income—you can quickly and easily do it yourself. Go online to www.irs.gov and fill in and file form 1040EZ or 1040A and then file a simple version of your state return. Another option if your income isn't too high (current cutoff is $56,000) is that you may be eligible to file your federal taxes online for free using either the forms or software program of the Free File Service at www.irs.gov.

If you are not in the above group, but still have a fairly straightforward financial picture, and are not self-employed with employees, you definitely still have the option of doing your tax return yourself. If you do, I'd suggest using one of the major tax return systems such as TurboTax that includes both federal and state forms. I would, however, have a tax professional check your return the first time you do this and also do the same thing every three to four years. The likelihood is that he will catch things that will more than pay for what he charges you.

Here are the pros and cons involved in choosing to use one of the major do-it-yourself tax return systems:

Pros:

- They do a good job of explaining your options and guiding you through the process.
- Your return preparation cost is likely to be a little (just a little) lower than hiring a professional.
- You are likely to develop a better understanding of how to minimize your tax bill going forward.
- Such systems automatically save all previous years' data. This makes doing the next year's returns a lot easier and it also helps remind you of every deduction you took last time, so nothing much slips through the cracks.
- If you try to go this route and it's not working, you always have the option to turn to a professional.

Cons:

- It won't work well if you are someone who has trouble following instructions and explanations or feel you have weak analytical skills.
- It may take more of your time than using a preparer and you will, at times, have to do a little homework on your own. This isn't that big a factor, however, as the overwhelming majority of the work involved is in the gathering and maintaining of the information and records needed, regardless of whether you do your return yourself or not.
- Certain states such as California have somewhat more complicated returns and the extra effort involved should be taken into consideration.

If you are either self-employed with employees or not self-employed but have a complicated financial picture, I believe you are best off hiring a professional. (You probably qualify as possessing a complicated financial picture if any of the following apply to you—extensive investments, rental property, investments in limited partnerships, foreign income, or you have lived in more than one country in the last year.)

Your choice will either be a national tax return franchise (i.e. H & R Block), an online service, or an individual local tax professional such as a CPA or an enrolled agent (tested and background checked by the IRS). My advice is to go with an individual local tax professional. (If you have a retirement program that includes your employees, a highly experienced local professional is a must.)

Here is why:

- The difference in fees is likely to be fairly small.
- The return preparers provided by such companies are usually part-timers and likely not as well trained and knowledgeable as the average CPA or enrolled agent.
- Franchise and online preparers are less likely to be available for any questions that might arise during the year.
- The turnover of franchise and online preparers is quite high, thereby reducing the chances you will have someone familiar with your tax situation on an ongoing basis.

Should you choose to go the route of using a local individual tax professional here are a few additional suggestions.

Despite the similarity of fees you will encounter, it will still pay to negotiate for the best price. Also, once you have someone you use regularly, here's a good tip for after your taxes are done. Tell the preparer you need to know the price for the next year. You'll often get a committed price and at the same amount you just paid. If you don't do this, there is a 50/50 chance that you'll find the price bumped a little come next year. Further, the first year you use someone it's more work than it will be after that. Use that situation to try to negotiate a lower price then and there for the next year by saying something like, "I can appreciate that it's more work the first time you do someone's return, but then somewhat less time consuming after that. What will it cost me next year?"

Seriously consider using tax preparation software first by yourself before you turn over your information to your tax preparer. Many find this to be a very valuable extra step as now there are two sets of eyes looking at the data from every angle to maximize deductions and minimize the hit. Also, you'll end up with a better understanding of how to minimize your tax bill going forward.

To get your money's worth, give everything to your tax preparer in early February, as soon as you've received the remaining documents needed. Any later and you enter a period of greater stress and a higher probability for both error and lost opportunity. Don't risk filing late. If you do, you'll almost certainly pay more taxes due to rushing errors and not having the time to get supporting documentation—and that's before adding in the late filing penalties involved of about 4.5% per month.

It's possible that you might run into someone who bases a fee on a percentage of the amount of your refund, who claims the ability to obtain larger refunds than other preparers, or who asks you to sign blank forms to be filled in later. All three of these things are red flags warning you to never to use that person. Regardless of who prepares your return, you are the one responsible for paying the taxes actually owed. If someone improperly does a lowball return you not will only end up having to pay the correct taxes, you'll also end up paying a penalty.

Learn from what happened to me and do not become complacent. Periodically review your decision, including the possibility of talking to and getting quotes from other providers.

Estate Planning

Estate planning is the setting in place of your wishes regarding the disposition of your assets and the handling of your personal affairs after you die. It also makes clear what you want done should you become incapable of handling your affairs at some point during your lifetime, which is a situation faced by millions of people every year.

To accomplish these things everyone should consider at least having a will, a living will, and a health care power of attorney. Some people may also want, at some point, to create a revocable living trust and possibly an irrevocable trust in certain circumstances. The first three documents are quite straightforward and are usually available for free or for a nominal sum. Revocable and irrevocable trusts are not simple and you may need the assistance of an attorney who specializes in estate planning.

Here is an explanation of each of these documents:

Will

A will states what you want done with your assets when you die, your wishes regarding the guardianship of your minor children, and funeral plans. It can be altered or replaced at any time you wish while you are alive.

Everyone should have a will. If you die without one the courts will decide who gets your major assets and who is appointed as the guardian of your minor children, based on the laws of the state where you live. You do *not* want to have the court make such a decision and affect the future of your children in ways you would not choose without your input. For many people, the laws of their state will result in the distribution of their assets to the members of their family as they would in their will anyway. However, there are situations in which you may want to leave your property to someone outside your immediate family or distribute a greater share of your assets to one heir compared to another. Possessing a will allows you to make such decisions for yourself. If you die without a will, it is possible that more of your assets may be lost to the expenses and charges involved in probating your estate than if you had a will. For many people, simply having a will is not enough, as wills can also have some serious drawbacks. There are ways around these problems and they will be explained below.

Living Will (also known as Advance Health Care Directive)

A living will specifies your wishes regarding your end-of-life decisions and the receipt of medical treatments in the event you are not able to speak for yourself. Generally, it describes certain life-prolonging treatments and identifies which treatments you do or do not want. A living will does not become effective unless and until you are incapacitated. Also, it usually requires a certification by your doctor and another doctor that you are either suffering from a terminal illness or permanently unconscious and unable to make your own decisions before it becomes effective. This means that if you suffer a heart attack, for example, but otherwise do not have any terminal illness and are not permanently unconscious, a living will does not have any effect. You would still be resuscitated, even if you had a living will indicating that you didn't want life-prolonging procedures. A living will is only used when your ultimate recovery is hopeless.

Health Care Power of Attorney (*also known as a Health Proxy*)

To cover those situations where you are unable to speak for yourself, but your illness is not so severe that your living will would take effect, you should also consider having a health care power of attorney. A health care power of attorney gives someone you choose the authority to make health care decisions for you in the event you are incapacitated but not terminal. The person you designate needs to understand what you would want, so be sure to talk it over with them. It may be a difficult conversation, but being clear about what you want will lessen the burden for that person should the need to make decisions ever arise. Should you have questions regarding the different situations that might be involved, ask your doctor.

Durable General Power of Attorney

There may be many situations that arise where you may need to execute legal documents but you are unavailable to do so due to travel, illness, or other reasons. In order for such documents to be executed in a timely and efficient manner, you should consider having a durable general power of attorney prepared. As with many of the other documents discussed in this section, you'll need to identify a person (or persons) who you trust to handle your affairs with honesty. It should be someone with some level of financial competence. Forms for such powers of attorney are readily available on the internet.

Revocable Living Trust

A revocable living trust is a document that gets its name because it can be amended or revoked at any time while you are alive. It is a common and often very good way to avoid the cost and hassle of probate or where just having a will is not enough. (Probate is the process where the courts of the state in which you live review and approve the execution of a will. Unfortunately, all wills must go through this costly and delay-laden process. The costs—including legal fees, appraisal fees, executor's fees, court filing fees, surety bond fees, and accounting fees—usually run between 2%–7% of the value of the estate.)

While you are alive, you control the trust and the assets held therein, and you can use and deal with those assets in whatever manner you wish. After your death, the assets held by the trust pass directly to the beneficiaries you have designated at the times and on the conditions you have stated. Such transfer of assets may be immediate, or your trust may state that the assets are to be paid out over time. Or the trust may state that the assets are to be held until certain events take place, for example, a child reaching a certain age. And, again, this will happen without incurring the time and costs of probate court proceedings. The person you've appointed to handle the trust after your death (your "successor trustee") simply transfers ownership of the assets to the beneficiaries you have named in the trust. In some cases certain revocable living trusts can also reduce federal estate tax. On the other hand, there are some assets, such as your IRAs, that should not be held in your trust as that may cause them to be taxed when they shouldn't be.

Unfortunately, a revocable living trust may be fairly complicated to set up if you do it yourself, and expensive to set up if you pay someone, such as an attorney specializing in estate planning, to do it. It also requires additional paperwork whenever you buy or sell something that is in or will be going into the trust. It is also critical to remember that simply creating a trust and even stating in the trust that you want your assets to be held in and owned by the trust, is not enough. An "unfunded" trust is essentially invalid. You have to make sure that the title to the assets you want to be held in the trust is actually transferred to the trust or your wishes may not be carried out.

Even if you set up a revocable living trust, you may still want a will to cover anything not covered by the trust, including personal items, funeral wishes, and such. This is frequently called a "pour-over will" because it "pours" the assets that were not owned by the trust into the trust after you die. In other words, it provides that any such assets should be treated like they were held in the trust.

Irrevocable Trust

This document is of value should you have substantial assets and also hold a sizeable insurance policy or policies. By placing the policy or policies in an irrevocable trust you insure that the proceeds can never be taxed. However, you should be very careful about creating an irrevocable trust and transferring your assets to such a trust. Once an irrevocable trust is made, it may be very difficult to remove those assets in the event you wanted to sell them or change your mind about who is to receive them. As with many of the decisions you will need to make, you should consult with appropriate professionals before proceeding.

How to Proceed

Let's start with the simplest situation and build from there. First, everyone should have a will for the purposes of distributing personal possessions and items of sentimental value, providing for future care of minor children, and stating funeral wishes. Your assets, however, should not be in a will, if at all possible, as your heirs will not have access to those assets for many months while the probate process proceeds and the fees that may be charged can be substantial. It is also worth noting that many people believe they need to have a will to avoid probate when, in fact, the opposite is true. If all of your assets are held in your own name when you die, your estate will have to go to probate if you have a will or not. However, at least if you have a will you can dictate who you want your assets to go to through the probate process. Shockingly, about half of adults do not have a will. Whatever you do, don't be in that group.

When getting your will prepared, you must select an "executor" or a "personal representative." This is the person who will be in charge of carrying out your wishes and handling whatever needs to be done after your death. Think this through very carefully. You need someone you can trust, who has the skills and personality necessary to do the job. You also will want to select someone who will be around after you die; this makes the selection of a parent to serve as executor a potentially unwise decision.

Everyone should take the time to create and sign a living will and a health care power of attorney. In some states these two have been combined into one document called an "Advanced Health Care Directive." Both of these forms are fairly straightforward and can usually be obtained for free or at a nominal cost. Ask your health care provider about them or, if necessary, you can find them online.

Property held in joint ownership, such as your home (if you're married) and joint bank or brokerage accounts are essentially available immediately to the surviving party at no cost whatsoever. In addition, any account where you've designated a beneficiary, sometimes called a "payable on death" or POD account, is treated in the same way. There are no fees and the account is immediately available. Further, as a general matter, the ownership of any and all tax-free/tax-deferred accounts automatically goes to the surviving spouse unless you designate otherwise, and without any taxes having to be paid at that time.

Wherever possible you should have a joint or POD arrangement in place so that as little of your assets as possible needs to go through probate, whether or not you have a will.

If you own a small business that is worth a relatively small amount, the action is quite simple. If it's a corporation or a limited liability company (LLC), just identify in the minutes of the corporation who takes it over should anything happen to you. If you don't do this, the operation of the business could be damaged or even destroyed as the normally lengthy probate process unfolds. Personally, I would never want to allow that, even if it's only a small personal business. If, on the other hand, you have a company of significant value, you should probably consider creating a revocable living trust and placing the ownership into the trust.

A mix of the above approaches should satisfy the needs for well over 80% of the population. It does leave a loophole, however, should you have minor children and there is neither a surviving parent nor another person who would automatically receive the assets from your estate needed for the support of your children. If you are facing this situation, or wish to cover the highly unlikely but not impossible situation where both parents die at the same time, you need to seriously consider setting up a revocable living trust.

If your estate has a substantial value (for example, a couple of million dollars or more), you need to learn whether or not you will be better off setting up a revocable living trust. There are several ways to proceed.

One approach is to go to my website where you will find links to sites, articles, and books that can help you. Included in the links are one or more sites that let you prepare most of the paperwork for free so you can see if you're comfortable doing it yourself. This can be a good first step. Even if you do end up retaining an attorney to assist you, you will learn quite a bit about what is involved and what you want out of the process. Sometimes just being familiar and comfortable with the terminology (the "legalese") can make all the difference. Another thing you can do is to attend one of the many free seminars that are offered all over the country on the subject; such seminars can often be quite informative. If you do, and are impressed with the person or group giving the seminar, do *not* just select them to help you. The person or group is only a candidate, nothing more, and you need to go through the complete selection process as covered in the section on Guidelines for Hiring Financial Professionals (see page 179).

If you decide that you are among those needing a revocable living trust, you can either prepare the paperwork yourself utilizing free services or the links on my website, or you can have it drawn up by an attorney specializing in estate matters. The fees to have it done by an attorney can range anywhere from several hundred to thousands of dollars, depending on the complexity of your situation.

If your situation is complicated or you are dealing with a very large estate, you're probably best off paying to have it done by a professional. In such a circumstance there are also several additional options for tax minimization and other estate planning mechanisms that you should discuss with your advisors and consider implementing. If your estate is not that complicated, you may very well be able to do it yourself online for a couple of hundred dollars. The paperwork is somewhat challenging and if you or someone you trust to help you aren't good at such things, you are, again, probably better off paying someone to do it.

Lastly, I'll restate the warning that you should never ignore: Over 50% of the revocable living trusts that are set up are never funded with the assets that were supposed to go into them. In such cases, the trust will have been a waste of time and money and will not control who receives your assets after your death. Be extremely careful in deciding whether you do want a trust and that you will do the work of putting the assets into it.

Other Considerations

Whenever you leave considerable assets to someone, you *must* think about how responsible that person will be in handling what they are given. This is particularly true if you are planning on leaving your assets to your children, more so if they are still young. Is it really best to give it all to them at once? If you do, is there a good chance they will waste an awful lot of it right away? If you see this as a real possibility, you should consider creating a structure that gives them the money gradually over a number of years. If you have a trust this is an easy thing to do. If not, there are usually some other ways to do essentially the same thing. If you have any questions or would like to learn more about your options, please go to my website for links to that information.

One of the additional steps you need to take, both for yourself and certainly for those you leave behind should anything happen to you, is to organize all your important documents and put them in one location. Create a set of folders for these documents. Then add a list on your computer listing the contents of each folder with a brief explanation next to any item needing clarification. At the end of your list, put any additional information your family or your executor needs or may need to know that isn't specifically stated in your will or other documents, but will be easy to spot by using the files. Print out the list, put it in the first folder, and update it whenever necessary. It should be a "living document" that will grow and should be amended as time goes by and your life and estate change. Do not be intimidated by this task and decide to do it "later." It really doesn't take that much time to do. Besides, you'll get an immediate payoff, because a lot of stress involved with staying on top of things into the future will be removed.

The list of folders and relevant documents are:

- **Asset accounts**—The most recent copies of all bank, brokerage, and retirement account statements. If they are paperless, print out and file copies of your account statements semi-annually and identify where the latest statements can be found online.

- **Debts**—Copies of any mortgages, notes, credit cards, or other agreements and obligations and the current balances due on all outstanding debts and loans; also include the payoff documentation on all closed loans. If they are paperless, print out and file copies of your account statements semi-annually and identify where the latest statements can be found online.

- **Family legal documents**—The originals or copies of all other family legal documents, for example, birth and death certificates, marriage certificates, divorce settlements, passports, etc.

- **Estate planning**—Copies of all will(s), trusts, living wills, health care powers of attorney, and general powers of attorney.
- **Insurance**—Copies of all insurance policies.
- **Taxes**—Copies of tax returns for at least the last five years, statements, receipts for deductions, proof of payments, etc.
- **Titled property**—Originals or copies of all deeds to homes or other real property, titles to motor vehicles, and any ownership documents to other assets with titles,
- **Social Security and Medicare/Medicaid**—Cards, benefit printouts, etc.
- **Business legal records**—The books and minutes for any corporations, LLCs, or partnerships.
- **Other**—All documentation regarding any other assets or liabilities, location of and access to lockboxes or storage units, lists of people to be notified, and anything not covered above, which you feel is important and which would be necessary for your executor and/or heirs to review and use when you pass away.

There are likely other folders you will think to create which would be helpful but these will get you started.

Legal Matters

In this book I have touched on the subjects of lawyers and legal advice only if and when it related to some aspect of personal finance, such as estate planning. Anything more would be outside the scope of this book. I will take a moment, however, to provide some brief thoughts regarding legal matters. I am not an attorney and cannot give legal advice, so what I offer here are my personal observations and opinions and they should be considered as such.

I feel it is very important to *prevent* legal problems from happening in the first place. The expression that "an ounce of prevention is worth a pound of cure" could not be truer when it comes to legal matters. This starts with paying attention to what's going on around you. By doing this over the years I've come up with a couple of rules I now follow quite religiously.

The first is whenever I begin to realize that someone is not reliable, I eliminate any dependence on them for anything significant. If they are part of my circle of friends, I do not count on them to make arrangements for any important events, and I am very careful about including them in any business ventures or opportunities. Such persons may earn the right to be included again in the future but until they have proven themselves, I've learned that being cautious works best for me.

A second rule I follow is if I see someone repeatedly mistreating or taking advantage of other people, even though they may treat me just fine, I cut them out of my life. I've learned it's usually just a matter of time before they will almost certainly mistreat me the way they've mistreated others. I'm talking about simple acts here. Maybe they're unnecessarily rude to a waitperson. Their actions may seem harmless, but they're not. Good people don't do that. When it happens, that's one strike. They do it again, that's two and now I'm really on the lookout. Three strikes and I'm gone or, more correctly, they're gone . . . from my life and my business. I didn't begin to understand the importance of this rule until I was in my late thirties and boy did I learn it the hard way. Since then I have had plenty of opportunities to observe the value of this rule.

Both of these rules have helped me avoid getting into legal disputes. However, sometimes you will need an attorney and, when you do, a good lawyer can often prove to be a very valuable asset. I believe, however, that you should go out of your way to avoid the use of attorneys whenever possible. I say this not because I am against lawyers. As with any profession, there are some very good and some very bad ones. My problem is that I believe the true costs involved, especially in initiating a legal action, frequently make such actions not worth the time and cost involved. A couple of times in my life I have thought about suing someone because I was very upset. I ended up concluding that I was dealing with the same situation covered in my investment rules: Do not let your emotions affect your better judgment. Once I was able to pull back from the emotions involved and review and consider the situation from a cooler, more reasonable viewpoint, I easily concluded that suing was a bad idea.

By watching others during the course of my business career, I came to believe that if the amount of money to be collected by suing is under $20,000 or so, it's not worth initiating a legal action. Here are some of my reasons for feeling this way:

- It has been my observation that the fees involved usually end up being far higher than the original estimate provided by an attorney.
- Pursuing legal action may require that you invest a lot of your time (in addition to your money), and the stresses involved can often substantially damage your quality of life.

- Even if you win, the probability is you'll only get a portion of what you felt you were entitled to, as the overwhelming majority of lawsuits are negotiated settlements ending up somewhere in the middle.

In certain situations, you may be able to take advantage of mediation services or pursue your claims in small-claims court. These procedures also offer the opportunity to vent and at least tell your story. However, if you add together all the downsides to filing a lawsuit, you are usually better off learning an expensive lesson from the experience and getting on with your life. However, if what is at stake is a lot more than $20,000, that's another matter. And if that is the case you should consult with a good attorney.

Next is the subject of contracts. A contract is an extremely common everyday thing. It exists whenever there is an offer and an acceptance, even verbally, between two or more parties about almost anything you can think of. Most sizeable consumer purchases require that you sign a contract. You signed one for every credit card you have, probably every bank account, every insurance policy, and so on. Contracts provide a very valuable function in that they spell out what the parties are agreeing to. They should be used to avoid misunderstandings between the parties, and can serve as a vehicle by which one can attempt to enforce one's rights.

If the agreement is a very commonplace one, such as a contract to purchase a car, and any risk to you involves only a moderate amount of money, I am of the opinion you do not need the advice of an attorney. You also have the alternative of using stock forms from internet sources for such things as wills or routine business agreements. It is my observation that these resources usually work well in most instances and are the norm these days.

However, there are times when you either need the help of an attorney or, at a minimum, should at least talk to one, including:

- You are being charged with a crime.
- Someone initiates a suit against you and you can't immediately resolve the situation on your own.
- You are involved in a divorce where you are unable to amicably separate your affairs on your own, and significant assets or children are involved. If you are in this situation, it is strongly advisable that you sit down yet again and do all you can to compromise and bend over backward to reach an agreement, especially if there are children involved. The involvement of attorneys should be a last resort as there is a high likelihood of polarizing things farther yet, with a very significant risk that both parties end up losing.
- If you intend to enter into an agreement that is not a routine everyday contract and it involves either the potential loss of a large amount of money or very valuable property, or places you at substantial risk of being sued some day.
- If you are purchasing real estate for investment or business use.
- If you are investing in someone else's business.
- Initiating certain estate planning strategies (described on pages 190–194).

As to selecting an attorney, follow the same directions outlined earlier in the section on Guidelines for Hiring Financial Professionals (see page 179). Obtain referrals from people you trust and first have a no-obligation conversation with potential candidates about your case, their experience in the specific area, and their attitudes about litigation and alternative dispute resolution procedures, such as mediation and arbitration, before making any commitment.

CHAPTER TEN

When to Invest—
A Critical Key to Success

There are two fundamental decisions when it comes to investing: *when* to invest in a given investment market, and *what* to invest in. The financial industry's standard response to the question of *when* to invest in the stock market is this: "Always invest for the long run. It's the only way, and you'll always win if you stay the course." When it comes to the real estate market, the standard advice is pretty much the same. As I have already shown you in chapter one, this mantra, which is repeated endlessly by the vast majority of the world's financial "experts," is just not true!

When to invest (when to buy and when to sell) is an extremely critical decision you can and must make. The tricky part is how to go about making that decision.

Buy at Fair Value or Below, Sell When Overpriced

In chapter one I showed you graphs on pages 11, 12 and 17 that document that the U.S. stock and residential real estate markets go through long periods of substantial over- and underpricing; that there were long periods of time when everyone was pretty much guaranteed to lose money, and other times when everyone was pretty much guaranteed to make money. You will find these patterns, alternating between overexuberance (greed) and fear, apply to pretty much all investment markets—commodities, foreign stock markets, commercial real estate, etc.

The "experts" do not understand this. They didn't need to, as the soaring stock markets of the 1980s and 1990s and the tens of millions of new 401(k) accounts made everybody a winner. It was the greatest price explosion in U.S. stock market history. How could anyone lose during this period? To keep alive the myth that they know how to invest, the financial industry "proves" what a good job they are doing by selecting the time period when things were good for the entire market. I'd like a nickel for every stockbroker and financial planner who used 2002–2004 when the market went up 67% as "proof" of how well they are doing for you. Why didn't they use 2000–2002, when the market dropped 40%? Or, to be fairer, even 2000–2004? For the four-year period of 2000–2004, the market's total return was a loss of 17%.

Almost all markets will experience a number of these major cycles in your lifetime. The upcycles usually take the market to where it is eventually way overpriced, rather than just a little, as human nature causes people to stay greedy longer than is wise. This is especially true of the professionals in that overpriced market. When a market is overpriced these professionals will be at their worst, selling with a non-stop genuine excitement as they are very caught up in it themselves. As a result, they are almost always great lagging indicators, not leading indicators.

To make good decisions about when to buy, hold, or sell investments in a given market, you must be paying attention to where that market is at any given point in relation to its fair market value. This means that when a market such as the stock market is overpriced it makes sense to move your money into another market that is underpriced or fairly priced, such as fixed investments, and then return to the stock market when it is fairly priced or, even better, underpriced. Pure and simple, it's all about the value of the investment, which is what something is *actually worth*, not what people will pay for it at a point in time.

The bottom line strategy is really very simple: When something is underpriced, buy it; if it's fairly priced, maybe buy it; but if it's substantially overpriced, sell it and invest elsewhere. I provide an estimate of the current market value of each of the six major investment markets: residential real estate, investment real estate, U.S. stock, foreign stock, fixed income, and commodities markets.

Once you've identified approximately where you are in the overall cycle of a market, here are some guidelines for what to do next. As you proceed, keep in mind that you will never get all the gains or avoid all the losses, nor do you need to. The key is to avoid the majority of the losses and get the majority of the gains—and that you *can* do. Remember, this is not market timing. Instead it's about assessing the market's *true worth*. It's about buying when you can pay a fair price, and selling when others will pay you more than what it's worth.

If you determine that a market has become moderately overpriced, stop buying but don't sell. Provided the overpricing is modest, wait for it to get worse, as it probably will. Then sell half of your holdings and move the money to another and better market. If the overall pricing of the market still continues to rise, and it often will, then sell the other half. I'm sure you'd like some hard numbers here, but it's difficult to provide them without knowing the specific circumstances. Here are some rough guidelines. I don't buy when a stock or **commodity** market is overpriced by 15% or more. I begin selling once the stock or commodity market is overpriced by 25% to 30% and I get out completely when it is overpriced by 40%. For investments in the real estate market, I stop buying at 5%–10% overpriced and get out at about 25%. For more specific advice regarding the approximate current value of the various markets and the actions to consider, go to my website to see my opinion, as well as that of others.

When markets drop, human nature causes people to overreact out of fear. As a result, the major downcycles tend to take the market to where it is substantially underpriced. It will also usually stay negative for quite a while, so don't pressure yourself into worrying about missing out. Begin modestly reinvesting once the market is no longer overpriced, even if it is still dropping.

Because it sometimes becomes extremely overpriced and dramatically underpriced, the stock market can be particularly frustrating. The market history I provided shows that you may well end up selling some day when the market is 40% overvalued, only to see it go up a lot more. Or you might buy at fair value and see it go down another 40%. The only logical approach is to accept this situation, as there is no timing what are essentially random, emotion-dominated events. You will almost always start to buy and sell somewhat too soon or too late and that's okay. Should you ever happen to hit the exact top or bottom it's just a lucky accident, nothing more. In the winter of

2000 I appeared to be a heck of a smart guy as I essentially caught the top of the market. Not true. The decision to sell out was a smart and well-informed decision. Happening to catch the top was dumb luck, nothing more. I could have just as easily caught it a bit before peak or a bit after. The point is that either way, I was selling in a substantially overpriced market relative to true value.

Let's take an example to show how this process can work. Say you re-entered the stock market in early 2003. The market bottomed at 7,900 and you bought 12% higher at 8,850. In 2007 the market peaked at 14,000 and you sold a lot sooner, say 12,000 on average. You made 35% in four years, which is about 8% a year, compounded. This sure beats the heck out of **buy and hold**, where you would've *lost* money (and a lot of it), if you had continued to hold onto the shares for the next couple of years. Notice that a lot of profit was given up due to buying too late and especially selling out at 50% overpriced, which turned out to be too soon.

The following are a few additional points to be aware of as you evaluate what is going on in a given market.

When one market is overpriced it is common for another to be underpriced because too much cash has been siphoned off to feed the overpriced one. This couldn't be better, as it opens up the opportunity to sell out of the overpriced market and buy into the underpriced market. My move from the stock market to the real estate market in early 2000 was a good example of this.

The pricing of stock and commodity markets is based heavily on people's expectations as to what the market will soon be worth, not on what it is worth now. This means that the market falls once enough people *believe* an economic problem is coming, like a recession, and not when it *actually* arrives. Conversely, these markets will begin to rise as soon as recovery is expected and not when it arrives. I tell you this so you are aware of how most everyone else is thinking and reacting.

It is useful to understand the impact of a drop versus a rise in value of a given market or investment. If a stock goes up 100%, say from 30 to 60, how much drop wipes out the entire gain? The answer is 50%. A 50% drop takes you back to 30. Even if you then go back up by 50% to 45, you are still 25% below your last high of 60.

Do Not Try to Make Money by Trading

Trading is the rapid buying and selling of stocks, commodities, currencies, etc. to make money on the small shifts in market prices present in almost all such investments. For many, it involves many buys and sells in a single day. For others, it's buying and selling based on chosen price points, where the transactions might be daily, weekly, or perhaps somewhat longer.

I strongly advise that you do not get involved in any form of trading. If someone tries to convince you otherwise, be careful; this person likely has a vested interest and there are quite a few trading scams out there. In an administrative complaint filed in 2009 against a now-defunct day-trading firm, Massachusetts securities regulators alleged that only one of the branch's sixty-eight accounts made money. From my experience, this company is the rule rather than the exception. Further, an article in the *New York Times* (8/1/1999), states that "Day trading has exceptionally high 'washout rates' and 'regulators who have examined the books of day-trading firms say that more than 9 out of 10 traders wind up losing money. Because most of these people disappear quietly when their cash runs out, few who replace them in the trading rooms know about them or their failures'."

A very small percent of day traders actually do make money, but it is dangerous to assume that you will be one of them. If you think you might be that exception, that you possess the nerves for the game, the mind and the willingness to risk the likelihood you could very well lose a lot (perhaps all) of your money, then I suggest you first trade on paper for six months and see if you make money. If you did and feel you want to trade for real, I recommend investing only a modest amount of money. That's because you're still probably going to lose it. The odds are that bad.

Do Not Listen to the "Experts"

When to buy and when to sell are among the decisions you must personally make. As you make those decisions, do not be influenced by what the "experts" say. One of their worst shortcomings is that they almost always react to what has already happened and, as a result, are usually lagging indicators. A leading indicator gives an early signal that something is likely to happen. A simple example would be that when your car's low fuel light comes on, you're going to run out of gas soon. The light is a leading indicator. A lagging indicator is the opposite. It confirms something after the fact. In this example, the car stops. This is a very good lagging indicator about how much gas is left because you just ran out! Obviously, leading indicators are very valuable, while lagging indicators are usually pretty darn worthless. Imagine if you thought something was a leading indicator when it was actually more of a lagging indicator and you made some serious decisions under that false assumption. If you did, you, my friend, would *not* be a happy camper.

Unfortunately, the overwhelming majority of financial "experts"—the financial media, stock brokers, real estate agents, and financial advisors—are usually fairly reliable *lagging* indicators. This is because they usually react to events well after the fact. They aren't very good at being leading indicators because most of them don't know how to make money reliably through investment in the first place. Instead, they fall back on responding to the motions of the market and the rest of the industry.

Time and again the experts will say, in words or by their actions, "The market has been rising. Great! It's a good time to be investing." The higher and more overpriced the market becomes, the stronger they will beat the drums. If the market begins to fall they'll stay positive and say it's a buying opportunity. They try hard to always remain positive because they need people to buy. Invariably, at some point the investing public hits a point of panic as they watch their balances sink and they will start selling, big-time. By doing so they are almost certainly selling at exactly the wrong time! They are selling too late, when, at that moment, they should probably be holding pat or selectively buying. Around this time, the experts start to turn negative (they will use words like "it's time to be cautious") and the level of their hold recommendations starts to rise which causes more selling in return. When things reach that point you are probably looking at a buying opportunity (but be sure to double-check with my website). It all comes back to Warren Buffet's advice: "Be fearful when others are greedy. Be greedy when others are fearful."

This "after the fact" approach to investing also applies to individual investment recommendations of these "experts" and not just to their attitude toward the overall market. The price of a stock has been rising? Their attitude will frequently be that it could well be a good thing to buy it. Oh, the price has dropped a lot lately? Well, let's' drop it to a "hold" as it's probably a good idea to sell it.

As an example of this process, the chart that follows shows how a group of investment analysts reacted to a stock I happened to be watching in 2008 because one of my sons was considering working for the company. The experts were all happy to recommend investing in Salesforce.com in the spring of 2008 at a per-share price of $56 on up to $72. A few months later the price dropped to $36. All of a sudden they started shifting their advice on this stock to hold, sell, or underperform. (Understand that "hold" is almost always a signal that they view the investment as a likely underperformer. They just can't bring themselves to say the "s" word.) After the stock had already gone up a lot they recommended buying it and after it dropped by 40%–50% they went to hold or sell. Guess what happened next? In less than twelve months the stock was back to over $60!

Unfortunately, what you see here is extremely common, especially since the investment banking profits most firms make from the very same companies they follow frequently warps their investment recommendations to the public. If you had followed their advice and invested in Salesforce.com, how would you feel? Talk about being a lagging indicator, eh? By the way, I didn't just select certain firms to make the point. According to www.yahoofinance.com, the recommendations I show for Salesforce.com include every single significant Wall Street recommendation during that time period. Notice that there was not a single underperform or sell until *after* the stock had already tanked. Studies have documented that this unwillingness to recommend selling a stock is the norm and to a degree you almost can't imagine. For example, a Zach's Investment Research study covering the first three months of 2001 reported that only 87 out of 12,339 stock rating reports were sells. These numbers are dramatic proof as to how badly they want you to keep buying and to always stay invested.

History for Salesforce.com (stock symbol CRM)
*January to October, 2008**

STOCK PRICE		DATE	RESEARCH FIRM	RECOMMENDATION	FROM	TO
Jan	$57.76	Jan 7	UBS	Upgrade	Neutral	Buy
Mar	$57.85	Mar 14	Broadpoint Cap	Initiated	---	Buy
Apr	$63.26	Apr 9	Bernstein	Downgrade	Outperfm	Mkt perfm
	$66.73	Apr 22	Piper Jaffray	Initiated	---	Buy
May	$72.31	May 22	Jeffries & Co	Upgrade	Hold	Buy
June	$68.23					
July	$63.79	Jul 11	Credit Suisse	Initiated	---	Neutral
		Jul 22	Citigroup	Downgrade	Buy	Hold
Aug	$56.02	Aug 20	Kaufman Bros	Initiated	---	Buy
		Aug 21	Piper Jaffray	Downgrade	Buy	Neutral
		Aug 22	JMP Securities	Upgrade	Mkt perfm	Mkt Outperfm
		Aug 26	Citigroup	Upgrade	Hold	Buy
Sept	$48.40					
Oct	$35.94	Oct 3	UBS	Downgrade	Buy	Sell
		Oct 7	Roth Capital	Downgrade	Buy	Hold
		Oct 7	Jeffries & Co	Downgrade	Buy	Underperfm

Source: Yahoofinance.com

Once again, this demonstrates that the stronger the financial professionals are beating the drums to buy, the more cautious you should become. When the advice begins to shift to saying it would be "wise" to protect your assets or that they believe an investment is likely to "underperform" it means you should be checking out fair market value and considering doing some buying.

Remember, I am not talking about market timing. Nobody, and I mean nobody, can reliably time markets or even individual investments. You can, however, identify in a very general way whether a market is noticeably over- or underpriced and this is what you must do. Fortunately, this is something you'll probably have to act on maybe a couple of times in a decade. Whenever you wish to know more about *when* to invest in a given market, go to my website, where I will provide my best estimates, along with those of others, about where we are in the cycles of the stock, fixed income, and real estate markets.

Finally, should you have any lingering thoughts that you can rely on the "experts" to provide stock investment recommendations, take a look at the following example. On the next several pages is a list of every buy-and-sell recommendation on that same stock I just talked about, SalesForce.com (symbol CRM), for a period of forty-eight months. Let your eyes wander down this list and keep in mind we're talking only forty-eight months, a reasonable length of time to invest. Notice how the same firms frequently switch their recommendations. Can you make any sense of what you see?

Should you feel this might be an isolated example, go to www .yahoofinance.com and enter the name or symbol of half a dozen large company stocks of your choosing. Click on "analyst opinion" then click on "more upgrades and downgrades." Then check the list of investment recommendation upgrades and downgrades.

Upgrades and Downgrades—Source: YahooFinance.com

DATE	RESEARCH FIRM	ACTION	FROM	TO
24-Nov-09	Wedbush Morgan	Upgrade	Neutral	Outperform
13-Nov-09	UBS	Initiated		Neutral
13-Nov-09	Caris & Company	Upgrade	Average	Above Average
11-Sep-09	Wedbush Morgan	Upgrade	Underperform	Neutral
21-Aug-09	FBR Capital	Upgrade	Underperform	Mkt Perform
21-Aug-09	Piper Jaffray	Upgrade	Neutral	Overweight
28-Jul-09	Soleil	Downgrade	Buy	Hold
22-May-09	Citigroup	Downgrade	Buy	Hold
13-Apr-09	UBS	Upgrade	Sell	Buy
9-Apr-09	Wedbush Morgan	Downgrade	Hold	Sell
7-Apr-09	RBC Capital Mkts	Upgrade	Sector Perform	Outperform
26-Feb-09	Roth Capital	Downgrade	Buy	Hold
21-Nov-08	Robert W. Baird	Upgrade	Neutral	Outperform
21-Nov-08	Caris & Company	Initiated		Average
21-Nov-08	Roth Capital	Upgrade	Hold	Buy
23-Oct-08	Jefferies & Co	Upgrade	Underperform	Hold
15-Oct-08	Soleil	Upgrade	Hold	Buy
13-Oct-08	AmTech Research	Initiated		Buy
7-Oct-08	Jefferies & Co	Downgrade	Buy	Underperform
7-Oct-08	Roth Capital	Downgrade	Buy	Hold
3-Oct-08	UBS	Downgrade	Buy	Sell
26-Aug-08	Citigroup	Upgrade	Hold	Buy
22-Aug-08	JMP Securities	Upgrade	Mkt Perform	Mkt Outperform
21-Aug-08	Piper Jaffray	Downgrade	Buy	Neutral

DATE	RESEARCH FIRM	ACTION	FROM	TO
20-Aug-08	Kaufman Bros	Initiated		Buy
22-Jul-08	Citigroup	Downgrade	Buy	Hold
11-Jul-08	Credit Suisse	Initiated		Neutral
22-May-08	Jefferies & Co	Upgrade	Hold	Buy
22-Apr-08	Piper Jaffray	Initiated		Buy
9-Apr-08	Bernstein	Downgrade	Outperform	Mkt Perform
14-Mar-08	Broadpoint Capital	Initiated		Buy
7-Jan-08	UBS	Upgrade	Neutral	Buy
12-Nov-07	Piper Jaffray	Upgrade	Market Perform	Outperform
1-Nov-07	Wedbush Morgan	Downgrade	Buy	Hold
15-Oct-07	Cantor Fitzgerald	Downgrade	Buy	Hold
11-Oct-07	Lazard Capital	Initiated		Buy
10-Oct-07	Canaccord Adams	Initiated		Buy
6-Sep-07	KeyBanc Capital Mkts	Initiated		Hold
11-Apr-07	Cowen & Co	Downgrade	Outperform	Neutral
11-Apr-07	Bernstein	Initiated		Outperform
22-Feb-07	WR Hambrecht	Downgrade	Buy	Hold
20-Nov-06	Lehman Brothers	Initiated		Equal-weight
9-Nov-06	Cantor Fitzgerald	Initiated		Buy
8-Nov-06	Caris & Company	Downgrade	Above Average	Average
6-Oct-06	Banc of America Sec	Upgrade	Neutral	Buy
29-Sep-06	Friedman Billings	Downgrade	Mkt Perform	Underperform
13-Sep-06	CIBC Wrld Mkts	Initiated		Sector Perform
22-Aug-06	AG Edwards	Initiated		Hold
17-Aug-06	Caris & Company	Upgrade	Average	Above Average
1-Aug-06	Prudential	Initiated		Underweight

DATE	RESEARCH FIRM	ACTION	FROM	TO
28-Jul-06	Caris & Company	Initiated		Average
9-Jun-06	Friedman Billings	Upgrade	Underperform	Mkt Perform
5-Jun-06	UBS	Upgrade	Reduce	Neutral
11-May-06	Matrix Research	Initiated		Hold
28-Apr-06	Wedbush Morgan	Initiated		Buy
25-Apr-06	Citigroup	Initiated		Buy
7-Apr-06	Morgan Stanley	Initiated		Underweight
23-Feb-06	Piper Jaffray	Initiated		Market Perform
14-Feb-06	First Albany	Upgrade	Neutral	Buy
10-Jan-06	Friedman Billings	Downgrade	Mkt Perform	Underperform
9-Jan-06	Robert W. Baird	Downgrade	Outperform	Neutral
6-Jan-06	CSFB	Upgrade	Neutral	Outperform
19-Dec-05	UBS	Downgrade	Neutral	Reduce
16-Dec-05	Banc of America Sec	Initiated		Neutral
12-Dec-05	Susquehanna Financial	Downgrade	Neutral	Negative
12-Dec-05	Jefferies & Co	Downgrade	Buy	Hold
2-Dec-05	Prudential	Downgrade	Overweight	Neutral
29-Nov-05	Citigroup	Initiated		Hold

CHAPTER ELEVEN

Evaluating Your Investment Alternatives

If you haven't already done so, read chapter five, "The 10 Rules of Investing Successfully," along with the section on Understanding the Numbers in chapter nine (see page 164) and chapter ten, "When to Invest," before reading this chapter.

There are many choices regarding where to invest your money. The following list shows the most common alternatives. All of these alternatives, with the exception of investing in your home (see page 272 in chapter twelve, "Buying and Selling a Home") are covered in this chapter. Also, please remember that except for the money you put into tax-deferred accounts, always pay off any and all debt, excluding your home, before investing in anything else. *No* investment is likely to produce anything like the guaranteed return and peace of mind you will get from debt elimination.

Some of the investment alternatives I will recommend that you avoid completely. Further, should you ever be offered investment opportunities not covered below, especially those that seem almost too good to be true, please be sure to check my website, www.MoneySmartOnline .com, where I maintain information and references regarding many of the investment traps and scams that are out there. These situations are *extremely* common, so do *not* let your guard down!

Investment Choices

Fixed-income Investments

Fixed-income investments provide a fixed (pre-set) rate of return. They include bank accounts, **money market accounts**, CDs, **treasury bills**, and bonds or bond mutual funds. A **bond**, as you may know, is a fancy word for a loan to a business or government body. (Annuities, also sold as fixed investments, are covered on page 228.)

The bottom line return from fixed investments is generally very low. After you account for the impact of inflation and taxes, fixed investments will usually make only a small amount of money if they are in a tax-protected account, and will probably lose a little money if they're not. Historically, the average rate for fixed investments has been around 5% versus around 3.5% for inflation. Having such a small gap between the fixed-income rate and inflation has always been true. Even in the early 1980s, when CD rates were at 15%–16%, inflation was 11%–13%.

Is this bad? Not really; it's just the way it is. Despite the lack of return, it's smart to put a portion of your investments in fixed income precisely because they *are* usually risk-free and provide protection from the more pronounced fluctuations of other markets. In return, there should be little or no risk involved, so stick to very low-risk fixed-income investments only. That means no high-risk bonds, etc. Fixed income is a bad place to take any significant risks. Later in this chapter I will cover the subject of asset allocation and provide some guidelines on what portion of your assets might best be served in fixed-income investments versus those with greater risk.

Fixed investments serve many purposes. They are useful for the money you may need now, in the months to come, or even in the next year or two. The cost of buying and selling other investments, the risk of short-term loss, and, in some cases, the difficulty of selling them make it far better to keep the money you expect to need in the near future both safe and available. You may also be a person who cannot handle the pressure of the risk involved with other investments. Perhaps you have enough money and would rather keep it safe and give up any additional return. There is nothing wrong with that. Peace of mind is a very valuable thing. At no point, however, should you lose sight of the bottom line. If you need or want to grow your money, you have no choice but to take on some degree of risk for a significant portion of your assets.

Are there any other reasons why you would use or expand your use of fixed-income investments? Possibly. One of the most common reasons is if you are in or are approaching retirement. In that circumstance, reducing your level of risk makes sense, especially if you have accumulated enough assets. The other major reason is as a safe alternative during those times when the stock market is significantly overpriced. Periods of truly high overall stock market risk will almost certainly happen a number of times in your lifetime. The winter of 2000 and the fall of 2007 are the latest examples. In this situation, you should consider protecting your stock market gains by moving those investments to the safest of positions, which means to high-quality fixed-income investments. When doing such a move you want to have planned ahead in order to minimize the tax hit involved from such selling. The subject of **tax minimization** is discussed toward the end of this chapter (page 263).

To illustrate the value of such a move, look at the last ten years. On December 31, 1999, the DOW Industrial Average closed at 11,497. Exactly ten years later it closed at 10,428. The inflation rate for those ten years totaled 28%. This is a net loss, in real dollars, of 34%. During that same time, the average return for a two-year CD was about 4.3%, a net gain of just under 1%. Yes, this is a very poor return, but it sure beats losing 34%. Also, as already discussed in chapter ten, "When to Invest" (page 207), there was a clear opportunity to go back into the market during that time and make some money.

Should you ever feel you are facing such a situation, go to my website where my input on the status of the stock, fixed income, and real estate markets will be available.

As you evaluate your choices regarding various specific fixed-income options, here are a couple of additional ideas to assist you:

- Don't keep significant amounts of money in regular savings accounts for any extended period of time as the yields are just too low. With money funds and money market deposit accounts, it is always well worth your time to do a periodic search for the best rates. For all of your other investment accounts do your best to keep them with companies with a reputation of solid finances, low rates, and discounted brokerage commissions.

- Build your position in fixed-income investments by using CDs, long-term treasury bonds (also municipal bonds if you're in a fairly high tax bracket) and high-quality individual corporate bonds rather than bond funds. By using individual investments of this nature, there are no fees, fund expenses, or end-of-year capital gains taxes. Plus you know the exact price you are paying and the interest you will be receiving. With a bond fund, the value of your investment and the interest you get is not fixed and will almost certainly bounce around.

- On principle, I wouldn't put more than 20% of your total assets in any one investment (other than your house), or in any one institution no matter how risk-free it may appear to be; that includes U.S. Treasuries. The only exception to this is if you have only a small amount of money saved and it's invested primarily in fixed-income investments such as CDs, Treasuries, etc.

Whenever you might wish for more information regarding fixed-income investing, see my website for some links to sites, articles, and books that can help you.

Banking Relationships

Any discussion of fixed investments should probably include the subject of banking relationships. You will need to establish a relationship with one or more banks, credit unions, credit card companies, brokerage firms—basically businesses that can provide any or all of the services that follow. The first six services are those normally provided by banks, savings and loans, and credit unions. The remaining services were not included in their service offerings in the past but, more and more, they'd love you to use them for everything possible. That is in their best interest, but usually not in yours.

Traditional Banking Services

- Checking accounts
- Saving accounts, money market accounts, CDs
- ATM cards
- Credit cards
- Consumer loans—Cars, mortgages, home equity
- Business loans and services

Other Services

- Purchase and sale of stock, mutual funds
- Investment management, financial planning
- Various forms of insurance
- Other products and services such as travel, emergency roadside assistance, etc.

In choosing a bank or credit union you should look for:

- Financial solvency. Regardless of the financial strength of the institution, you should not exceed the maximum account balance insured by the federal government. The rules keep changing, so be sure to check. If you keep a lot of money in fixed assets, be sure to keep them at more than one institution. Should you have significant money in a brokerage or mutual fund money market fund, always ask if the account is federally insured. If it is not, either move it to an insured account or to a Treasury market fund.
- Free checking with interest on your balance, free debit card, no ATM fees, and 100% coverage of fraudulent use of your debit card(s) over $50. Always ask about this and, if they do not offer it, switch to an institution that does.
- Easy to use, well-executed online services.
- Competitive CD and money market rates.
- Helpful and capable assistance.
- Convenient location(s) or phone and online access.
- Reasonable hold times for deposited checks.

If you are choosing your bank for personal and not business needs, be sure to talk to one or two local credit unions. Many times you will find them to be a very good choice, which is often overlooked as they usually don't advertise on a national basis. Be sure to shop your online choices, as the internet can be used to identify the institutions offering the lowest fees and highest savings rates. If you need business services and prefer not to go to a second bank for your personal accounts, then focus on choosing the best commercial bank.

As to everything else—credit cards, loans, investments, and insurance, etc.—your bank will go out of its way to talk you into "staying with the family." Do not do it. Go out and find your best deal, which will usually not be a bank. For loans, your assets and credit history will be the determining factor, not that you are a "member of the family." For other services, you will usually find a better solution elsewhere that includes no fee, 3%–4% back on gas credit cards, discount brokerage firms for your stock market related purchases, and so on.

If the product or service involved is other than a normal bank product, such as insurance or travel, it is reasonable to assume that the institution is acting as a middleman. Middlemen charge more and usually know less about what they are doing. I will caution you that this is especially true when it comes to investment management and financial planning. It is unlikely that your bank, no matter how large and impressive it may be, will be your best source for such expertise.

Annuities

An **annuity** is a contract that is sold by an insurance company and is designed to provide periodic payments to the holder, usually after retirement. Annuities and their earnings are tax-deferred. They cannot be withdrawn without penalty until a specified age, unless you are hit with something like a true health emergency. Fixed-income annuities guarantee a set payment amount. Variable-income annuities do not, but have the potential for greater returns. Both are relatively safe, low-yielding investments. An annuity has a death benefit equal to the higher of the current value of the annuity or the amount the buyer has paid into it. If the owner dies during the accumulation phase, his or her heirs will receive the accumulated amount in the annuity. This money is subject to ordinary income taxes in addition to estate taxes.

There are two primary types of annuities. One is an immediate annuity, which pays out like a pension. The other is a deferred annuity, which lets users invest money on a tax-deferred basis. Deferred annuities can be in investments that pay a fixed amount or in mutual funds that vary with the stock market or in some combination of the two. Deferred annuities often come with insurance that protects the money against losses, as well as payments to heirs in the event of death.

The benefit of an annuity is safety and, if it's a fixed-income annuity, a guaranteed income stream. There is also the option of having an annuity that appears to protect you from inflation. People who like annuities argue the expense is justified for the peace of mind, and the protection allows users to invest the rest of their money more aggressively in order to generate higher returns to offset those fees. The drawbacks are cost, rate of return, the impact of inflation, and lack of liquidity. Annuities often come with fees and costs that can be as much as 3%–4% a year. As for the impact of inflation, annuities adjusted for this circumstance do not solve the problem. The monthly payments start far lower than a regular fixed-income annuity, and if you add up all the payments, they are unlikely to exceed what you would receive from the regular annuity during your lifetime.

Despite the fact that they are *not* life insurance policies, annuities will usually be recommended by insurance salespeople or insurance companies. They are investment contracts. Their primary benefit is that the income you make is tax-deferred. For this reason buying an annuity in an already tax-protected account makes no sense at all, even though such sales are very common. If I had a financial advisor that recommended such a move to me, I would fire him.

I believe that fixed-income annuities are a bad idea in almost every instance. There are some limited situations, however, where a variable-income annuity may be a good idea. Usually they involve a person that is at, or very close to, retirement age, is afraid of losing money, and is willing to give up quite a lot to be protected. They can also sometimes be of value in certain unusual tax circumstances. It takes a very knowledgeable person to spot when they are desirable and an extremely honest person to sell them only when they should. Unfortunately, there are waves of commission-driven salespeople who will try to convince you to buy an annuity when you should not. Many have very limited knowledge regarding investment and don't know how destructive their recommendations really are. What they do know is that the commission for an annuity is very big. That commission will come from your money. Unfortunately, whether or not an annuity is right for you, many salespeople will rationalize their advice and lock in on the money at stake for themselves.

The best advice I can give is this: Do not purchase an annuity unless you are willing to do enough research on your own first to learn how they really work and whether they might be good for you. On my website I provide a list of sites and articles that can help you.

Whatever you do, do *not* listen to an insurance/annuity salesperson. The subject is complicated, with some of the difficulty added intentionally to make it harder for you to follow. Most of the salespeople are well trained to "prove" what a great thing the annuity is and how right it is for you. Unless you've done your homework, you are very unlikely to spot the huge, fatal flaws in his or her logic, which are likely to be there. Make your own decision. If you decide that you are the exception and that you should consider investing in one, then buy a no-load annuity and save the commission. If you aren't willing and able to do the homework I am suggesting, the decision is simple: Don't buy annuities.

For those of you who have already invested in an annuity, I advise you to do your research before the surrender (penalty) period is up. A lot of the time you will end up deciding to cash it in.

Mutual Funds

A **mutual fund** is an extremely large pool of money invested in a related group of individual stocks and/or various fixed-income investments. A management team makes all the buying and selling decisions within the fund. When you buy shares you own a tiny proportional percent of the whole fund. Your performance will exactly match that of the fund, minus the management fees involved. The fund might be all stocks, all fixed income, or a mix of both. It might be based on geography, i.e. U.S. investments, worldwide, Asia, Brazil, etc. Some funds focus on specific business sectors such as energy or technology, while others focus on company size or company growth potential.

There are a lot of choices, including:

Traditional Mutual Funds. A **traditional mutual fund** either has a commission to buy into it (a load) or it does not have a commission (no load). Sometimes a commission is paid to buy the fund but is not required to sell the fund (front-end load), while others only charge a commission when you sell (back-end load). There are even some funds that are both front- *and* back-end loaded. All mutual funds have an annual management fee (annual expense) that you will be paying. For a "back-end" loaded fund or the "B shares" of a loaded fund, the commission is essentially still there in one form or another. If anyone tries to tell you otherwise, know that such a claim is untrue.

Index Funds. One common type of stock-based mutual fund is an **index fund**. An index fund will own a statistically representative sample of the stocks in a specific portion or sector of the overall market, such as banking, manufacturing, or health care. Each stock in the index is assigned a percentage of the overall holdings in the index fund, which is identical to the size of that company's total market value as compared to the combined values of all of the companies in the indexed sector. By doing this, the fund's performance becomes the same as the entire sector. The most popular of these index funds is the S&P 500 index fund. This fund buys every stock in the S&P 500 index, which represents the five hundred largest companies and therefore the majority of the total value of the U.S. stock market.

ETFs. Another type of mutual fund is an **ETF** (exchange-traded fund). Each ETF represents a large number of individual investments that are all in a specific business area, such as building company stocks, bank stocks, oil company stocks, corporate bonds, etc. ETFs can focus on a market index, such as the S&P 500, or even a specific commodity, such as oil or agricultural products. ETFs can be bought and sold daily just like stocks, and will go up or down in value based on the change in value of their underlying asset group. For example, should the value of bank stocks drop on any given day, a bank stock ETF will drop by the same percent as the overall drop in bank stocks.

ETFs can be attractive as investments because of their low costs, tax efficiency, stock-like features, and—especially—the ability to invest in a whole business arena without being tied to the fortunes of a specific company or set of companies. Annual expenses for ETFs run about 0.4% versus about 1.5% for the average managed fund. As their holdings have a low rate of turnover, the annual tax hit for money not in a tax-protected account will be a fraction of the hit from the average managed mutual fund. Not surprisingly, ETF assets have jumped from $74 billion at the end of 2000, to over $700 billion by the end of 2009 and are now the fastest-growing segment of the mutual fund industry. Unfortunately, ETFs are complex and hard to understand and they often come with large hidden fees and costs. You must do your homework thoroughly, and very carefully research any ETF you consider. I believe the bottom line is that most people should not invest in ETFs.

Here is what I recommend for all of your stock and fixed-income market investing, both planned and existing.

Invest *exclusively* in no-load (no commission) index funds with an annual expense of less than 1% a year. For the portion of this money that you choose to invest in the U.S. stock market, I would put a good percent of that money into an S&P 500 index fund. Such a fund is likely to beat about 80% of all managed mutual funds. Additionally, even if you were good enough (or lucky enough) to have picked one of the 20%, remember that the list of the funds that match or beat the S&P 500 index changes every year. It's not the same set of funds. Makes it pretty simple doesn't it? To their credit, many of the popular financial self-help authors of the last five to ten years have been saying much of the same thing. Most recommend that you invest primarily in no-load index funds. Unfortunately, the marketing effectiveness of the financial services industry has continued to be a far more powerful influence.

Why is it that index funds usually outperform the "pros"? Here's why:

- **Fund managers are usually lagging indicators in their investment decisions.**
- **Fund managers try to time the market.** Mutual fund managers like to keep about 10% or more of their money in cash at any given moment, thereby trying to time their purchases and sales; this is something nobody can reliably do. An index fund, on the other hand, is always 100% invested and as the market, on average, is more likely to be rising over time it usually ends up beating the manager's cash.
- **Lower operating expense.** Index funds usually carry a noticeably lower operating expense as there is nothing much to manage. Managed funds, however, require teams of people out investigating and monitoring the companies they are invested in or are considering investing in. On the other hand, the average managed fund turns over something like 85% of its holdings every year. Studies have concluded that the average U.S. equity fund has annual trading expenses of

about 1.4% and an annual expense ratio of about 1.3%. By comparison, the Vanguard S&P 500 expense ratio is 0.19%. These two factors—higher trading costs and elevated operating expenses—combine to create an expense gap of about 2%, on average, between a managed fund and an index fund.

■ **No commissions.** Many mutual funds are loaded funds with a commission to buy and/or sell the fund. For an equity (stock) mutual fund this commission is likely to run, on average, about 4%–5%. Many investors also end up paying an annual advisor's fee of 0.75%–1.5%, and sometimes a lot more than that.

As you can see in the following chart, the absence of the fees alone creates a dramatic difference over time, especially when you consider that you are dealing with an average market return of 8%–10% a year and net returns, after inflation, in the range of 4%–6%.

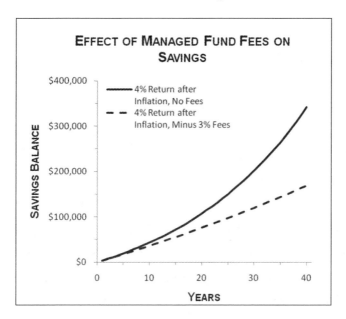

Graph is based on a monthly investment of $300 at an annual return of 8% and an inflation rate of 4%.

To give the illusion of narrowing some of this performance gap, did you know that the mutual fund companies normally do not include the funds they discontinued, usually the losing ones, in their long-term results? Further, something like half of all of the new funds that are opened are discontinued within three or four years. This has a big effect on the numbers they report. Let's say I have six funds and the returns over three years are 15%, 11%, 10%, 7%, 3% and -3%. That's an average performance of 7.2%. But if I close the two worst performers, my track record jumps to an overstated 10.7%. Since the worst funds are gone after a few years, the survivors all look pretty decent; some even look terrific. But it's just dumb luck. What happens next is that the funds with the recent hot track record almost never stay that way.

Let's look at what happens to the average investor, with or without the help of a financial advisor, when it comes to picking mutual funds. A common reaction is to consider what the financial media has to say. In chapter one (pages 6–15) I explained how unreliable the financial media has been in its advice on mutual fund selection. The most common source of advice regarding the selection of mutual funds, however, is not the media. Most investors, as well as most financial professionals, look to the advice of a mutual fund rating service called Morningstar.

Morningstar ratings run from one to five stars. It should be no surprise that 80% of the new money is invested in the four- and five-star funds. The problem is that most of those funds will subsequently underperform and drop to less than four stars, and do so quite quickly, within three years or so. The investors, unhappy with the performance they got, pull their money and move it to the next four- to five-star fund, which then usually repeats that same pattern. Here are several quotes worth thinking about when it comes to making investment decisions based on the Morningstar ratings. Note that the last quote is from Morningstar itself.

> Despite the focus on the stars, there is scant evidence that the stars accurately identify future top-performing mutual funds . . . the results of the study suggest (that) the stars are not useful in identifying future top performers within asset classes.
>
> —*Journal of Investment Consulting*

> Probably the single most potentially dangerous action a mutual fund investor can take is to pay attention to "top performance" lists.
>
> —John Markese, president, American Association of Individual Investors

> If you ask us, star ratings are overrated.
>
> —*Morningstar's Fund Investor* (Morningstar's own newsletter)

The point of all this isn't to keep bashing the "experts" but to point out that it is extremely difficult to pick a fund, especially a stock fund, that is likely to perform well for the next five to ten years; very few people can do it reliably. Further, the most common investor result is dissatisfaction with underperformance, which is followed by churning of their money from fund to fund, which just leads to additional fees.

Should you still harbor any lingering doubts as to what to do regarding managed mutual funds, here's some more to think about:

- You'd think that the mutual fund managers invest a sizeable amount of their own money in the fund(s) they manage, right? I certainly would expect that. Well, Morningstar studies show that over half of the mutual fund managers they track have *none* of their own money in the funds they manage. *Zero!*

■ How about the recommendations of the two greatest mutual fund managers in history? Peter Lynch says, "(Most investors would) be better off in an index fund." Warren Buffet says, "The best way to own common stocks is through an index fund."

By now I'm sure you see the truth. You will still need to be on guard, as the managed mutual fund industry—and all the brokers and financial advisors who currently make their livings from it—are not going to go away without a fight. They will try to do everything they can to reinvent themselves, recommending new and/or "better" alternatives; things like institutional funds, private investment groups, etc., that do "not" hide the problems that have now come to light. Don't you buy it! Most of those same problems will remain.

Should you ever consider relying on the advice of any financial professional when it comes to choosing your investments, here is what I recommend. If you happen to run into that rare financial advisor who can provide you with a five-year or more record, *in writing*, of *100%* of his or her investment recommendations, and the years involved include both up *and* down markets, and the net return is even just a couple of percentage points better on average than the market, then you've found a source of advice worth listening to and paying for.

The same goes for a mutual fund. If you can find a fund that has kept the same manager for the last ten years or more, and he or she has provided a net return of at least several percentage points better than the market, then that is a fund worth considering. If you are not so lucky, which will almost always be the case, do it yourself by investing in no-load, low annual expense index funds. Then periodically go to my website to insure that the market or markets you are in have not become substantially overpriced.

Also, do yourself a favor and do not follow any of these investments or the markets in general on a daily or weekly basis. By doing so you will learn little to nothing and decrease your quality of life by creating unnecessary stress. Also, if you do, you are more likely to shift investments when you shouldn't.

At the end of this chapter I cover asset allocation and the kinds of index funds to consider.

Individual Stocks

Even if you have the knowledge and ability to invest in individual stocks, ask yourself: Is closely following stocks the most enjoyable and profitable way to spend your free time? It can be very time consuming and it's often stressful. Perhaps 10% of you can, and perhaps should, invest in individual stocks in addition to mutual funds. Even if you feel you are in that group, the majority of your money should still be in index funds.

Before I go any deeper into this subject I must again caution you that most people should *not* be investing in individual stocks. For those of you who wish to go deeper yet into this subject despite this warning, you need to be an experienced investor and/or be willing to spend the time necessary to ensure success. For openers, if you haven't already done so, you need to read at least one good book that focuses on the basics of the operation of the stock market, one that explains the terms you will need to know, such as *price earnings ratio* (p/e), *market capitalization*, and so on. Once you have done this you are ready to proceed.

Let's start by considering several different scenarios where an individual stock investment may be brought to your attention:

- A stock is recommended to you by a financial professional or you read about a company or industry that is a "good opportunity" at the moment.

- You've been investing in and following the stock market for at least five years or more and you personally see what you believe to be a good investment.

- You work in a specific industry, know a lot about it, and see what you feel is an unusually good opportunity for growth and success of an industry participant.

- As a consumer, you see a company that looks unusually promising.

- Someone you know and respect suggests a company to consider and provides an attractive rationale for doing so.

Say a stock looks good and you're interested. If so, you must not just trust what you are told. There is a good chance you're dealing with incompetence, or a vested interest, or you're being fed an industry-prepared pitch. Remember that insiders aren't buying—they're selling. Do your homework and make your own personal decision. If you won't do that, don't invest! Once again, part of the reason it is so important you do your homework is this: You are less likely to sell out quickly, at a loss, should the price go down temporarily.

The next step is to do your homework on the investment involved. If you don't do so, and thoroughly, your chance of success will drop a lot. Here are some specific things to do or consider:

- **For each individual stock you are considering, read several analysts reports.** Try to read both a recommendation to buy and an underperform, "hold," or "sell" recommendation. Keep in mind that you're looking to learn things on your own. You are *not* looking to be influenced by their buy recommendations. As discussed in chapter ten (pages 207–220), they are almost always telling you to buy, not to sell.

- **Do not underestimate the difficulty of what you are trying to do.** Most of the information available about a company is already built into its stock price. What's usually missing is the next set of events that will affect the stock in the future and are difficult to predict.

- **Don't be influenced to buy a company because it's recommended by the financial media or by an "expert" of any sort.** Should you have any question regarding this advice, please reread the information provided in chapter one (pages 3–15) and in chapter ten (pages 207–220).

- **Do not invest in a company you wouldn't want to own for at least five years.** Often you think you can time the buying and selling of what you see as a short-term winner. This is a bad idea, as things will probably go differently than you think. Stick to companies that appear fundamentally good for the long term, even if you plan on owning them for a much shorter period. Keep in mind you are really investing in a business, not a "stock," and it should be a business you're willing to own for a long time.

- **Don't invest just because the price seems to be a bargain.** It's far better to buy an excellent company at a fair price than a fair company at an excellent price.

- **Consider buying only a third of what you want.** Wait a little while, and if you still feel good about it, then buy the rest. Lastly, if you like an industry but aren't sure exactly which company or companies to go with, consider buying the ETF for that industry.

- **Be extremely thorough with your homework for stocks priced under $10.** If you can't do that, don't invest in them. Low-priced stocks are an area of much greater risk and one where too many other people are likely to know a lot more than you do about what's going on.

- **Be extremely thorough with your homework on a stock where the p/e ratio is greater than its growth rate, or greater than thirty regardless of its growth rate.** The same goes for any investment with an expected return of over 15% per year. An abnormally high return is a warning that you are now in dangerous territory, so you need to have a compelling case for owning them.

- **Don't confuse brains with a bull (upward) market.** This long-standing Wall Street expression talks about the loss of reality that hits both individual investors and professionals during "booming" markets. Be especially careful to not be influenced by the "experts" who will be the worst of influences at such times.

- **Understand that institutional/mutual fund managers dominate the market.** When the TV news and the daily shows are saying "investors stepped in today" or "investors were selling today" it wasn't individual investors, it was the institutional managers. What they do will usually be *the* dominating influence at any given moment. Never forget this—and also never forget they are usually lagging indicators.

- **If a stock is going up, is this a leading or lagging indicator?** Often it's a lagging indicator, especially if it's been going up for a while, because the industry professionals are the ones doing the buying. Should a stock be dropping, again be careful. A lot of the time the drop is based on things you don't know. Given this, your best bet might either be a stock that dropped a good bit but has now stabilized or a stock whose growth, to this point, has been fairly steady.

- **Never assume a company's stock will withstand a bad market.** When a bad market hits, it takes most of the stocks down with it. Why is this so? Because the institutional managers own most of the stock and they *will* sell, either because they are doing their lagging indicator thing or because they are forced to by redemptions (individual investors selling out of their fund).

- **Try to be properly diversified.** This means owning several industry segments and several stocks, but not too many. How much is enough is a subject of great debate. First, don't own what you aren't confident about and can follow thoroughly. That alone will limit you greatly, both in finding enough stocks you are confident about, and in limiting the number you can thoroughly follow. I'm hesitant to name a number but, again, I know you need something, so here goes. I'm sure I'm going to shock the "experts" when I say that maybe it's one stock. Why? Maybe that's the only stock you feel confident about right now. I see nothing wrong with that as long as you do not have more than 10% of your stock market investment in a single company. It would be better to hold more than one, if possible, so I'll venture that a good number is between five and ten stocks totaling no more than about a third of your investment in the stock market. If it's more than that, I believe you can no longer do the job involved unless you do it full time.

- **Be careful about owning too much of the stock or stock options of the company you work for.** Remember, your salary and your benefits are already dependent on your company. Do you really want to add more eggs to that basket? Diversification suggests you invest in stocks elsewhere. You may feel extremely confident your company will continue to do well, but you can never know for sure. Should you doubt that, Google the words *Enron* and *WorldCom* and see what happened to the employees of those companies who thought they knew the whole story. Further, I would not allow the value of your individual stock holdings to exceed 20% of your net worth (excluding your home).

- **Do not buy a stock at the moment, or within several days, of it being pitched in any way.** That includes TV shows, news stories, brokers, etc. Most of the time the stock will have risen by the time you can execute a buy. Within several days it will usually go back to its former price, as the people behind the promotion involved, or who knew about it before the public did, sell out and pocket their profit which, of course, is your money.

- **Don't underestimate the value of dividends.** They are not only for old people. A respectable dividend is an extremely desirable thing, provided you're comfortable they're likely to remain that way. If a company pays 4%, you just got half the 8% you're looking for right there. Be wary of extremely high dividends, however, as they are often unsustainable and can be a warning sign of pending trouble.

- **If one company buys another, think twice about buying stock in the purchaser for a while.** Their stock frequently goes down for a while because of the purchase.

- **Stick to common stock.** The other alternatives, like preferred stock, may appear better or safer but they usually are not.

- **Pay no attention to technical or pattern analysis (the study of patterns in buying, selling, and price movement).** Make no decisions based on it. It sounds great but loads of people do it full-time and still can't make it work reliably. If you question this, do some pattern analysis trading on paper and see for yourself how unreliable it is.

- **Don't let taxes keep you from selling when you otherwise would.** Every time I did so I regretted it. My favorite story is WorldCom. I owned it from its early days as LDDS-Metromedia. I made hundreds of percent on my investment so my holdings were essentially totally taxable. When I sold 70% of my market holdings in January 2000, one of the stocks I kept was WorldCom because I hated the guaranteed loss of the taxes. I talked myself into believing it would hold up enough in the coming storm. My brother, Ron, did the same thing. Not only was that not so, there were, as you may know, problems a lot bigger than taxes coming down the pike. Despite its huge size, top management had managed to cook the books. They were on their way to jail and brother Ron and I were on the way to a pair of six-figure losses in a single stock. We let the taxes influence us when, in our hearts, we knew we should've been selling. This is an extreme example, but the point still holds true in many cases.

- **Always remember and follow the advice of Warren Buffet:** "Be fearful when they are greedy; be greedy when they are fearful."

Before leaving this subject, I'd like to address the technique of **dollar cost averaging**. Dollar cost averaging means making a repeated number of stock buys over a period of time, usually at set intervals, instead of investing all at once. By doing this you get to buy more shares when the price is cheaper, and less at the higher prices, so you end up paying a lower average price per share. Most investment experts will tell you that it is the way to go. I don't necessarily agree. If you already have the money to invest and play this game, you are doing what the mutual fund managers are doing, which is staying in cash. As the market is, on average, moving up, you will on average lose by staying in cash like they do.

There are two exceptions to this. First, if you are investing into a mutual fund monthly (and the market is not noticeably overpriced), it's okay to do so. Second, if you have an unusually large sum of money to invest at one time, it's usually better not to invest it all at once. Invest a portion, maybe a third, and put the rest in a six- to twelve-month CD. Take the time to think things through and also to see how comfortable you are with the third you already invested. Such an approach is likely to lead to both a better decision and greater peace of mind.

Commodities

Commodities are consumable necessities such as agricultural products (like wheat, oats, and corn); metals (for instance, aluminum or copper); and energy (for example, oil or natural gas). Investing in commodities is attractive for several reasons. First, as Asia and other emerging economies continue to grow, there is likely to be a strong demand for commodities. Second, while global need is likely to expand, the supply of most commodities is somewhat limited. The third reason is that commodities are likely to offer some good protection against the U.S. dollar's continued deterioration, which is likely today given the unsustainable level of debt the U.S. government is currently holding.

If and when you invest in commodities, commit to doing so for a fairly long term. Commodities are often highly manipulated by traders in the short run and it's easy to think you know what's going on when you don't. If you're not committed to the long term, you're far too likely to sell out when you shouldn't.

Don't invest when you don't clearly understand the specific commodity market involved, especially when that market is substantially overpriced. My site, www.MoneySmartOnline.com, will assist you in determining if that is the case. Further, I very strongly recommend against buying commodity ETFs. Such ETFs must constantly replace their expiring buying rights with new ones and when they do, it is usually with a very large penalty. To understand just how bad an investment commodity ETFs are, Google the subject and start reading. If you want to invest in commodities, you are far better off buying stock in companies that are likely to benefit from the increase in commodity price. My brother, Ron, did that in 2000. He invested heavily in oil company stocks and made a lot of money over the next seven years. There is an added advantage in approaching commodities this way. Stock is taxed at the lower capital gains rate for holdings of twelve months or longer. Commodities, on the other hand, are taxed at a mix of regular and capital gains rates.

What about gold? This precious metal is a very heavily pitched investment, but is it a good place to invest? In other than very unusual times, I don't advise it. The sixty-year record of the U.S. stock market and the gold market, adjusted for inflation, follows. You will see that the record for gold is poor when compared to stocks, as it is compared with most investments. Yes, there have been several periods of time, primarily fear-driven, where gold has been a winner, but, as you can see, that is not usually the case. How can you pick those times, and how can you know how long they are likely to last? The bottom line is that gold is either a trading vehicle where the risks usually outweigh the rewards, or a likely underperformer as a long-term buy-and-hold investment.

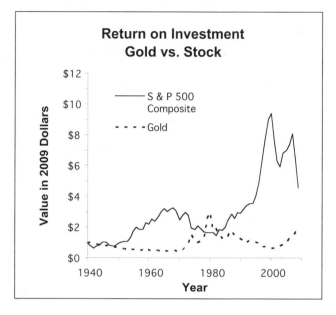

Austin Gold Information Network. 2009. Research – History of Gold Prices since 1793. http://goldinfo.net/yearly.html
Schiller, R. J. 2009. Information Site for Irrational Exuberance. http://www.econ.yale.edu/~schiller

The only possible exception is that gold *might* provide a hedge against extremely difficult economic times or unusually high inflation. The "experts" love to pitch you on that, but there are two problems. The first is that there is no clear evidence to support that gold will be a winner in extremely difficult times or even that it is a reliable hedge against inflation. Maybe it will be, but maybe it won't. The second, and worse, problem is that most of the time the probability of such a favorable time actually occurring is usually too low. Interestingly, as I write this in the spring of 2009, we might be looking at such an exception occurring in the not-too-distant future for maybe the second or third time in my lifetime. Should you ever believe that, be very careful, as history has shown that as soon as the fear involved begins to abate, the price of gold is likely to drop hard and fast. Even if you do someday believe you are looking at the probability of extremely difficult times or unusually high inflation, and have seen enough to convince you that those events are actually starting, do not invest more than a small percentage of your assets in gold. Given that the demand is mostly fear driven, and with the unpredictable trading-driven patterns involved, it's wise to be very cautious.

Real Estate

This section is not about home ownership; that is covered in chapter twelve, "Buying and Selling a Home." It is about real estate investment in property other than your primary residence.

Historically, the vast majority of all fortunes have been made in two places—real estate and owning your own business. Real estate is a great place to invest, and I very much encourage you to consider it if and when you're ready. As with all investments, you should not invest in real estate unless you really know what you are doing.

Investing in real estate is a business. Many people think otherwise. Worse yet, there is no end to the people out there who would like to give you some advice and get some of your money in the process. These people will go to great lengths to convince you it is an easy way to make money. I'm talking about all those seminars, books, and infomercials on how to get rich in real estate. By now you know exactly what I think about them and what you should do. As I've already said, "easy" has a very clear message. It means run! If you think you can simply read a book or someone's "plan" and go out and succeed, you'll probably just end up losing a lot of money that goes into the pockets of others, making *them* rich.

It is not the purpose of this book to tell you how to start and operate a business. What I will do, however, is spend a few minutes to show you why investing in real estate is usually a business and why you better darn well do your homework very thoroughly before getting started. Real estate has historically been one of the greatest sources of wealth, but it is also one of the most dangerous places to lose wealth when you don't know what you're doing. The stakes are extremely high.

So what do you have to do to succeed? Let's start by listing the most common investment choices followed by the fifteen decisions you're going to have to make—and make correctly—in order to be successful. Then I'll give you some idea of how much you must know to make those decisions. By the time we're done I hope you will begin to appreciate what type of research is required and possess some idea of how to proceed.

There are ten choices for real estate investment. By the time you hit number 5, you are involved in the running of a business. The possibilities, in order of difficulty, are:

1. A second or vacation home
2. A residential home or condo to rent out
3. A small multi-unit property where you will be one of the tenants
4. Land to hold for long-term investment
5. Land to subdivide and sell off
6. An apartment building
7. An office building
8. A mixed-use property
9. An industrial building
10. A shopping center

You can also own shares in a corporation or limited partnership in any of the above businesses. If you do, you are then depending on the expertise of those running that business venture. The same advice applies: Trust no one and do your homework. Listed below, in sequence, are questions to answer when buying:

1. Is the market's near- to mid-term future positive?
2. Is the purchase price right?
3. Is the structure of the deal right? Are the tax consequences minimized?
4. Is the estimate of future value well thought out?
5. Will the costs involved be about as expected?
6. Can you handle the costs if the market weakens and the vacancy rate rises?
7. Are there any significant hidden negatives that will hurt value?
8. If government approvals are required, will you get them, and approximately within your time and cost estimates?
9. For an income property, will the income be about as estimated? How about the vacancy rate?
10. Do you possess, or have at your disposal, the management skills and resources needed?

When it comes to selling, your success will again be based on the quality of your decision making. The questions to be answered are:

- Is this a good time to sell?
- Have you chosen the right asking price and terms?
- Have you chosen the right steps to prepare the property?

- Will the property sell within approximately the time frame, price, and terms expected?
- Have you made a good decision regarding who will sell it and how the agency and its representative will go about it?

Let's start with one of the easiest choices, a residential home or condo to rent out. If you've been a homeowner, you may feel you know what's involved. Have you ever been a landlord? Some of the people that will want to rent from you are trouble. They may stop paying the rent, damage your property, and/or do all they can to go on living there as long as possible without paying another cent. Do you know how to screen them out? Do you know the laws of your state regarding tenants' rights? It's likely that the bad tenants do. They know where the fine print is that lets them stop paying rent and get away with it. They know the energy and cost involved in collecting money via legal action.

Are you willing to give up the time, money, and loss of quality of life that might be involved in being a landlord? Do you really know the costs you will face to carry the property? How about the probable vacancy rate? So far we've covered parts of two decisions. What about the other eight? Are you well prepared to make them? You certainly can be. I just don't want you to underestimate the situation and get hurt. If you thoroughly research each of the questions above, real estate investment may well be a very good path for you.

How about buying some raw land to hold for long-term investment? That should be easy, shouldn't it? No, it isn't. Once again, you need the information to make those ten decisions. Here are some of the things you need to know:

- How is the parcel zoned, and what are the usage restrictions?
- What is the probability it will be unfavorably rezoned in the years to come?
- Can it be subdivided and, if so, what are the rules, the cost involved, and the value of the subdivided parcels you could get?
- What is the zoning of the adjacent and neighborhood land?
- Do you think the adjacent parcels and also the neighborhood will change noticeably over the next ten years and, if so, in what way?
- Are there any pending new public easements (legal right to use the property)?
- Are there enough good comparative properties to give a clear picture of the current value?
- What qualifies you to make these decisions and, if others are making them, what qualifies them? Can you trust in their honesty and competence? Do they make money off your decision?

If you look at the rest of the list of investment choices, you can see that both the complication and knowledge needed keeps rising. The bottom line is that to safely and successfully invest in real estate, you need to do a number of things. First, read up on the subject. Second, talk to people who have done it successfully. Third, go out and look at a lot of properties over a fairly long period of time—six months should be the absolute minimum and preferably a year or two. If possible, you or your spouse or partner should go to work full- or part-time as a real estate agent to list and sell the kinds of properties you are interested in owning. If you do that, you will learn the most of all.

If you aren't willing to do these things, you still have the alternative of entrusting your investment to others by taking a piece of what they do through an LLC or partnership of some sort. If you do, you still need to learn a lot about the subject, the properties available, and everything you can about both them and their business plan for the property or properties.

Please do not take anything stated here as discouragement. Real estate can be a terrific place to invest. I have been successful with it and you can be, too. The very things I learned and did, however, taught me to respect how much knowledge is necessary. Just make sure that you're really ready.

At this point you may be wondering about timeshares. I can give you one piece of advice: Do *not* buy a new timeshare! Not ever! Should you have any question about how bad a move this is, go online, Google the subject, and start reading. Among other things, you will discover that the average new timeshare loses at least 50% of its value the minute you own it.

I lived on Maui, where timeshare selling has been at epidemic proportions for decades. You can easily pocket hundreds of dollars for getting a prospect to visit a site. The timeshare companies can afford that because they are very, very good at what they do. They close sales with something like 30% of the people who walk in the door. The people who buy generally didn't have the purchase of a timeshare as a high priority before they got there, haven't done any homework on it, and therefore are extremely unprepared to spot the flaws in the seller's logic. Quite frankly, most people are sitting ducks in that situation.

The bottom line is this: *Never* attend a timeshare presentation. Do not let your ego ("You can't sell *me!*") do you in. Do not take the risk that they can find a way to get to you.

A key element in the pitch is to tell you that the timeshare will be a good investment. The truth is that timeshares are such a bad investment that many can't even be given away to charities. The annual maintenance cost versus the value of the unit makes them essentially worthless.

Should you ever feel that a timeshare has become a priority item on your wants and wishes list, go online and buy one of the tens of thousands of units being resold for a *fraction* of their purchase price by all those people who didn't follow the advice I'm giving you. You also might consider renting one of the thousands of units available; they are often dirt-cheap. By renting you pretty much get to go where you want, when you want, with no restrictions.

Starting or Buying a Business

Small business drives the U.S. economic engine, and millions of small businesses are successful. It is historically one of the two great sources of wealth, the other being investment in real estate. The intent of this section, however, is to provide information on the investment aspects of owning a business. Such subjects as career selection, starting, and successfully running a business are whole books in their own right. I am, however, a big fan of owning your own business, provided it's the right thing for you and provided you prepare yourself thoroughly for such a challenging step. For this reason, I will go a little bit farther than just looking at the investment aspects involved. To get you started, here are some of the key things to consider and/or do.

Do you have the necessary skills and a very strong desire to run a business? Are you willing to work long hours? Don't buy into the illusion that it will be easier when you work for yourself. Expect to work long, hard hours for at least the first two years and probably a lot longer than that. Can you handle the pressures and the risks involved? Do you have the necessary skills?

If you answer yes to these questions, you might want to double-check yourself by asking people who know you what they think. If you find you hold significant doubts, don't start a business until and unless you resolve them. Starting a business is always challenging. Nothing is simple, so do not underestimate what will be involved.

Plan for the work to start a new business to be twice what you estimate, because it will be. The same goes for the start-up capital involved. Do your best to estimate required start-up costs, then double that figure. If you can't handle that then don't do it, because the figure will almost certainly be double. The average successful full-time business start-up loses money the first fifteen months. Don't assume you'll be any different.

If possible, start the business part–time while keeping other employment, preferably something that provides health insurance for you and your family. If you happen to already work in the same business or business area, it will really help you with your homework and decision making.

Thorough homework is absolutely critical. This means getting a good understanding of how the business works, your chances of success, how to succeed, and how to prepare. Remember the keys to success, which are hard work, believing in yourself, and never quitting. Boy, are they ever the keys here. Most people do not do enough homework.

They think a few hours does it, when what's needed is a few hundred hours. If you don't do your pre-start-up homework thoroughly, your chance of failure soars. Most of the time you will learn that your idea is not likely to work. Don't let that discourage you. For most successful people, such events turned out to be the necessary steps that led them to the right idea. It was how they learned. So do your homework. Here is what you have to do:

- Read at least one good book on starting your own business.
- Read everything you can about the specific business you are considering.
- Make a thorough list of what you want to know.
- Talk to several different people whose business will not be your competition because they are in another city, retired, etc., who have done it successfully.
- Go to trade shows and talk to people.
- Talk to potential suppliers or businesses that will be supporting you in some way.
- Work part-time in the same business, if possible. This will be a huge advantage if it can be done.
- Do a thorough search for pending new competition and trends or new innovations that will change and/or damage the business you are considering.
- Create a file on every significant competitor. Study each one to learn all you can about them.
- If there are a limited number of potential customers, create a file on each one. If that's not the case, such as in a retail business, create a profile of each customer type.

- Create a file on everything that can help in getting started, e.g., how and where to advertise, marketing ideas, using the internet to attract customers and drive sales, etc.

- If you are considering buying an existing business and a real estate agent or other such middleman is involved, be sure to read the explanation on selecting and dealing with a real estate agent in chapter twelve, "Buying and Selling a Home" (see page 271). Trust no one, and independently verify everything you are told, especially the reason given for selling. An awful lot of the time the reason given is not true and they know something you don't. The reason could be new competition, zoning changes, loss of key personnel, pending big increases in costs, changes in technology, etc.

As to investing in an ownership position in someone else's business, the risk you will lose your money is very high, especially if it's a new business. If it's a new business, I would advise against it. If it is an existing business, however, maybe it *is* something worth doing. In that instance most of the homework listed still applies.

If you like what you learn from your homework, create a thorough, written start-up plan. Identify your capital needs, the products and/or services you will offer, your customer base, specific goals and timetables, assessment of competitors, and pricing strategy. Do not skip this step! If you can, get an experienced person to help you. Most new business start-ups fail. Thorough homework and a well-prepared plan will cut those odds a lot.

Don't let the length of this list discourage you. Once you get into it you'll probably find it a pretty enjoyable thing to be doing. Also, don't feel you must be perfect "or else." You'll often find that if you miss something in one place it will just pop up someplace else.

There is one more piece of advice. Do *not* participate in a multi-level marketing business of any kind! I am talking about a business where there are master distributors then sub-distributors, then sub-sub-distributors, etc. Most of the people who participate in such ventures end up losing and are sold a distorted bill of goods that only benefit others. The odds are absolutely awful. You will be told of people making terrific money. Are there such people? Yes, but they are a tiny minority who are usually doing it at the expense of others.

If at any time you consider doing such a thing, I urge you to first go to the internet and Google the name of the company and read everything you can. Be careful that the source is reliable and not a setup. This is anything but a new game. I remember my first boss almost lost his house because he bought loads of multi-level marketing product he couldn't sell—and that was forty-five years ago. There is a term for most of these schemes. They're called *pyramid schemes*. Go Google that, while you're at it.

Collectibles

In 1962 I decided to try to make some money buying and selling coins, specifically uncirculated rolls of some of the harder-to-find U.S. coins. The trade paper in those days was *Coin World*. Every week it would have a large number of dealer or speculator ads on buying and/or selling. Many were half- to full-page ads. What I discovered was that many of the ads were exactly the opposite of what they seemed to be.

Take the following ad: "*Must* buy 1950-D nickels. *Any* quantity!" When I called the day the paper came out I was told, "Sorry, we just bought all we can handle this week. Try us again later." I came to learn that for many of the ads there *was* no later. Every week they continued to run their ad, and every week they "just bought all they could handle." It didn't take a lot of digging to learn the truth. These people weren't buying 1950-Ds; they were *selling* them. The advertising campaign was designed to keep the price as high as possible. Pretty clever, eh? In the stock market, the government polices such activity and it is illegal. But since there is no oversight in the collectibles markets, there is no buyer protection in place.

I tell you this story to illustrate a point about collectible markets in general. They are a lot more risky than you may think. It is extremely common to be led to believe you can sell whatever you are buying at a nice profit when it's just not so. There are certainly some very nice and capable people involved with collectibles. I've met a number of them, and they would be among the first to tell you to be extremely careful.

Can you make any significant money at collectibles? Yes, but you better be really, really good at it. Be careful that you are in that elite group. Also, be honest about how much time it takes to make any money. If you enjoy yourself, great; that counts for a lot. For the other 99% of you, my advice is to not invest in collectibles, as you will lose money. For example, did you know that the FBI reported in 2003 that at least half of the items sold in the one-billion-dollar-a-year autographed sports and celebrity memorabilia industry were fake, including forgeries so good that even the best of experts were often fooled by them?

If you do dabble in collectibles, perhaps as a hobby, look out for the "phony price" game. The experts appraise what you are buying, even what you've already bought from others, and show you the money you've already made. Ask them to buy it from you at that price. Surprise! They will have a very good reason why they aren't buying "right now." So what's the game? The game is to get you into a frame of mind where you don't want to sell and won't even try. You'll be happy to hoard your good fortune and wait for the even greater gains they tell you are "highly likely." Better yet, they'd love to sell you even more of those "good" investments.

A variation of this game is part of the sales pitch for an awful lot of the diamonds that are sold. The salesperson convinces you that you're getting such a low wholesale price that it will appraise out for a lot more than you're paying. For diamonds, it's a sales pitch. After all, who's going to sell her ring? For other collectibles and investing in them, however, it is a lot more than that. This leads me to make a further observation: Almost everyone who collects never sells. How much is something worth if it's never sold?

Another sales ploy to look out for is the "phony market." Technically it's called a Ponzi scheme. Here is how this game is played. You are told that a hot new artist has emerged. You love his work and buy one of his originals or a limited edition print. You can't wait to hang it in your living room. At that moment, the gallery will tell you the price of this guy's work is starting to skyrocket. You just made a terrific last-minute buy. Several weeks later, the gallery calls. The prices on his work are shooting up. Maybe they will tell you of some event that caused it, maybe not. You can sell your painting for a lot more than you paid for it, right now. They ask you "Would you like to sell it?"

The question is a setup. They already know you won't sell. Why should you? The price is rocketing up and you bought the art for your living room wall for you to enjoy. Either on that call or the next one, the game escalates. As one of the artist's early supporters, you will be given "an opportunity" to buy more of the artist's work as an investment that is "almost guaranteed" to make you a *lot* of money.

So what's the catch? The catch is that there almost always is no real market, just a temporary one created by the game. Just like musical chairs, when the music stops, guess what? Those holding the paintings can't sell them at anything like they paid and will lose, big-time. Understand that this is a sophisticated game. The gallery will buy back some of the paintings when they have to, as part of keeping the game going. Such minor losses have little impact on their overall profit. Feel like playing this game? I sure don't.

In summary, unless you are in that rare, extremely knowledgeable group and are happy with your pay-per-hour of time spent dealing with collectibles, and/or the enjoyment you get, don't invest in them. Collectibles are a hobby, not a sound investment.

Other Considerations

Tax Minimization

Because taxes are such an important factor when investing, you want as much of your investments as possible to be in a tax-protected account. For any portion of your money that is not in a tax-protected account, please keep the following in mind as you decide how to invest:

- Investments held twelve months or longer (long-term investments) are taxed at the capital gains rate, which is typically quite a bit lower than the tax rate you normally pay on investments held less than twelve months (short-term investments). Currently, short-term investments are taxed at the same rate as your regular income (ordinary income).

Paying at the reduced tax rate has a significant impact over time, as you compound not only your base investment but also the extra dollars you got to keep.

- The profit on your managed mutual funds is essentially taxed every year, and the majority will be at your ordinary income rate. This is because the average fund manager sells a very high percentage of his investments each year, thereby creating a lot of short-term investments. If there's a loss for the year you get to claim the loss as a deduction. However, long-term losses cannot be deducted from anything but long-term gains. It is not uncommon to have more long-term losses in any given year than long-term gains. Long-term losses can, however, be held over for several years and eventually paired against long-term gains. Some of your short-term losses (currently up to $3,000) can be used to offset ordinary income. Short-term losses can also be paired against long-term losses but this is usually a bad idea, as the tax rates are different and you will not receive the full benefit of reducing the higher tax rate gains.

- The annual tax on index funds and ETFs is generally minimal until and unless you sell. So, while it's best to own individual stocks and managed mutual funds with your tax-protected dollars, your index funds and ETFs can be in accounts that are not tax protected.

- Should the market get badly overpriced and you need to sell a lot, try to do so in the following sequence: First, sell stocks that are not in tax-protected accounts that have losses; then sell the ones with small profits; then sell stocks held over a year for the capital gains tax rate; and, finally, stocks with substantial short-term profit. You probably can't pull this strategy off 100%, but get as close to that as you can.

■ Remember that if an investment needs to be sold, don't pull a "WorldCom" and let tax decisions stop you from selling. The odds are you'll lose more money yet if you do.

The information provided in this Tax Minimization section is based on IRS rules as of 2010. Substantial changes to the tax laws are tracked on my website.

Asset Allocation (Diversification)

Asset allocation is a fancy term for how you choose to diversify your investments. The decisions involved are highly personal ones based on the size and nature of your assets, how financially free you are, your age, your tolerance for risk, what opportunities are available to you, and how good you are at evaluating and executing those opportunities. It also depends on where you are in your overall plans, as your allocation will need to shift both over time and as your assets grow. The types of investments that might typically be involved include:

■ A home (primary residence)

■ Cash or its equivalent: CDs, money markets, treasury bills, etc.

■ Corporate or municipal bonds

■ The U.S stock market

■ Foreign stock markets

■ Commodities

■ Other investments such as real estate, a business, etc.

I will repeat what I told you under Investment Rule #10: Diversify Your Investments. The success of the market in the 1990s and the brain-washing that you will "always win in the long run" has truly twisted so many heads when it comes to the importance of investing in the U.S. stock market. Investing in the U.S. stock market can be a *component* of your long-range financial plan but it must never *be* the plan. Your plan should include many components. These components should include such items as no debt whatsoever, owning your home free and clear, fixed-income investments, investment in the U.S. stock market, and investments in the markets of other countries. Additional possibilities include commodities such as grain and oil, real estate, a small business, and so on. True diversification requires you to develop and maintain a plan that includes a number of these components and to never over-rely on a single one.

Always start by eliminating your debt and maximizing your tax-protected contributions. Then, if you haven't already done so, buy a home, provided the real estate market is not noticeably overpriced.

As a general approach to how to allocate your tax-protected accounts, if your investment horizon (the number of years before you need the money) is ten years or more and the stock market is not noticeably overpriced, I would allocate about 70% to no-load stock index funds and 30% to fixed-income investments. If your horizon is shorter, increase the percentage that is in fixed income. Similarly, if your overall assets are modest, and you will therefore need those assets quicker than if you had deeper pockets, you must increase the percent of fixed investments. When you do, remember that fixed-income investments make little or nothing in real dollars after inflation is taken into account. Unless you are fortunate enough to have all the money you'll need for your entire life, the best bet is usually to remain actively invested in stock, provided the market involved is not noticeably overpriced.

For the portion of money you allocate to stock funds, stocks, and commodities, I suggest you invest a good portion of it in foreign markets. Although the S&P 500 index will give you some degree of international investment, I'm recommending you go a lot farther. The U.S. economy is fairly matured and is unlikely to grow as strongly going forward as it has in the past. Other economies, especially those in Asia, continue to emerge and are likely to grow at a decidedly better rate over the next twenty years or so. Also, the U.S. government has a huge and ultimately unavoidable debt problem, and one must expect that the U.S. dollar will eventually depreciate a lot. By owning foreign investments you are likely to both benefit from greater growth and reduce the hit from the depreciation of the U.S. dollar. The greatest single risk of overseas investments is political risk so be vigilant to such possibilities and diversify by investing in multiple countries, perhaps by using a non-loaded regional fund.

When you make overseas investments try to make them for the long run. They are not short-term bets. Also, stick to investing in no-load international funds as you are very unlikely to know enough when it comes to picking individual stocks.

The following is a basic guide to help you with your asset allocation. Once again, I offer these suggestions *only as a basic guide* as they must be tempered by your personal situation, including the amount of assets you already own, your age, and your tolerance for risk. For example, if you already have what you need and are uncomfortable with risk, why take any? Also, if you are in or are close to retirement you should consider lowering your level of risk by increasing the percentage in fixed income, etc. Lastly, be prepared to shift your percentages when specific markets become substantially over- or underpriced. This is something that is likely to happen only a few times in a decade. Again, my website will keep you informed about these markets.

1. If you start with only a small amount of money I'd consider putting it all in an S&P index fund.

2. Your next step would be to begin to put some money in an international stock fund or funds. Be careful to select an international fund, not a global fund. Global funds often have big positions in U.S. stocks, while international funds do not. If you invest in a global fund, you could be duplicating investments and may not get enough non-U.S. investments. I especially like Asian markets as a long-term bet, but I must caution you that those markets often get wildly overpriced and then drop a lot. Whenever you are considering investing in them, be sure to visit www.MoneySmartOnline to see my opinion of market value, along with links to other sites offering some good input on this issue.

3. Your third step would be to grow your fixed-income position to about 30% of your total. As I've already said, build your position using CDs, long-term treasuries (if you're in a fairly high tax bracket), and high-quality individual corporate bonds, rather than by using a bond fund or funds. By using individual investments of this nature, there are no fees, fund expenses, or frequent end-of-year gains taxes. Also, you know exactly the price you are paying and the interest you will be receiving. With a

bond fund, the value of your investment and the interest you get will almost certainly bounce around a lot.

4. Once you are saving the maximum tax-deferred amount allowed by the IRS, I recommend that you begin to pay off your mortgage, if you have one, fairly aggressively. The return is guaranteed at the interest rate you pay for your mortgage, less any tax savings you are getting by deducting the mortgage interest. For example, if you are in a 28% federal tax bracket and have a 6% mortgage, you would be saving about 4.3% net after taxes. This isn't that much less than the historic return of 5% on fixed-income investment, plus there is the benefit of additional peace of mind. You'll know you're on the way to owning your home free and clear.

If and when you get to the point where you've done these things, a good mix might be something like:

- 30% in fixed income: money market funds, CDs, treasuries, corporate and municipal bonds.
- 40% in an S&P no-load index fund. (I'd keep at least half of this money in an S&P 500 index fund.)
- 30% in international no-load stock fund(s).
- Zero debt
- A home you own free and clear

That's about as far as you should ever really need to go. This approach keeps things simple. You don't need to get involved with decisions like growth stocks versus value stocks or income stocks. These categories don't really vary on overall return that much anyway over the long run. You will notice I did not recommend using a mixed-asset fund (one that invests in both stock and fixed income). Mixed-asset funds don't let you control your diversification preferences, as these funds can often shift quite wildly in their mix of stock versus fixed income.

Please, do not throw up your hands and feel you cannot make these decisions. You can and should. Investing takes a little time and effort. In return, the payoff will likely prove to be far greater than anything else you could do with that time.

Lastly, I remind you of what I said under Investment Rule #10: Diversify Your Investments—that the outcome of investment decisions will never be 100% certain, and that's okay. You goal should be to diversify your investments into a number of things with a high probability of success. That is the best we can do and is also usually all we need to do.

CHAPTER TWELVE

Buying and Selling a Home

This chapter is about buying and selling your home. For all other investment in real estate, go to the section in chapter eleven, "Evaluating Your Investment Alternatives," regarding investing in real estate (see page 250). If you are considering buying a timeshare, you also need to read what I had to say about timeshares in chapter eleven before reading this chapter (see page 255).

For most of you, your home will probably be your biggest asset and the single biggest area of investment decision making in your life. It is easy to assume you know how to buy and sell a home but there is probably a lot you do not know, even if you are not a first-time home buyer. This chapter will cover whether and when to buy or sell a home and how to go about it. Let's start with the buying process.

Buying a Home

In the section on investing in real estate, you read that the buying process breaks down into a series of decision steps. It's the same here. Listed below, in sequence, are the questions to be considered, followed by a brief discussion of each decision area. It's best to follow the sequence shown below. If you do not, you will significantly increase the odds you will make bad decisions.

Question 1: Should you rent or buy?

Owning your own home can obviously provide a number of very desirable non-financial benefits. As for the financial benefits, it's said that a home is your best investment. Is that true? If you look at return on investment, residential real estate tends to roughly track the rate of inflation and little more. Even after factoring in the tax savings involved, a home is not a very good investment unless you happen to buy at a low point in the pricing cycle. Nevertheless, owning your own home is a very good financial idea for most people, but not because it makes you a lot of money.

The first reason buying a home is usually a good financial idea is because most people are not disciplined at saving money, and a mortgage payment forces them to save. So if you are like most people then, yes, a home is your "best" investment. The second reason is that, for most people, owning their home free and clear is a very desirable component of achieving financial freedom. Add up the reasons and you'll see that owning your own home is usually a very good idea.

Buying a home is not a good idea if you are uncertain you will live in the same area for at least the next four to five years, unless the market is substantially underpriced. The transaction costs and effort involved in the purchase and sale are too much to justify the purchase in this case. A short window of ownership also increases your exposure to market risk. The longer the time period, the more likely the ups and downs will average out in your favor.

Other reasons to postpone buying a home include if your employment and income are uncertain, if your relationship situation is shaky, or if you do not have a sufficient emergency fund in place. You should have a five- to six-month emergency fund and be essentially debt free. If 25% or more of your net income is going to debt payment other than an existing mortgage, you cannot afford to buy a home until you change that situation.

Next, you need to be honest about your ability to handle the total expense load involved. Total expenses include your mortgage payment, taxes, insurance, maintenance, association fees (if any), and a somewhat higher level of utility costs than is normally associated with a rental. If there is a significant risk that you cannot handle this new level of expense keep renting for a little longer, save more money and, if you can, increase your income level a little farther.

Lastly, homeownership is a big responsibility. If you are not sure you want to take it on at this time, don't do it. Instead, save and invest the extra money so you have the option to change your mind in the future.

Assuming you do not have any of these issues that would prevent you from buying at this time, the advantages and disadvantages to owning your own home are listed below. Be sure to think through each of these factors very carefully. Even if you are better off being a homeowner, it may well be that it's not yet the time to do so.

The Advantages of Owning a Home:

- You are assured a permanent home.
- You have a greater selection of living environments and homes to choose from.
- For many, homeownership offers a sense of pride and accomplishment.
- You are free, the boss of your world, as you can alter your home and property in whatever manner you wish, can afford, and the law allows.
- Buying a home creates forced savings. For most people this is a *very* big benefit.
- It is a key component for most people in achieving financial freedom.
- It removes some of the pressure to invest your money wisely. A big portion of the decision has been made and your investments are also now more diversified.
- Although maintenance and taxes will continue to rise with inflation, your mortgage payment will not, provided you get a long-term fixed-interest mortgage. If you rent, 100% of your payment is likely to rise with inflation. For many, the inflation protection provided by owning a home offers a lot of peace of mind.
- It's possible you might get some added tax savings, but be sure to calculate your taxes both ways, that is, standard deduction versus itemized deduction to understand the true impact. For most people, these tax breaks don't add

anything much, as the interest and taxes most people incur turn out to be somewhat similar to the amounts provided by the IRS standard deduction.

- Many will say that investment return should be on the list of benefits of home ownership. History has shown, however, that the value of your home is likely to increase at about the rate of inflation and little more, making it likely the investment will underperform your other investment choices, such as the stock market. The only exception would be if you happen to purchase at a low point in the residential real estate cycle. (The eighty-year history of the U.S. residential home market is provided in chapter one. See page 17.)

- If you withdraw money later in life from a tax-protected account, 100% of that money will be taxed unless it's a Roth IRA, where the money is taxed before it goes into the account. The same goes for the profit on any and all investments you make using non-tax-protected money. The profit on a home, however, is much more protected from such taxation up to certain limits. Hopefully that will still be true in the future; nonetheless, I would plan on such tax protection becoming a lot more heavily tied to your income and assets. Make too much or have too much and it's likely you'll also end up being taxed at some point in the future on most or all of the profit from your home, should you sell it.

The Disadvantages of Owning a Home:

- As already stated, alternate investments, such as a long-term investment in the stock market, are likely to beat owning a home quite substantially over time. This financial gap becomes a lot bigger yet if you are willing and able to pay a very low rent and save the difference.
- It is likely to require a lot more money out of your cash flow every month than you would pay for a rental.
- It adds a number of responsibilities, will probably require a decent amount of work, and take from your free time, especially if it is a detached single-family dwelling.
- It limits your ability to move elsewhere, except at a substantial cost of time, money, and disruption.
- You have a large ongoing financial responsibility you may not be able to able to get out of quickly, except at great cost.
- It may tie up a lot, or perhaps all, of your otherwise free money, thereby limiting your financial options going forward.
- If you're away a lot for business or other reasons, owning a house may create additional pressures and responsibilities you may not want. If this is the case, a condo may be a better choice.

Question 2: Is this a good time to buy?

Chapter five, "The 10 Rules of Investing Successfully," dealt with understanding and acting on market cycles. This is a good time to reference that information and go to my website, where I do my best to give you an idea of where we are in the residential real estate cycle at any given moment. One of the key ways I do so is by calculating the affordability of the current price levels. As an example, if mortgage rates are at 5.7% and the median family income in your area is $50,000, then median home prices should not be noticeably greater than four times family income, or $200,000. The higher the multiple is, the greater the probability that the value of homes in your area cannot be sustained by the household incomes in your area.

After checking my website, you should still do some additional homework regarding the status of your specific local market, as compared to the national, regional, and major metropolitan area pictures covered on my site. It's really important to always do these things, as you do not want to buy real estate if the market is substantially overpriced. Resist any pressure you may feel to jump into a significantly overpriced real estate market. Do not do it! Be patient and keep saving. You'll get your chance and probably a much nicer house.

What if the market is only slightly overpriced? In that instance, go buy your home if you're ready to do so and it's what you want to do. If we were talking strictly investment, then that's another matter, but a home is a lot more than just an investment.

Even if the real estate market is at an acceptable level, there may be another factor that may mean you should delay buying. That factor is your credit rating (FICO score). If you have a low FICO score you will end up paying dearly for it in the form of a substantially higher interest rate. It is not uncommon for the difference to be as much as 2%. On a $200,000 mortgage, this translates into a loss of up to $4,000 a year or $3,000 if you itemize your tax deductions. It would be far better to hold off buying for a little while and do all you can to first raise your FICO score. For more information on this subject, see my website for links to sites, articles, and books that can help you. Additional information on raising your FICO score is available on my website under debt elimination.

What is the best time of year to buy? Sixty percent of all sales occur in the spring. Does that mean it's the best time to buy? Unfortunately, the answer is a mixed one. The biggest selection is in the spring, but the best prices are in the fall, as the remaining sellers are now much more receptive to taking a lower price rather than holding on any longer.

Lastly, if you already own a home you must not be obligated to buy your next until you've sold your old one, unless you are fortunate enough to be able to make the purchase independently of the sale. Yes, I know this is a big problem, but it's one that almost everyone has to deal with. The purchase of your next house *must* be contingent on (subject to) the sale of your current one. Although you can usually avoid it, you must be prepared to store your stuff and rent for a while if necessary. At times you may think you can get around this by finding someone willing to enter into a contingency contract when your current home is not already under contract. This is usually a bad idea as you can pretty much bet the selling price involved will be noticeably higher than they would have otherwise taken.

Question 3: What can you afford to buy?

Write down the amount of your monthly net income after taxes and IRA contributions. Then add up all monthly debt payments, excluding your existing mortgage payment if you have one. Once again, if 25% or more of your net income is going to debt payments other than an existing mortgage, you cannot afford to buy a home until you change that situation.

Assuming you don't have that problem, your next step will be to identify the amount you can put down and the monthly payment you can afford. A lot of people assume all that's needed is to pay the monthly mortgage payment but, as you are about to see, you will need a lot more than that.

To figure out the monthly payment you can afford, start with what you identified as free money in your Spending and Saving Plan back in chapter six. Add to that all of your current monthly housing costs. Make a reasonable estimate of your new property taxes, insurance, maintenance and homeowner's fees, and additional commuting costs, if any, and subtract them from the total. Add back in the tax savings you expect to receive from being a homeowner and you have the monthly payment you can afford.

To figure out the amount you can put down, start by calculating the total amount you will have available. Available savings should not include any of the money in your emergency fund. Emergencies will happen and it will be even worse if you're a homeowner and you don't have an emergency fund. You can probably borrow additional money from your 401(k) but I recommend you do not do so. The money you take will be taxed twice, when you loan it and again when the money comes out again in the future. Also, if you lose your job or are fired you must repay the loan immediately. If you have a Roth IRA you don't have these problems, but I'd still be cautious about taking from your savings for the future.

Once you know how much savings you have available, subtract from it all of the miscellaneous costs involved in buying a home. These costs usually range from 3%–6% of the purchase price and include such things as loan origination fees, up-front "points" (prepaid interest, where each point equals one percent of the loan amount), application fees, appraisal fee, home inspection, survey, title search, title insurance, recording fees, transfer fees, and attorney's fees.

When calculating the mortgage payment and down payment you can afford, do not borrow money beyond what you have saved. A family member may offer to loan you money so you can buy a better house. First, it's not a good idea to borrow money from anyone other than a bank. Second, you now have an extra financial burden of the additional payment that must be made sooner or later. Third, you just used up your best backup should trouble, such as the loss of job or a major illness, arise in the future.

The minimum you should have available for a down payment is 20%. After all that has happened with bad mortgages, you will find that most lenders now require at least 20% down. If you can't do that but can readily make the monthly payment, can put down 10% or more, and the housing market is not overpriced—and you must meet all three conditions—then it's probably okay to go ahead.

At this time your only source for a loan that requires less than 20% down is likely to be an FHA loan. Such a loan has two substantial extra costs. The first is the fees charged tend to be higher than for a conventional mortgage. The second is that when you put down less than 20% you are required to pay for private mortgage insurance (PMI). The amount involved tends to run somewhere between three-eighths and three-quarters of a percent of your loan amount per year. Should there ever be any payoff on this insurance, it will go to your lender, not to you. Once your equity is over 20% you can get it removed, but it will take many years to increase your equity.

By the way, it is common in the mortgage industry to say that the monthly housing cost you take on should be based on a percent of your gross pay. The most common of such rules is that your payment (principal, insurance, and taxes) should not exceed 28% of your gross income, and 36% when all debt payments are included. The implication is that if you are within these ratios that all is okay. Such rules are usually outdated when it comes to today's world. What matters is the amount you can reliably afford to pay each month and your personal comfort zone.

If you find that the results of these calculations don't provide enough to purchase a home that you would like in your area, you must decide if you should move to a less-expensive area or delay the purchase of a home. Once again, there is nothing wrong with waiting and building your savings to increase the odds you can buy in the area where you wish to live.

Question 4: Where do you go for mortgage approval?

The next step is to get your mortgage approval. By this I mean full pre-approval, not just getting pre-qualified. Do not break the sequence. Do this first before proceeding. You will increase the odds you'll pick the right house and it will also give you a necessary edge when you make an offer. Deciding where to go for your mortgage isn't easy. As I write this, there are lots of mortgage company commercials advertising "4.25% first mortgages!" At this moment the banks are paying that same rate on their CDs. As no financial institution loans money without a profit, the rate can't be right. Still, millions of people will call on those commercials every year. But that will not happen to you because you remember the rules: Always tune out service advertising, and, if it seems too good to be true, it's not true.

So what's the catch behind those 4.25% ads? It could be a lot of things. Maybe it's the fine print at the end of the commercial that "restrictions apply." Those restrictions likely apply to 95% of the callers. What happens if you are one of the 95%? No problem; they have something else to sell you that's "better." It's a "bait and switch" sales tactic, where they draw you in with something they never intend to sell you, and then sell you on what they wanted to in the first place. Should you be one of the lucky 5%, they don't want you and know a lot of ways to get rid of you.

Here's another peek under the tent of the mortgage industry. I once briefly co-owned a small mortgage company. I learned that a lot of the time the agents played a game, one that is quite common in the mortgage broker industry. The agent gets you to go with his company by offering a rate he knows they can't deliver. Two weeks or so before the closing the agent calls, pretending to be all upset, and tells you the loan has been denied for some reason. It's easy to come up with something on almost anybody. They probably saw their loophole the day you filled out your application.

Imagine your reaction. You've sold your house, packed up everything you own, and altered your life, all on the premise that you would buy this house. You're trapped! The agent tells you that he is "upset" with what happened and tells you not to panic. He'll "see what he can do." He hangs up, the performance over. A couple of days later he calls you again to tell you that all is okay, almost. "We got it! It's approved!" He then adds, "The rate had to be a little higher under the circumstances but we got it!" What a hero! He probably made hundreds of dollars more from the higher cost they just hit you with.

So what do you do? The answer is simple. Do not deal with a mortgage source unless it is very large and you Google it and check that it has a good reputation. Get several quotes from large established sources like Costco, use the internet, get a quote from a local credit union, and then take the best offer from an institution with the reputation of delivering what they commit to. When it comes to getting the best rate you will find, if you work at it, that the industry is quite competitive and that the truly best rate is available from a number of sources. Here are a few more things to consider:

- You should carry little or no debt. If you do you will pay more in interest and are more likely to get into trouble and forced to sell the house, quite possibly at a loss. Clean up any errors on your credit report and, as already discussed, make sure you've done everything you can to raise your credit rating (FICO score) as high as possible. (See my website for more information.)

- Get three offers and be sure to let the lenders know they're competing. The difference in interest over the years can add up to a *very* big number. Use the crash course on negotiating (see page 335) to help you. Make it clear they are not to pull a credit report on you until you say so, as extra credit report pulls may lower your credit score. It is best to avoid even giving them your Social Security number until you have done your homework and you're ready to commit. They may pres-

sure you, but be tough. They don't need your Social Security
number to give you a quote and if you give it to them, more
likely than not, they'll pull your credit score anyway.

- Do not take either an ARM (adjustable rate mortgage) or
balloon mortgage. They are too much of a gamble when it
comes to your home and your financial solvency. As I write
this, mortgage rates are unusually low, which only adds to
the risk involved.

- Do not take out a second mortgage or home equity line
of credit "just in case." Millions of homeowners lost their
homes for this reason over the last few years.

- As to taking a fifteen-year-, instead of a thirty-year-mort-
gage, I recommend you do not do so. The benefits are a
lower interest rate, a greater rate of forced saving, and a
greater likelihood you will pay off your house sooner. The
disadvantages, unfortunately, are usually greater. They
include reduced financial flexibility, no added tax advantage
(principal payments aren't tax deductible), and a slightly
lower rate of return on the additional money you invest
than you're likely to get elsewhere. Further, you increase
the risk you won't be maximizing your tax-free/tax-deferred
savings over the ensuing years.

- Check to insure there isn't a prepayment penalty clause in
the mortgage you select.

- Do not purchase mortgage life insurance or accelerated payoff programs. If you feel you need insurance, go buy some
term life insurance. It's a lot cheaper.

- There are people and institutions that will readily approve you for a mortgage that is higher than you can handle. Do not take a larger amount than you can afford! Millions of people lost their homes over the last few years, and in many cases went bankrupt, trusting in that kind of thinking. Only *you* must decide what you can and can't afford, and what you are, and are not, comfortable with. If it means you have to wait to buy, then wait. It's far worse to commit to something you can't handle yet and sabotage your life as a result.

Question 5: What neighborhoods should you consider?

As the saying goes, there are only three things that matter when it comes to real estate: Location, location, and location. Well it's *true, true,* and *true*! Most people have a tendency to lock in on the property with a quick, "I like it and I want it," but the rush of owning a nicer home will fade very quickly if you buy in the wrong location. If you want to be happy with your home, both as a place to live and as an investment, do *not* focus first on the home. Focus first on the neighborhood and the schools, then on the home. These are also the same things that will usually determine the success of your home as an investment. It's supply and demand, pure and simple. Most home buyers have children. Most homebuyers, especially repeat home buyers, *are* focused on the location, the neighborhood, and the schools. So, start by deciding on the location first and then work from there. Admittedly, sometimes the school system will not be that important, such as in an area where everyone sends their kids to private schools, or perhaps a retirement area. Such exceptions are easy to spot.

If you are relocating and are not familiar with the area it may be better to select a real estate professional to help you. Assuming that is not the case, drive around on your own and identify the neighborhoods that might be your best choice. Do not go into any open houses or talk to any realtors until after you have completed this step. Trust me that this is a superior process in leading you to the best result. Find out where the good school systems are, even if you don't have kids. Talk to people in the neighborhoods you're looking at, as they will usually know and be willing to share that information. Average test scores and API ratings of schools are available online as well. If you have children who will be going to the local schools, it's a good idea to visit those schools and talk to the staff. After you've done that, go to the internet and study the homes currently on the market in those neighborhoods. Today almost everything is online, virtual tours and all.

Again I will remind you not to take on a much longer commute for a bigger, better house, as it is usually a bad path to take, damaging both your own quality of life and that of your family. If, however, you feel it is necessary to insure good choices for your children's schools then that is another matter, and the decision admittedly becomes a lot trickier and a lot more personal.

Question 6: How do you select a real estate agent?

Regardless of his or her title and experience, your agent is still a salesperson. In chapter five, "The 10 Rules of Investing Successfully," one of the rules is to not trust the advice of people who make money from it. No matter how likeable they are, regardless of who may have referred them, you cannot just trust them unconditionally. Should you at any time doubt this advice, remember that I hired, trained, and managed over a hundred agents over a ten-year period. I've seen it and lived it. Do not get me wrong. A good agent can be a great asset. You just need to always be very careful in assessing the advice you are given.

In selecting an agent you are looking for three things. You want solid professional knowledge, very good knowledge of property availability, and, hopefully, the ethics to put your interest ahead of theirs. Most people end up going with someone either from a referral or from a random event such as walking into an open house or real estate office. When you walk in you will be assigned to whoever is on floor duty at that moment. You don't want that because you don't want such an important decision to be made randomly. Be wary of referrals by people or companies unless you are confident they have nothing to gain. Be careful, as most of the time this is not the case. A referral from someone you know who used the agent to purchase their house is probably the best referral you can get.

Take notice of the companies that seem to have the most listings in the neighborhoods in which you're interested. Do not be influenced by the agent name on the sign, as they may be primarily a listing agent working with sellers.

Next, call each of the real estate agencies active in the neighborhoods you're interested in and ask to speak to the manager. Describe what you are looking to buy and ask the manager to select an agent he or she feels is best suited to help you. The manager knows the team, wants the business, and is likely to pick someone good. You can't be sure, however, so don't assume so. Get the name and number of the agent and say you'll call as soon as you're ready to start looking. You don't want to talk yet. If you end up on the phone with the agent, politely state that you're not ready to start yet and will call back as soon as you are.

There is yet another good source for choosing a candidate. At this point there is nothing wrong with going into open houses in the area(s) you're interested in and checking out the agents you meet, provided you do *not* give them your contact information. Remember, no matter how nice they seem they are only possible candidates. Do take their cards. Later on you can decide whether or not they are among the people you will interview.

It's important to find at least three agent candidates and this process should provide you with at least that. The next step is to call each one. Keep in mind that you will be picking only one of these people, as it's best not to work with more than one agent unless you're looking in more than one geographic area. Do not make an in-person appointment with anyone until you've first called all of the referred names. Tell each one you've had several referrals and decided to have a short phone call. Give them an idea of your interests and needs and then conduct what is no less than an interview. Your questions should include things like:

- Why do you feel you'd be a good choice for me to work with?
- How do you work with a client?
- Do you work with a partner or an assistant? If so, what are the roles of each person?
- To what degree do you work as a buyer's agent versus a seller's agent?
- How long have you been in the business? (You do not want a rookie.)
- Do you have any training or designations beyond that? (An agent who is a realtor with some additional legitimate

professional designations after her name, and has been in the industry awhile, increases the probability she'll meet your first two requirements.)

- How many buyers bought properties through you in the last twenty-four months? How many properties did you list and sell during that same period? How many listings do you have at this time? (If you ask if they're full-time you'll usually get a yes, even if it's not really true. The level of business they've done will tell you a lot more.)

- Have you worked for any other firms before this? Why did you change companies? What did you do before becoming a real estate agent?

- What are your thoughts on the market and on the current property availability situation? (Specifically, be sure to ask about the neighborhoods you're interested in. How familiar are they with those areas and how much have they listed or sold there?)

- Can I see written testimonials from past clients and the names and phone numbers of at least ten clients from the past eighteen months? (Does their firm conduct client satisfaction surveys? If so, you want to see the results for both the firm and for them.)

- Is there anything else about you or your firm I should know?

After you have completed your telephone interviews, if you are comfortable eliminating anyone, do so. Then go online to the Department of Commerce and Consumer Affairs for your city or state to see if there are complaints or lawsuits against either the agents or the firms. The final step is to meet and talk to each remaining candidate in person. Before you're done, have them play back to you their understanding of your needs and interests. Such a step is often quite educational. At times you will find they did not pay very close attention to your concerns and interests.

Make no commitment until you've met all the remaining candidates. When you're done, make your selection. As you work with them continue to pay close attention. If a relationship is not working do not hesitate to change agents. Should anyone try to get you to sign an agreement making that person your exclusive buyer's agent, do not do so.

If your mortgage approval is for more than you have decided to spend, be very firm in telling the agent that you will not spend more than you have decided to, despite the approval for a higher amount. This is especially important when it comes to negotiating the price on your chosen property, as your agent may assume the extra money is there for the spending. That assumption can undermine your negotiating leverage. If you are buying the house with a spouse or other partner, select one of you as the person who absolutely will not budge on the upper price limit.

Does this sound like a lot of work? Actually, I think you'll find it's really not that bad. Remember that your agent can often make or break you on one of the biggest decisions affecting both your money and the quality of your life. Do not skimp on your homework. Only you must make all decisions. That does not mean that your agent is not a valuable source of information and assistance, as he or she can and should be. An agent's negotiating skills can also mean a lot to you. The only caution, and it is a big one, is that you cannot just take what you are told at face value. You must fully understand and/or personally verify every piece of significant input provided.

Once you have made your decision, your next step is to meet with your chosen agent before getting started. You have now entered a working partnership, so you need to be open regarding your expectations and concerns, what you hope to achieve as a final result, and any ideas and opinions you have as to how best to go about it. Listen carefully to what your agent has to say in response, as he or she has dealt with most of these things before. Ask your agent to fill you in on the common practices for the areas you are concentrating in, as every area is a little different from the next. That includes things like who normally pays for what, how many days you're likely to have to inspect the property before completely committing to the purchase, whether lawyers are involved in the closing, and so on.

Conducting a productive meeting up front that covers every aspect of the process to come will often prove invaluable to insuring a successful working partnership and to optimizing the probability of a successful end result.

You will probably hear the terms *buyer's agents* and *seller's agents*. Now, it is very common to find an agent who specializes in both the buying and selling process. Most agents routinely do both. If you are a buyer and an agent works with you, he or she becomes, for your transaction, a buyer's agent and should be representing your interests only. If you are selling and list with an agent then, for that transaction, the agent has become a seller's agent and should represent only your interests. Should the situation ever arise where your agent is selling a property that is also his listing, have a frank talk. If, after that, you are at all uncomfortable with the potential conflict of interest involved, tell your agent you would be more comfortable having his manager assign another agent to handle your end of the transaction.

You will be told that the agent representing the seller will try to get the client the best deal and that the agent representing you is trying to do the same for you. Maybe that's true and maybe it's not. If you pay $300,000 a normal commission is 6%, or $18,000. Each agent makes maybe 60% of half the commission, about $5,400. If you pay $325,000, they make $450 more. It's obvious that $5,400 or $5,850 beats zero every time, so you must assume they both have pressure on them to push both parties as far as they can. This may very well create a conflict of interest that keeps them from fighting to get you the best deal. Always be on guard for any sign this may be happening. If you suspect it you have no choice but to become your own advisor when it comes to what to offer.

It should be noted that there is a positive to what I've described. If the agents didn't push both ends, they would both lose sales for the homeowners and frequently lose good home purchases for the buyers. The parties do usually need to be pushed to a fair compromise. This may especially be true for you, the buyer. In many cases, you really want this property and paying say $10,000 more than you "should" may well be a better decision than losing it. You just need to remain very aware of all that is taking place.

Question 7: How do you choose the right property?

At this point you should have already selected a few neighborhoods that are acceptable, feature good schools, and offer a price range you can afford. Do not let anyone and/or your emotions take you beyond the amount you've decided upon. Next, evaluate your needs five to ten years out. After that, count the things you like and value most, such as a great backyard, a quiet setting, a view, a big kitchen, being able to walk to things, etc.

Do not buy a house that is bigger than you need. How much extra size are you drawn to want, and for what reason? Is some of it that you feel more successful, or that you will live better? Well these things don't actually change; it only seems that way. Worse yet, you're breaking the rules! You want life to become better as you go forward, not worse. If you take on too much unneeded house, you will probably end up regretting it. Be patient; your house will show up.

Once you think you've found a good potential home, talk to the neighbors. You will learn a lot. Go by the house both at night and on the weekend and drive or walk around the neighborhood. Sometimes you'll find that the neighborhood that was so nice during the day or during the week turns out to be anything but during those times.

Lastly, here is a checklist of things you don't want in a home. If you choose to accept any of these things, then you should be paying a lower price as they affect both value and resalability. You don't want:

- The biggest, most expensive home on the block
  or in the neighborhood.
- A property backing up, adjacent to, or close to industrially
  or commercially zoned land or a trailer park.
- To live on an active road. Even a moderate amount of traffic
  is not good. You want it quiet, with a low volume of immediate neighborhood traffic. Do not underestimate this one.
  It can prove to be very nasty, especially when you try to
  resell it someday.

- To live in a higher-than-normal crime area, or need to drive through one on your way in or out. The website of the local police force usually has this info. If there are any questions about this, go into the station and ask what you want to know.
- An unusual architectural design. It will be very hard to sell.
- An area of high noise, such as airplane flyovers, trains, industrial and traffic noise, especially at night. Hearing the sound from a high-speed highway at night is a definite negative.
- An area prone to flooding when it rains.
- To live within a mile or two of a landfill.
- A neighborhood that appears to have no code enforcement regarding the parking of trucks, mobile homes, trailer homes, boats, etc.
- To live adjacent to a multi-unit rental property.
- A corner lot. This is a subtle one. You will have a more spacious setting but less privacy and more traffic exposure.
- To live near a school where a lot of kids walk by every day.
- Any kind of flat roof, such as on an addition, makes it harder to sell.
- A one-car garage, versus a two-car garage, is also harder to sell.
- A tiny master bedroom.
- A neighborhood with high homeowner's association fees.
- To live on a steep hill in an area where you get ice and snow.
- A location that gets the headlights of cars coming into the house at night.
- A neighborhood where property values have not increased much. Provided it's a positive market, this should never

happen to you. If it does, you did *not* pick a good neighborhood in the first place. This is a fatal error. Do not buy that
house or anything in that neighborhood!

If a property must be altered to meet your needs, have your agent check
with the appropriate local zoning office to insure you will be allowed
to make the intended changes.

There is one more important suggestion for finding the right house.
Some of the very best properties sell immediately because experienced
buyers and/or buyers who've been shopping are now clear about knowing them when they see them. Do not depend on your agent calling
you the minute a new property hits the market. Have your agent set
you up to receive automatic e-mail notification of every new property,
price change, contract, and closing in the neighborhoods you're looking at. If and when you see a potential hot candidate, call your agent
that minute and see the property that day if possible or, failing that,
the next day.

Finally, let's consider the factors involved in buying new construction.
The houses are fresh, modern, and very appealing. They contain all the
features you're looking for. The neighborhood looks like it will turn out
very nicely. Yes, new construction has a lot of advantages. Before you
sign on, however, be sure to weigh the disadvantages:

- The house is likely to cost substantially more per square foot.
- Your negotiating room is usually greatly limited.
- A new house seldom comes out like you picture it.
- There are often a number of things that need fixing, and
  you are at the mercy of the builder to some degree, certainly

on how quickly things get done. Always read the warrantee very carefully.

- You might be living in a construction zone for several years or more. Dust and noise will be common.
- Much of the new construction these days is in areas, such as flood zones, that were formerly considered undesirable or even unbuildable. Learn a little about the area and its history, but not from your real estate agent or agents representing the builder.
- You will probably be getting an un-landscaped or under-landscaped house. Before you buy, get a rough professional estimate of what it will cost to give you an attractive setting. You can expect that the cost will end up somewhere between 10%–20% of the price of the house.

Sometimes there will be a period, such as the one we are currently in as I write this, when the builders have been caught by a shifting market and forced to cut their prices a lot. In such a situation, the first two disadvantages listed above no longer apply.

Question 8: How do you make a winning offer?

- **Listen to what your agent has to say.** Evaluate your agent's comments cautiously. Follow what you learn from the crash course on negotiating in chapter fourteen (see page 335). Next, you *must* be willing to lose the house. Do not get into the mindset that this is *the* house, the *only* house. That is almost always not true, so don't go there. This means you don't want to let time pressure you too much. Be willing to hold your fire and to walk away if you feel the price is bad. So that we're clear here I am not talking about the situation where you've done your best, you're at the end of the road on negotiating, and the difference is small. As I said, in that instance it may well be a good decision to pay the difference if you really like the house a lot. Properties tend to fall into three categories. You "must" have it; you love it, but not at that price; and you like it but have no problem walking away. Don't let yourself fall into that first category.

- **You *must* personally understand the comparative properties (the comps) that have recently sold or are on the market now.** They will give you the overriding data on what the property is worth. Did the property or any of the comps receive offers that didn't fly? What were they? Use everything you can to understand what the property is currently worth. Your offer must be based on a realistic price and you need to have a pretty good sense of what that number is.

- **Do not negotiate directly with the seller.** First talk it through with your agent and listen very carefully and open-mindedly. Most of the time it is a very bad idea to negotiate directly.

- **You agent should have a copy of your mortgage approval letter and proof of cash funds.** Without it you've weakened both your position and your agent's negotiation efforts on your behalf. Give your agent the phone number of the financial source involved so that he or she can arrange to fine-tune the approval letter to the offer.

- **Always sleep on it before you make any offer or counter-offer, even in a hot market.** The human mind is amazing as to what it accomplishes while we sleep. Get it on your side by deciding in the morning. Yes, there's a small risk you'll lose the house by waiting twelve hours and your agent will almost certainly try to scare you, but do it. The risk of loss is small, the benefits great. Ask your agent to alert the sellers that he or she expects an offer in the morning; that should freeze the situation for you. In most cases it will also strengthen your hand as even a slight delay is likely to place additional pressure on the seller.

- **If the market is not real hot, time will probably be in your favor.** The sellers do not know how much you want their house or what you're willing to pay. They, on the other hand, probably feel a pretty strong pressure to sell, especially if the house has been on the market awhile. They have only one house to sell, while you have many to choose from. This means that you should offer a good bit under what they're asking and wait to counter them. Use some of the tactics in the crash course on negotiating in chapter fourteen (see page 335). When I say a good bit under, I do not mean a lowball offer. If you come in way too low, there is a substantial risk of turning them off. If you believe their price is way out of line, then do it, but your agent must be prepared to make a very good case that their asking price is indeed way out of line when the offer is presented.

- **All houses sell.** If a house doesn't sell within a reasonable period of time it usually means that the asking price is too high for the current market. If a house has been on the market for over ninety days without a price reduction, you should assume that the asking price is too high for what it is or where it's located, and take that into consideration in your offer. Conversely, if a house is brand new to the market you will probably have to pay closer to the asking price than you normally would, as the buyers are not likely to be very flexible during the first thirty to sixty days or so. This means you have to be extra careful in evaluating its likely selling price versus the comps.

- **How much should I offer?** I'm a little hesitant to give you any numbers about what is normally a smart amount to offer. Keep in mind that these percents swing a lot depending on how hot the overall market is and on the specific neighborhood and house involved. Most of all, you really *must* have a good idea about how fairly priced it is. The fairness of the asking price will and must be the *number one factor* in determining what you offer. Given that the asking price is set fairly, here are some guidelines. In a really hot market you should not offer much less, maybe 2%, than the asking price. Most of the time your initial offer will need to be at full price. In a normal market, about 5%–6% below the asking price is a good guideline. In a weak market, maybe 8%–10% below the asking price is the way to go.

- **What should I expect to pay?** Expect that you'll end up actually purchasing at around 4% off the asking price in a normal market, 6%–7% off the asking price in a weak market, and paying full price in a hot one. Remember, these are general guidelines. If you have reason to alter them, do so. If not, let them be your guide.

- **Read the seller's disclosure carefully.** By law, the sellers have to disclose everything negative they are aware of. This is a starting point, so also always have a home inspection done. Some owners will not disclose a problem with the idea that they can, if necessary, later claim they "didn't know" about it. Fortunately, anything they don't list will usually be caught in a competent home inspection. If the inspection uncovers things of substance you weren't aware of, you should ask for and expect that the selling price be adjusted accordingly. Never accept any inspections paid by the seller; always acquire your own independent inspections.

- **In those states where you are required to have an attorney, I recommend you not use someone suggested by your real estate agent.** It's best to be very cautious here and avoid the possibility of getting too much of a rubberstamp approval.

Selling Your Home

Just like with buying a home, your decision whether, when, and how to sell will be based on many factors. The questions to be answered are listed below. A lot of the answers to these questions were already covered under the section above on buying. If you haven't already read it, stop and do so before you proceed. It will also give you a good feel for the mindset of your buyers.

Question 1: Should you sell, and if so, when?

It is possible that you might be forced to sell your home right away for serious reasons such as job relocation or financial problems. If not, what is your reason for selling? Is it to get a bigger or smaller home? A better home? A better neighborhood or community? A home is a very personal thing. With all of the emotional elements that are likely to be involved it is easy to make the wrong choice on what is often a really big life decision. You need to challenge yourself to be fully honest in comparing the benefits to the drawbacks. For example, if it's to get a bigger house, is it really a good idea? So often it is not. Do you really need the extra space? Do you have children who will be leaving at some point in the not-too-distant future? Can you afford the larger mortgage if your finances were to change due to professional or health situations beyond your control? Would you be improving your commute or making it worse?

With the size of the decision and all of the emotional elements that are likely to be involved, you need to be especially careful and thorough in thinking through your reasons why you should or should not sell. If you are at all uncertain as to what to do, please be sure to talk it over with someone you trust and respect.

At times your decision whether and when to sell can be greatly influenced by where the real estate market is in its cycle. My assessment of the real estate market is on my website, www.MoneySmartOnline .com. Use it as a starting point as you research the status of your specific local market. What you learn may not change a decision to sell, but there is the possibility it could greatly influence when and how you go about it. It may also influence any buying decision that you may be making at the same time.

A substantially overpriced market can prove to be a very difficult situation to deal with. On a strictly financial basis, the decision is obvious. Sell and prepare to become a renter for at least a few years until the market has corrected enough. This is what I did in 2006 and now, three years later, I'm still happily renting. For me it was an easy decision. We had already made the decision to relocate and really didn't care that much whether we owned a home for a while. We were happy to take a temporary break from the responsibilities of home ownership, reap the financial rewards of selling when the market was overpriced, and wait to buy until a good deal could be found again.

If you are not satisfied with your home, I think selling and renting during an overpriced market makes a lot of sense. If, however, you are happy with being a homeowner and like your home, neighborhood, and the community where you live, your best decision may well be not to sell. But do not underestimate the long-run benefits of selling and waiting until the market is fairly priced to buy a home again. The benefits of such a move could be buying a much better house later, or becoming financially free a lot sooner in life. These are highly personal tradeoffs and only you can make the decision. I just caution you to think your decision through carefully.

If you are in an overpriced market and want to sell in order to trade up and buy a more expensive home, you are looking at paying a premium on the difference in price. In a substantially underpriced market, selling to buy a more expensive home is much smarter, as the reverse is true. The difference in price between the two homes will get you the full benefit of the underpriced market.

In a noticeably underpriced market scenario, if you sell but do not plan to buy, you will likely lose money by waiting to buy. If buying another home is not an option at this time, consider renting out your current home rather than selling it.

A fairly priced or slightly under- or overpriced market will not greatly influence how much you will make or lose. In that instance, the personal factors—apart from the financial ones—can more strongly dictate your decision in this type of market.

The spring is the best time of year to sell as 60% of all sales occur then. It is best to list your house early, in late February to late March. If you do sell by summer or need to list your home in the fall, understand that it will be somewhat more difficult, on average, to get your best price at that time. The homeowners that didn't sell in the spring are, by fall, more willing to negotiate a lower price, and many fall buyers expect that to be the case.

Question 2: What do you need to know about real estate agents?

It's really not much different than the process laid out under buying a house other than that it's preferable to get someone who primarily functions as a seller's agent. Dig out the candidates and interview them on the phone. Do your homework thoroughly or you may end up losing a *lot* of money unnecessarily. Here are some specific do's and don'ts, and things to consider in relation to real estate agents.

Almost every agent will act as though the commission is set in stone and that to lower it will cause the other agents to sell another house rather than yours. This is usually not true. The "standard" commission is usually 6%, with 3% to the agency that listed the house for sale, and 3% to the agency that sells it (and represents the buyer). Most of the time there will be two different real estate agencies. For openers, if it were my house, the first thing I would do is ask for a commission of 5%: 2% to the listing agency, and 3% to the buyer's agency. Keeping the buyer's agent's commission at 3% insures there is no disincentive to that realtor as he is still getting his normal full commission. (To assist you in getting the best deal regarding the commission, read chapter fourteen, "How to Negotiate." See page 335.)

You *can* sell your home yourself. About 15%–20% of the homes sold each year are done so by the owners. If you choose to go this route and do not have enough information to be confident regarding your asking price, hire an independent professional appraiser (this costs about $300) and be sure you thoroughly understand the comps they provide. Most sellers hurt themselves the most by setting a price that is either too high or too low. Provided you've priced it appropriately, you can always shift to listing the property with a realtor after a reasonable period of trying to sell it on your own.

Please be aware that you should not opt for exclusive listings or listings that do not go into the local multiple listing service (MLS) immediately! Everything must go into MLS, and immediately. It is common for an agent to sell the benefits of their firm's website as a way to sell your house. For the most part, that's usually just a sales pitch and little more. MLS, and not their site, is going to sell your house.

Many brokers will tell you they will hold an open house and act as though it is a valuable step. It is for them, but probably not for you, so don't place any weight on this in selecting your agent. The National Association of Realtors estimates that only 2%–4% of all sales are made that way. This doesn't mean you nix an open house. Just understand that it's probably more of a favor to your agent than it is to you. The "open house" that really matters is when all the realtors caravan your house (visit as a group). That visit is extremely important and your home needs to be standing tall that day.

Most residential listing agreements include a clause that clearly states that all offers must be presented in a timely manner. If it's not clearly stated in your listing contract, make sure it is added. Supply your agent with your mobile phone number and make it clear that you will expect an immediate phone call with any and all offers.

A good partnership with your chosen agent requires a thorough kick-off meeting to get the collaboration started on the right foot. Presenting all offers should be part of that discussion. There are times when the seller either does not hear about an offer or doesn't hear about it as soon as he should have. Unfortunately, sometimes agents delay presenting an offer from another agent. Sometimes they do this because they're trying to get one of their own buyers, or a buyer of an agent in their group, to make an offer first so that they or their associates can get the whole commission, rather than half. Sometimes the first offer is very low and your agent is convinced you can do better. This still does not mean the first offer should not have been presented. A good partnership is one that has a clear understanding on this issue.

As part of this meeting you should cover with your agent that you may not respond to offers on the spot and may also delay your response over night, or even by a day or more. However, if your home has been on the market for an extended period of time, agree that you will respond more quickly. You should also instruct your agent that when an offer does come in, you expect that the other agents with interested clients will be told that an offer has been received. Always remember that if a second or third offer comes in, you can consider all offers equally no matter which one came in first.

One of the most common myths in real estate is that the "first offer gets considered first" and that "you are obligated to work through the first offer before considering the next." Even though this may be a common and customary practice in some areas, it is not binding on you and will in most cases cost you money if you allow it to happen. If you are fortunate enough to receive two or more offers on your property, instruct your agent to give all offers what is known as a multiple counteroffer. Multiple counteroffers are worded to allow you to accept whichever final offer you wish.

Question 3: How do you choose the right asking price?

You determine the price by choosing a good agent and then personally taking the responsibility to thoroughly understand the comps, or the similar properties that have recently sold or are on the market now. If you do not clearly understand how each comp compares to your property, or how the value of your home is being arrived at, keep asking questions until you do. If you feel that the price has been set improperly, hire a professional appraiser on your own to double-check the price before placing the property on the market. It may well prove to be the smartest $300 or so you'll ever spend, and will leave you with a very clear mind when it comes to negotiating the final price with your buyer.

Question 4: How do you properly prepare the house?

The selection of a good agent will help a lot. Basically you, the agent, and anyone else you can trust to be candid, must get into the head of the buyer and do a walk-though. Anything not working properly and any type of damage must be fixed; there are no exceptions. Beyond that, everything—and I mean everything—needs to feel fresh and "new." This includes paint, carpets, and the landscaping. Make sure the kitchen and the bathrooms are standing especially tall, even if you have to spend a little money to do so. Also, like it or not, you need to mute most of the décor as much as possible with a lot of off-white walls. Are there exceptions to this? Yes, but you better be sure the real estate agents and the prospective buyers will see whatever it is as a positive. Remember, it's all about what *the potential buyer* thinks, not you.

Fresh and new throughout the house also means getting rid of all clutter and streamlining the furniture. Every extraneous object should be put into storage. Think of what a model home in a new development looks like. That's what you want—clean and sparse. You even want a little staging of the home, adding fresh flowers, live plants, and other décor touches to liven up your home. This is not the time to make a significant renovation to the house to enhance the sale or increase the selling price because the odds are high you're throwing away money. If there are any doubts, ask your agent.

Question 5: How do you negotiate a winning sale?

This has pretty much been covered under the buying process, except now you're on the other side of the table. The crash course on negotiating in chapter fourteen (see page 335) will provide guidance on this process as well. There is, however, one more critical piece of advice that is worth repeating. The same rule applies to sellers as it does to buyers. You must not be obligated to buy your next home until you've sold your current one, unless you are fortunate enough to be able to make the purchase independently of the sale. The purchase of your next house *must* be contingent on the sale of your current one. Although you can usually avoid it, you must be prepared to store your stuff and rent for a while if necessary. At times you may think you can get around this by finding someone willing to enter into a contingency contract when your current home is not already under contract. This is usually a bad idea as you can pretty much bet the selling price involved will be noticeably higher than they would have otherwise taken and there is also usually an "out" for the seller if you don't go ahead with the purchase fairly quickly.

CHAPTER THIRTEEN

Choosing Insurance

The purpose of insurance is to pay a reasonable amount of money to someone else on an ongoing basis for the guarantee that they will, in turn, pay all or most of certain unexpected major financial losses or costs should those expenses hit you at some point.

Here are the insurance terms you should know:

Liability—To be liable means to be legally responsible for an injury to someone else or to be responsible for loss or damage of his or her property.

Premium—The monthly, quarterly, or annual amount you have to pay for insurance.

Deductible—The amount you will be required to pay for any claim before your insurance coverage kicks in. It can either be a set dollar amount or a percent of the claim total. Deductibles often have annual limits beyond which you do not have to pay anything more, even if you file additional claims during that year.

Copayment—The fixed percentage of the claim that you are required to pay after your deductible has been subtracted from the total amount of the claim. Copayments often have a maximum amount (a cap) after which you are no longer responsible to pay anything more, unless the maximum limits of the policy have been reached.

Ratings—There are four ratings services that rate the financial strength of insurance companies: A.M. Best; Standard & Poor's; Moody's; and Fitch. Ask any company you are considering to provide you with their ratings and do not do business with any company that does not have a good rating from all four services. Also, always be sure to use the internet to check the company's reputation for handling claims quickly and fairly.

Be aware of a key truth: *The more expensive a type of insurance is, the more important it is that you have it.* If it's cheap, it says that the insurance company knows there's a small chance you'll end up collecting on it. Otherwise the company wouldn't price it so cheaply. The most expensive insurance coverage these days is health insurance, and I don't have to tell you that it is the policy you are far more likely to need and collect on than any other.

Always buy an insurance policy based on a combination of price and terms, never just on price alone. Terms include the definitions used for whether you qualify for being paid, size of deductibles, limits on payments, non-cancellation, inflation protection, etc.

Always try to go with the highest deductible amounts you can possibly be comfortable with. The odds are likely to be in your financial favor when you do. For example, on the comprehensive portion of your auto insurance policy, raising the deductible from $200 to $1,000 usually saves an average of 40%, or $100, per year. In the same vein, consider self-insuring (taking on the financial risk yourself) when the amount at risk is something you can cover. Pay your insurance bills annually, or at least semi-annually if a discount is given for doing so. Don't file claims unless they are twice your deductible or more.

The price of insurance can vary a lot so you absolutely need to shop it. If you are, or have been, a member of our armed forces, or are a dependent of someone who was, I recommend including USAA in your shopping list. The company is extremely strong, handles claims quickly and fairly, and quotes some very good rates. Another company to add to your list is Costco as they will undoubtedly have partnered with a very strong insurance company and gotten some very competitive rates out of them.

After you've checked the offerings of these two sources don't stop there. Look at the quote services and the major company sites on the internet. It won't take much time and will probably be well worth the effort. As you proceed, remember not to break Spending Rule #4: Never Respond to Service Advertising or Infomercials. Always decide who to talk to by doing your own homework. As for walking into an insurance office or talking to an insurance salesperson, even on a recommendation I believe you'll find the major companies on the internet will usually beat them out, so I'd do them last, if at all.

If you do choose to contact an individual agent or company, I recommend doing it over the phone and not in person. They will hate that and do all they can to "sit down with you." If you hold firm, they will usually give in and work with you over the phone and via e-mail. This strips away a lot of the sales pitch and sales games, leaving you very much in control, a lot more focused on the facts, and not influenced by how "nice" or how "professional" that person is. If you end up feeling you can't make a good decision on something really complicated—such as long-term care insurance—on your own, it's possible to turn to a "fee-only" financial advisor highly familiar with insurance to help you. Such an advisor should not be affiliated with any particular insurance company and should not receive a fee or commission from any policy or from any company.

I will caution you that this is a risky situation. You may see ads, for example, stating that such an advisor can save you as much as 80% on your premiums. I looked into that kind of advertising far enough to develop the opinion that it was very misleading. All told, I believe it is far better you do it on your own if at all possible. Time and again the bottom line is the same: You and only you must learn enough to make your own informed decision and the time you spend to do so will be well worth it.

Worst case, if you do end up selecting someone to help you with your insurance decisions, do *not* let them talk you into using them for investment advice without first reading and following what I have to say in Do Not Listen to the "Experts" in chapter ten (page 213) and review the sections on mutual funds, index funds, and ETFs in chapter eleven (page 231).

There are quite a few different reasons why you may need insurance, both now and in the future. The following is an explanation and brief discussion of each of the eight major types of insurance you will need to consider at some point. After that is a list of common miscellaneous other policies that may come up from time to time, most of which are a waste of money. As you proceed with your life your needs will change, so make it a practice to review this list and your specific policies on an annual basis. There is a high tendency to ignore and just accept insurance bills. Don't do it. Things are always changing and the policies and coverage that were right when you got them may no longer meet your current needs.

Auto Insurance

The purpose of auto insurance is to cover damage to your car, the cars or properties of others, medical costs for injuries to yourself and others, and suits against you for pain and suffering. If you have a car, you absolutely need auto insurance. Auto insurance policies are made up of four different types of protection:

Auto liability—If you caused the accident, auto liability pays the medical expenses of anyone injured in the accident other than yourself. For a standard policy it also pays for the repairs to the property of others. Do *not* set the limits too low for this part of your coverage. It is one place where paying for high limits is a very good idea, especially if you have significant assets.

Medical payments—Medical payments coverage provides money toward your medical expenses and those of your passengers, regardless of who is at fault. The amounts provided are limited and cannot be depended on to pay more than a portion of the expenses involved.

Collision—Collision insurance covers your car, whether or not you caused the accident.

Comprehensive coverage—Comprehensive insurance covers your car if it is damaged or lost due to a cause other than an auto accident. The policy covers fire, theft, vandalism, flood, etc.

In addition to the above, you can also purchase uninsured motorist coverage that provides a degree of additional bodily injury protection should you be involved in an accident with an uninsured motorist. Once you've selected the company you will deal with, it's worth asking them about the pros and cons of taking on this additional coverage.

If you drive a fairly old car, consider dropping comprehensive and collision coverage completely and instead self-insure on the cost of any repair or replacement that might occur. One rule of thumb is to drop the coverage if the price you could get for your car is less than 10% of the premiums involved. Insuring your home and your car(s) with the same insurance company is likely to save you some money, perhaps 5%–10% or so. If you maintain a clean driving record, be sure to make that known to your auto insurance provider, as it is likely to reduce your premiums.

Lastly, there are a number of things you can do to avoid or reduce the risks and costs involved in owning and operating a vehicle. For starters, don't drink and drive, don't buy vehicles with poor safety records, always wear your seat belt, and insist your passengers do, too. Park in a locked garage or in a well-lit exposed area, don't license a teenager before you have personally decided he or she is ready and responsible, and *never* tailgate.

Homeowner's Insurance

The purpose of homeowner's insurance is to cover unexpected loss or damage to your home and its contents and to help cover suits arising from your ownership of the property. In addition to basic homeowner's insurance you may also need to deal with additional coverage for floods and earthquakes. You may be required to carry PMI insurance (PMI is required if you purchase a home for less than 20% down. Should you default, this policy pays the bank, not you, the difference between the amount you owe and the 20% down.) If you own a home, you need homeowner's insurance. If you carry a mortgage your lending institution will require it, but even if you own your home outright you need to buy this insurance. Basic homeowner's insurance provides four kinds of coverage:

- Damage to the home
- Damage and loss of personal possessions
- Liability protection: Should you be responsible for reimbursing someone for their loss or injury inside or outside your home, including limited medical expenses. (Your own medical expenses should be covered by your health insurance.)
- Rental or additional living expenses: Should you be unable to live in the home for a period of time

Here are some guidelines to assist you when obtaining homeowner's insurance:

- You will have a choice between an actual cash value provision that reimburses you for the original cost of your possessions, minus depreciation, or a provision that covers the actual cost to replace the items. For the most part you're better off with the replacement cost option.

- Make sure your policy adjusts for inflation.
- Once again make your deductibles as high as you think you can cover. Not only will you probably win by doing so, you also avoid the nuisance of having to file and justify minor claims that may end up causing a nonrenewal of your policy. The purpose of homeowner's insurance is to protect against big losses, not for amounts you can cover if necessary.
- Do not assume that you are covered by the amount of insurance your mortgage lender requires. That amount all goes to the lender, so you need a higher amount in order to cover your share of the dwelling, your possessions, etc.
- I recommend you take a video camera and videotape every room and each possession in the house. Then file the tape somewhere safe.
- Be aware that the following are undoubtedly excluded from your coverage: expensive jewelry, art, collections, boats, RVs, business equipment, normal wear and tear of the property, earthquakes, floods, termites, etc. Read the policy carefully and list those things that are excluded. A lot of what you own can probably be covered. Then you have to decide when it's worth the price. If you're in a flood zone, that decision is easy. Get flood insurance. For a boat or RV you'll need liability coverage for yourself, as well as others who use it. The rest is a personal call.

- If you own a condo or co-op, the insurance policy is pretty much the same as a homeowner's policy. The primary differences are that your property coverage ends at the wall of your unit and you probably need to include a generous amount to cover you should your condo association assess the owners for a major uncovered loss or liability. As part of choosing your coverage, be sure to identify what the association master policy does and does not cover

- If you run a business out of your home, be sure to identify what your homeowner's policy does and does not cover.

Renter's Insurance

Renter's insurance is essentially the same thing as homeowner's insurance except that there is no home to insure. Such a policy provides coverage of your possessions, liability protection, medical payments coverage, and contributes to your living expenses should something happen. If you can't afford to replace your possessions if something happens, this insurance is a good idea, again with the highest possible deductible. Further, what makes it a must for me is the need for liability coverage in today's lawsuit-happy world. A liability situation is quite unlikely to occur, but if it ever does, the results can be devastating if you are not covered.

Umbrella Insurance

An umbrella policy is an additional level of liability protection should a lawsuit exceed the coverage of your auto, homeowner's, or renter's policies. If you have a net worth of $1 million or more, or your future income is likely to be quite substantial, this policy is also a good idea.

The amounts covered by such a policy usually run from $1 million to $5 million. The premium averages about $150 to $200 per year for $1 million dollars of coverage, and $75 to $100 more if you go to $2 million. So, if you possess a lot of assets or earn a lot of money, I'd recommend you buy such a policy. To get such a policy, your best option is to get it from the company currently providing your homeowner's, renter's, or auto insurance coverage.

As you evaluate your choices of umbrella policies, pay careful attention to what your current insurance policies do not cover and how the umbrella policies do or do not fill in these coverage gaps. How well an umbrella policy covers the gaps may well turn out to be the most important selection criteria of them all. Also, if you are sure you will be getting an umbrella policy, you will gain more negotiating leverage if you buy it at the same time you purchase your homeowner's/renter's and your auto insurance.

Disability Insurance

The purpose of disability insurance is to provide you with a significant portion of your current income should you be unable to work due to illness or injury. It insures what is almost surely your greatest asset, that is, your ability to work and the money you make from doing so. It is far more important than life insurance, yet far fewer have it than pay for life insurance. One person in seven will be disabled for life before they turn sixty-five. It is *not* something you should ignore.

If you have been working for ten years or more and your situation meets their requirements, you are eligible to receive disability payments from the Social Security Administration. Further, should you be injured on the job you are probably covered to some degree by worker's compensation insurance. The problem is that these benefits are very limited and are very unlikely to cover your needs should something serious happen.

It's possible your employer may provide additional disability insurance beyond worker's compensation insurance, so you need to check whether or not that's so. Even if it is, you are likely to find that the coverage or the definition of *disability* are too limited and that it can or will be cancelled should you leave or get fired. The right thing for most people is to get a private policy to at least fill some of the financial gap should something happen.

If you do purchase a disability insurance policy, you want one that adjusts for inflation, includes a guaranteed premium amount, cannot be cancelled or altered on you, and that covers you for inability to work at your current occupation and not just at any occupation.

Unfortunately, most people ignore having this kind of insurance. I strongly recommend you take the time to look into this subject and be honest with yourself about the significant probability that you may need such insurance and think about what would happen if you didn't have it.

There are a couple of other cautions. The first is that these policies are usually based on your income from your current occupation. If you are considering changing from what you do now, things like becoming a stay-at-home parent or perhaps starting a business, you need to have a non-cancellable policy in place. The second is that if you are self-employed do not take the premiums as a business deduction. If you do, all disability payments then become taxable in full.

Health Insurance

The purpose of health insurance is to cover both routine health care and unforeseen major medical expenses.

You absolutely need health insurance. Yes, I know it can be very expensive unless your employer is providing it, but if you don't have it because you believe you can't afford it, you better think again. The truth is you can't afford not to have it. Without it, you are at great risk of financial disaster. According to a study carried out jointly by researchers at Harvard Law School and Harvard Medical School, illness and medical bills caused half of the country's 1,458,000 personal bankruptcies in 2001. Without health insurance, you and your family are also far less likely to seek preventive care, thereby greatly increasing the risks to your health and even your life. If necessary, pick the highest deductible, highest co-pay program you can find.

For most people the answer is to choose either an HMO (health maintenance organization) plan, a PPO (preferred provider organization), or a POS (point of service) plan. In an HMO you can only see the HMO's doctors. In a PPO or POS program the choice of doctors is broader and the flexibility is greater, but the premiums are higher.

Unfortunately, this is about as far as I can go on the selection of private health insurance. It is a personal decision that must account for the available options, income level, and personal preferences and needs. Be sure to ask enough questions and do enough research to fully understand and evaluate the insurance choices available in your area.

Once you reach sixty-five you are eligible for Medicare and Medicaid. In one sense, be thankful these programs are there, as the costs of purchasing health insurance once you are sixty-five-plus are astronomical. On the other hand, you must realistically expect that your benefits under this program will be reduced considerably over the next ten years or so and that the cost will rise considerably, especially if you continue to make a decent income. I say this because these programs are essentially broke. The people running our government (Congress) the last fifty years or so decided to spend the money you paid in. By doing so they had no choice but to depend on the new payments coming in each year to provide the payout money needed. Unfortunately, this scheme is starting to hit the wall, as the money coming in can no longer cover expenses. The same is about to be true of Social Security. What this all says is that you need to spend carefully, save aggressively, and insure that your future ends up under your control and not the control of others.

Briefly, here is what each of these programs cover:

- **Medicare Part A** covers hospital costs and, with limitations, nursing or hospice care (hospice is end-of-life care for someone terminally ill). This program rarely covers long-term care, hence the need for long-term care insurance (see page 326). There is no charge for Medicare Part A.

- **Medicare Part B** covers routine medical coverage such as physician's fees, outpatient hospital care, etc. As of 2010 the cost starts at just under $100 a month, dramatically lower than anything else you can get. The cost is indexed to your income, so if you earn a lot of money the payment goes up quite a bit.

- **Medicare Part D** is a program that covers prescription drugs.

- **Medicaid** is a program intended to provide medical care for the poor. To qualify you truly have to be just that. This is not a place you want to end up. There are a lot of shortcomings in the Medicare program, so you need to seriously consider also purchasing supplemental coverage (appropriately called **Medigap** policies) from a private insurance carrier to cover some of the gaps.

Be sure to do your homework and select your options before you turn sixty-five, as some choices become irreversible at that point. You can also expect to see a number of significant changes to these programs at some point in the years to come, so do your best to stay abreast of such changes.

Life Insurance

The purpose of life insurance is to cover the living expenses of the people who depend on you should you die. When it comes to life insurance, you should answer these four questions:

- Do you need it?
- If so, how much should you buy?
- How long will you need it?
- What type of policy should you get?

Do you need it?

If you're single with no dependents, you do not need life insurance. The same would be true if you hold substantial assets. If you do not fall into either of these categories, do you have children and, if so, how old are they? Does your spouse work? How much income do you bring home and what would happen if your income wasn't there? For most people the answer is "big trouble." If that is the case then you need life insurance.

If so, how much should you buy?

If you have children, how many years is it until they are on their own? Do you wish to cover their college expenses? Do you wish to provide your spouse the money to pay off the house? Ideally, why not leave them $1 million or more and do it all? If you do, however, you may well be into a heavier premium than you can afford or that makes sense. This is a highly personal decision. All I can suggest is this: Your current savings plus the amount of the insurance policy should be equal to at least six times your annual net salary, thus allowing your family at least that length of time to adjust to their new circumstances.

How long will you need it?

I recommend having it run until you can build up your savings adequately and/or your children are on their own. For most people a reasonable answer might be a term that covers your children until the youngest one is eighteen or twenty-one.

What type of policy should you get?

Although there are many variations of policies available, at root there are only two basic types—term life and whole life. A term-life policy covers you for a set amount of years. It may be one year at a time, and it is renewed annually. It might be five, ten, twenty, or even thirty years. A whole-life policy (alias universal, variable, or cash-value life) covers you until you die. To me there is only one policy that makes any sense for almost everybody, and that is a term policy.

Term policies are a *lot* cheaper than whole life and do what the real job should be, which is to cover your dependents until they are on their own. The secondary reason why whole-life policies cost so much more is that they cover you for life, which is something you should not need if you save properly. The primary reason is that they aren't solely insurance policies. Whole-life policies are part life insurance and part investment vehicles.

Whole-life policies seldom perform as promised. More importantly, like annuities, they are, with rare exception, a much inferior investment when compared to your other choices. The bottom line is never buy insurance as an investment. Be forewarned that insurance salespeople receive big commissions for selling whole-life policies and are very adept at convincing you it's your best option. They are so good at it that most of the life insurance policies in existence today are whole life. Do not fall for it.

Should a salesperson try to raise the subject of whole-life life insurance to you, cut the person off by making it clear that it is *not* an option. The arguments are endless: "Be sure of your financial safety forever." "Guarantee an income stream when you're older." "Protect your assets from unnecessary taxation." "Leave a special gift to your loved ones." "We have a whole new approach to this kind of policy." And on and on. Buy the term amount you need and invest the difference in the premiums. The only exceptions I can think of to the above involve very large assets, protecting sizeable business ownership interests, etc. If this is the case you are dealing with an estate-planning issue, and you should be seeking the advice of a good estate-planning lawyer, not someone in the insurance industry.

In general, if you already own a whole-life policy you are probably best off cancelling it at your first opportunity to do so. You might find it interesting that about half of all such policies end up getting cashed in during the first seven years, even though a lot of the money paid in is lost due to the huge up-front commissions and fees involved. Even if you lose a lot of money, by investing whatever you get plus the premiums you will otherwise pay in the years to come, you are highly likely to end up better off. Remember: Never cancel any policy until you take a thorough physical and have your replacement policy in place.

There are three choices for term insurance:

- An annual renewable policy where the premium rises each year
- A level-term policy with the same annual payment for the life of the policy
- A decreasing term where the payment stays the same but the death benefit decreases

A level-term policy will probably be your best buy and decreasing term your worst buy. Purchase only guaranteed renewable term products. If you have a group policy available, take the time to price out private coverage if the group policy can be cancelled against your will for reasons such as changing jobs. If that's the case and the price isn't a lot higher, go with the private policy.

You may be given the choice of adding an accidental death (alias double indemnity) provision to your policy. Such an option means that should you die an accidental death, your heirs get twice the payoff. This is fundamentally a bad deal, as you are unlikely to die in that manner. A better use of the money, should you feel compelled to get more protection, would be to increase the size of your policy amount a little more or, maybe, buy disability insurance if you haven't already done so.

Long-term Care Insurance

The purpose of long-term care insurance is to cover the major new medical and living support costs that will probably occur should you at some point become unable to take care of yourself on your own. Once you're over fifty this type of policy should start to be given active consideration. If you're fifty or older, keep reading. If you're not, come back when you are.

Our culture used to be different, with children readily accepting responsibility for caring for their parents if and when they were too old to take care of themselves. Most women were stay-at-home homemakers and available to do the job. Life spans were a lot shorter. Medical costs, too, were only a fraction of what they are today. All of that has, unfortunately, changed—and quite dramatically. Although the insurance to cover this situation is quite expensive, it is not something to ignore. According to the U.S. Department of Health and Human Services, 70% of the people living today will end up facing long-term care issues. You *must* assume that you will be facing this need someday. It is the insurance you are far more likely to end up needing more than any other, and yet it is the one most people do not own.

If you possess, or expect to soon accumulate, the assets necessary to cover such a situation and don't mind the risk of your estate being reduced accordingly, then you probably don't need this insurance. Be forewarned that the amounts required are big. The average person entering an assisted-living situation today spends just under two-and-a-half-years in such a facility at a cost of about $70,000 a year (as of 2009). At an inflation rate of 3.5%, that amount will double in twenty years. In most instances, Medicaid will not pay for these expenses unless you are truly poor. And even if you are, you might not be too happy with the limitations involved. You are allowed to own a home, but only if your spouse is still living there. You can try transferring your assets or getting divorced and leaving everything to your spouse but these strategies are illegal and Medicaid is very well aware of these tricks.

The obvious alternative to buying such a policy is to look to your spouse or partner to take care of you should you hit such a point and for your children or family members to take care of them if and when they need the help. This all becomes a highly personal decision, as you have to evaluate how much assistance you are actually likely to get.

The best answer for most people these days who have not accumulated the assets to cover such a situation is to get such a policy. You must be certain, however, that you can continue to pay the premiums after you retire. If you can't, don't do it, as you're probably going to end up wasting all the money you pay in. In that instance you're better off investing the money you would have otherwise paid out in premiums.

The best age to initiate such a coverage is probably somewhere in your late fifties. After that, the annual premiums involved rise a lot as each year passes and there is a growing possibility of a health issue occurring that will deny you coverage. Insurance agents will encourage you to start sooner, rightly pointing out that the premiums are a lot lower if you start earlier and the likelihood you'll be disqualified for health reasons is lower. The drawback to their logic is that you are far more likely to make a better decision by waiting until your late fifties. By then you'll have a noticeably better handle on your assets, on whether you can self-insure, and, especially, on your ability to continue to pay the premiums after you retire.

The selection of a long-term care policy will require that you do a good bit of homework, as there are both a lot of options and also potentially a lot of pitfalls if you're not careful.

Miscellaneous (and Usually Unnecessary) Insurance

There is no end to the other situations where someone will be offering (selling) you a policy to insure something. Although there may occasionally be a circumstance where one of these policies may be a good idea, they are usually a waste of money.

Here are the most common offers you will encounter.

Life insurance for children—The purpose of life insurance is to cover the living expenses of the people who depend on you should you die. Unless you have a major child star on your hands, nobody is depending on their children for income. Millions of these policies are in existence. The people who sold them should be ashamed of themselves.

Warranty insurance and maintenance policies or programs—These policies cover repairs that are not covered by the warranty that comes with the product. The odds are in your favor if you opt to skip the insurance and just cover the expense should it arise. If you think that this isn't always true, that it's better to insure your computer, dishwasher, etc., I do not agree. In every instance you can bet that the company issuing the policy has done its homework and set the odds and the rate in their favor, even after paying all the expenses involved to market these programs, paying the sales commissions, etc. Also, should something happen, the amounts involved are something you undoubtedly can afford, especially once your emergency fund is in place.

Mortgage protection life insurance—The idea behind these policies is that your home will be fully paid off should you die. If you think about it this is really no different than life insurance, the only difference being that the premium will be a *lot* higher, sometimes by as much as 200% more. If you feel you want this type of coverage, increase the size of your term-life policy. It's a lot cheaper way to go and offers more flexibility for your family to use the money should something happen to you.

Travel insurance—Such insurance reimburses you should you be forced to cancel a planned trip, etc. This is almost surely a losing proposition. Insure this risk yourself by being willing to cover any amount(s) that might be lost.

Flight insurance—This is extra life insurance in case you're killed in a plane crash. Do you have any idea how few people are killed in the world this way each year versus the number of passenger trips taken? This is a terrible deal. Pass on it.

Travel and trip insurance—Travel insurance is life insurance should you die while traveling. It preys on people's fears and is the same bad deal as flight insurance. If you need life insurance, you should already have the appropriate policy in place. Betting that if you die during your trip your family can get more money is a bad bet, given the rates involved. Also, you'd be surprised at the loopholes in these deals regarding how much you'll get and whether you'll even get paid at all. As for trip insurance, this is a policy that reimburses you for lost expenses if something interferes with a trip you've already booked. Once again the amounts should be something you can afford and the premiums are way out of line for the risk involved.

Travel medical insurance—Travel medical insurance covers your medical bills (often with a lot of restrictions) up to a limit (usually a low one) for a fixed number of days when you are traveling. These are bad odds and therefore a bad deal. To make things worse, it probably duplicates the coverage already provided by your health care insurance policy. If you are traveling out of the country, be sure to call your health care provider to understand its rules and restrictions, if any.

Cancer insurance—This is a relatively new insurance product. The coverage can vary a lot from plan to plan. Medical expenses covered can include co-pays, extended hospital stays, medical tests, and other specific cancer-related treatments. Non-medical expenses can include things like home health care and loss of income.

You are already covered for cancer by your health care insurance, so the real question is: Where are you not covered? The answer is usually if care for cancer exceeds the maximums of your health care policy. Your first step should be to compare such a policy with the benefits and coverage of your current health insurance to see the degree of overlap and where this type of coverage would kick in. Most health insurance policies contain a clause that says they won't cover expenses that another plan does. This alone can mean that a cancer policy is not a good way to go. Also, even if you experience a coverage shortfall it may cost less and provide a wider range of benefits if you upgrade your current health care policy. The bottom line is that most people are probably better off passing on this type of policy. Lastly, if you do not carry disability insurance and have a goodly number of years left to work, ask yourself where your dollars are best spent. Is it on extra cancer coverage or on disability protection? For most people it will be the latter.

Car rental insurance—This one is also a little tricky, as you do need liability insurance coverage for the rental and maybe collision, too. Before you rent a car for the first time call and find out what your auto insurance policy does and doesn't cover and also whether you have a credit card that covers collision damage on rentals. You'll probably find that you're already covered on liability and likely on collision, too. Unfortunately, some rental companies are now tacking on new clauses for extra nuisance fees, such as for their inability to rent the vehicle while it's being repaired, that your policy may not cover. If there is any doubt, read their clauses before you rent and/or call your insurance company to find out if you're already covered.

Tuition insurance—This kind of policy reimburses you if you've paid your child's tuition and he or she gets sick or injured and can't continue with their education. The odds are greatly in your favor if you self-insure, and the school involved will often work with you in such a situation.

Wedding insurance—This covers the added cost that might occur should the wedding be postponed due to illness on the part of the bride or groom, missing vendors, damage to the reception site should the place not have its own insurance, etc. Once again, the insurance company will have done its homework. What is covered, and the rates charged, makes it a winner for the company, not you, even given all of the marketing and selling expenses the insurer pays out. By the way, these policies do *not* pay off if either the bride or the groom changes her or his mind.

Credit card theft insurance—Federal law limits consumer credit card liability for unauthorized charges to $50. These types of insurance are normally pure scams. The FTC (Federal Trade Commission) singles out credit card theft insurance as the biggest type of scam out there today. But there is a loophole. The $50 liability limit does not include debit cards (nor does credit card theft insurance). Most financial institutions also cover you on your debit cards but, to be sure, call and find out. If they do not cover you, move your money to an institution that does.

Identity theft insurance—For the most part, these plans do not reimburse you for the money you lost, just for the expenses incurred if your identity is stolen, such as phone calls, copying fees, and lost wages. By and large they probably aren't worth it.

Credit life insurance/credit card balance insurance—These policies pay off your credit debt if you die. This is that same situation where the premiums are ridiculously high compared to term-life insurance rates. This is another attempt to play on your emotions or take advantage of your good will toward your family.

Pet health insurance—For most people, purchasing a health insurance policy for a pet is yet another bad deal, where the companies pay out a big percent in up-front commissions and know from their analysis of a zillion past experiences that they still win. So which side of that bet do you want? Still, there can be an exception. If you're one of those people who would do anything, at any cost, to save your pet, then this insurance might not be such a bad idea.

CHAPTER FOURTEEN

How to Negotiate

Negotiating is an enormously valuable skill. Just knowing the basics is likely to save you big dollars when you buy a car or a house, invest in real estate or someone's business, or negotiate for a pay increase. When it comes to negotiating, my brother, Ron, is a master. The information in this chapter is mostly his. He's trained dozens of executives over the years in these skills, so you can count on what we'll teach you. Good negotiating ability is not a common commodity and there is quite a bit to it. Here is a quick crash course to acquaint you with the basics and give you some tactics to use. There are three keys to successful negotiation: knowledge, time, and options.

Knowledge

The saying "knowledge is power" is never more true than when it comes to negotiating. What follows are some key things you need to *know* before you start any negotiation.

- Know exactly what you do and don't want. You must be very specific. Some of your wants are "gotta haves" while others may be less critical "niceties." By prioritizing your wants, you will know whether to dig in your heels or give something up as a trading chip.
- Know what you can realistically afford, including the ongoing expenses involved. For example, a vehicle needs fuel, insurance, maintenance, storage, etc.
- Know your timeline. When do you want or need to acquire the goods or services? For how long will you need them?
- Know your choices. What are the track records of each party? Try to find out what you can short of calling the referrals provided as such referrals are unlikely to be other than complimentary.
- Know what the other party wants to get from the deal. You often won't know and end up making assumptions. Ask questions and carefully evaluate the other party's responses in order to get a true understanding of the person's objectives. It is easy to overvalue things like the price, and undervalue other things, such as a quick sale or a reliable party with whom to do business. Sometimes liking and/or being comfortable with the person you are doing business with can make a big difference. I've seen a number of instances in real estate where the simple fact that the buyer really liked someone's house and taste went a long, long way. Because the sellers learned that the potential buyers "loved" the

house and wished they could pay what the sellers were asking but just "couldn't," the buyers were willing to negotiate a noticeably better price.

- Know the other party's desires and time constraints. As an obvious example, think of home sellers that have already found the next house they definitely want to buy. Do you think they're now more motivated to sell?

- Know the track record of any business you're dealing with. This is especially true if you will be dependent on it for a period of time (warranty, service contract, etc.). Is the business financially sound?

- Know if there are any new or emerging products, services, or trends that are or will be influencing the situation. If so, there is frequently a competitive advantage for those who recognize that change has happened or is about to occur.

- It's important to insure that the person you are negotiating with has the authority to make the deal. For example, a sales manager at an auto dealership has the authority to do so, while the salesperson probably does not. In a large corporation an officer has the legal ability to bind the corporation while someone under officer-level does not. Although you always want to negotiate against the decision maker, that is not always possible. Ask the other party if he has the authority on his own to agree to a binding deal. If he does not, you gain an advantage. From that point on treat the person as someone who is helping you by relaying your offer to the decision maker. Never forget that you are actually negotiating against someone else.

Time

All things being equal, the person with the biggest time constraint is at a disadvantage. Can you delay purchasing until competitive conditions improve? The option to buy now or later is very valuable. If you are not able to walk away from a deal, it's a clear disadvantage.

If a business is involved, keep in mind that the people there are usually working toward a quota and are under pressure to "make the numbers." If they believe you don't have to buy now, they will be under pressure to sweeten the deal. For some businesses such as the automobile industry, this can become particularly useful toward the end of the month.

Options

Competition is your strongest ally. The more options one has the better. You need to try to understand where both sides are regarding this issue. Usually, the pressure is greatest on the person doing the selling and you should assume this is so, unless you have a good reason not to. If the competitive element is in your favor it's important the parties involved become aware of that. Subtlety is key. Don't overdo it. If you do, they'll decide you're not serious and turn off and wait for someone who is.

When negotiating, whether for a lower interest rate on a credit card, a major purchase, or a sizable business agreement, there are a lot of different tactics that may be used. Here are some of the main ones to be aware of:

- For starters, choose the right person to be the apparent negotiator. As an example, a couple is trying to buy a house and one of them is better at hiding his or her feelings. That person becomes the apparent negotiator and the other person makes it clear that it's that person's decision.

- Ask for everything you could possibly want at the start. You will never get more than you initially ask for by adding it as you go along without trading something away for it. Before you start, list the options you will ask for. Also make a list of the options that may be presented to you during the negotiation and how you wish to respond to them.

- Do your best to disguise your time and option liabilities. If you are short on time, see if you can't force the person or business you are negotiating with to an even shorter time. If you can do that you turn a liability into an advantage.

- Most negotiation involves taking turns. You go, then I go. This frequently results in the two parties ending up in the middle between their respective starting positions. There are times, however, when you can get away with getting the other party to go twice. When you do, the result is usually beneficial. Most people will not let you get away with this, but you never know. It's possible they're not good negotiators or may need the transaction more than you do, so give it a try. As an example, someone is selling a car and is asking $13,500 for it. Instead of making an offer, try to get the seller to immediately go again. Say something like, "It's a nice car but it's more than I can afford right now." Then wait. If the seller comes back with a lower price you did it. If that doesn't work, try the same exact thing again after you've countered and the seller comes back with the next number.

- Much of a negotiation is played out in the trading of concessions; they are used like trading chips. When you give in on a point you are entitled to ask for something in return. Use these moments to expand your knowledge about what is most important to the other party. The basic approach is to say, "I will concede X if you give me Y!" Don't be afraid to ask for a greater concession than you are giving. It may not matter that much to the party and you will be pleasantly surprised. Also, every time you are asked for something is an opportunity for you to ask for more in return. Learn to appreciate and make the most of concession trading.

- Take time before making a counteroffer or concession. Think out your position carefully. Once you say it, you cannot retreat from it without hurting your position. Also, if you respond to a request too quickly it will be assumed that it was easy for you to give something up and their demands will likely increase. A little play acting doesn't hurt. Try to make it look like the concession was painful. Purse your lips, slowly shake your head from side to side, let out a deep sigh, and *then* make the concession and ask for one in return. Sometimes it's a good idea to go a step farther and sleep on it.

- Never flat-out reject any request. Negotiating processes are very fluid. You never know exactly where they will take you. Do not close the door on anything until you are completely finished. Instead of saying no use phrases like "I can't agree to that at this time," or "I could only do that if . . ." and ask for a concession that you know is a deal breaker for them (usually cost). This is a good way to temporarily shelve the issue so that you can reintroduce it later in the process if it becomes desirable to do so.

- Don't over-focus on the dollars. Price is usually the single most important negotiating point and it is important to hit it hard and early. At some point you are likely to hit stiff opposition. Shift to non-price issues if they offer a significant opportunity to sweeten the deal. People often focus less on other areas than they should.

- Silence is very powerful. In most negotiations there will be a critical make-or-break moment. Be on the lookout for that moment! At that instant, remember that he who speaks first usually loses. I'm not kidding. Try it. Do *not* be the first to speak. You'll be amazed at what a great strategy it often turns out to be. By holding your silence, the other party often feels he needs to say something and that something could be a concession to your advantage.

- Throughout a negotiation, remember to be patient. It is a process. Many times you will reach an impasse in negotiations where everything stops. Wait. Let them get nervous. Most people will come back with concessions. If they don't, you have a number of options. If you are in a store or on the phone you can leave or try to leave, or end the call by telling them you'll think about it. To a salesperson, "think about it" is the kiss of death, and many times you will find they will make an additional "final" concession at that moment. If you do actually leave or end the call, nothing says you can't go back or call in a few minutes.

- Always be friendly. Don't try to beat on anyone. You're far more likely to win if you tone down any notion that this is a contest.
- Avoid reverse traps. A reverse trap occurs when the other party asks a question. If you answer it, your own words will be used to reduce your negotiating options. For example, say you're looking at a car and the salesperson asks you, "Just how much would you like to pay to be in this baby?" If you answer, you may well get a worse deal than if you don't. A good answer might be, "What can I get it for?" This tactic will force him to go twice.
- When you are not a repeat purchaser or do not require ongoing service after the deal is made, you can be as aggressive as you wish. If that's not the case, you want a motivated "partner" and should look to strike a "win-win" deal. Each party is entitled to a reasonable profit for their efforts. Also, do you want an ongoing relationship with anyone not smart enough to make a profit or that you're able to take undue advantage of? I wouldn't.
- Watch out for situations where the purchase is cheap but the follow-up costs are not. For example, copy machines, printers, and air cleaners are cheap. The profit is in the required supplies like toner cartridges, filters, and so on that you are later obligated to purchase. When you negotiate be sure to include the cost of any follow-up items and services.
- Especially in a business situation where you are hiring a firm to provide a product or service, complete *all* negotiations before selecting the winning vendor. Once you've

selected your vendor, and they know it, 95% of your negotiating power is gone. Many people will tell or signal the vendor they've decided to go with them and then continue negotiating. No way! Once you have eliminated the competition you are no longer in control. They are.

Should you wish to learn more about negotiating; you will find there are a lot of good books and courses available on the subject.

In Conclusion

The path to smart money management starts with a clear understanding of what you want and why you want it. To accurately identify your wishes, you must do all you can to shake off the commercial brainwashing that tells you what you should want, how you should look, what you should own, where you should live, what you should do, what you should be, and even how you should think in order to be happy. Once you push these false expectations aside, you and you alone will decide what you want, why you want it, and what you are willing to trade for it.

An important part of this process is to reject the idea that more money will always add to your happiness. It will not, if in order to get it you must trade away things like good health, special relationships, and enjoying how you spend your days—the things that matter most. Once the basics like food, clothing, shelter, medical coverage, and a car that runs are covered, money is unlikely to add significantly to your happiness. Sadly, money can, and far too often does, take away from contentment. As a source of stress or leading to feelings of not being successful enough, money can gnaw at you.

To take control of your finances—and your life—use this book and make sure that money adds to your life in meaningful ways. Dollars shouldn't drag you down. Think carefully about the balance between the time you spend making money and the time you give to your personal life. While saving for a good future is important, it is also crucial not to give up today for tomorrow. Today, just like tomorrow, is your life. Find the balance that will make for the most enjoyable and satisfying life now and still be fulfilling as the months and years go by.

As you travel the money-smart path, maintain a positive attitude and believe in yourself. Whenever your plans don't turn out as expected, understand that you're still stepping toward your goals. Going through some trial and error as you make your way is to be expected. The important thing is that you are still moving toward what is best for you.

So long as you are honest with yourself and willing to do what it takes to get the job done, you can achieve your goals. There is no having your cake and eating it too. The stock market of the future will not save you. You will not win a lottery. However, through planning and self-control you can use your money to create the life you want. Winning the lottery of life is not an accidental thing. You plan for it and earn it. So choose your goals carefully and then be disciplined in your pursuit of them. Do the things you said you would do to achieve them.

Now you know that personal money management is not too complicated for you to learn. Reject the lie that says it is. Take control of your money and understand that you can manage your money better than anyone else can. The tools to do so are in your hands. Always follow the rules of money and don't lose sight of your goals for achieving financial freedom and living the life you want.

Please trust that it really isn't how much money you make, but what you do with it that counts. The only real foundation for smart money management starts with the saving of a substantial percentage of your income. You can save a lot more than you probably thought and by that action alone ensure that money adds to your happiness.

By personally believing in and doing the things I have laid out in this book, I am living a life that is all I could ever have dreamed of. As you journey forward, I wish you the same success and a life you have both earned and feel honored to have received.

Finally, I would like to ask a favor. Once you have read the book, if you find that it was informative and helpful, I ask that you pass it on. It is my wish that that this simple, down-to-earth approach to money and personal finance will spread and become the new norm. I'd like to see the intimidation and confusion that so often hamper people's decision making become a thing of the past.

"Just-in-Time" Subjects List

Find these "Just-in-Time" subjects at www.MoneySmartOnline.com.

Bankruptcy

Children

Death of a spouse

Divorce

Financial scams and investment traps

Job loss

Marriage

Planning for the world of tomorrow

Tax law changes

Glossary

401(k)

A 401(k) is a government-qualified plan established by employers to help their employees save for retirement. Eligible employees may make contributions from their salaries on a pre- or post-tax basis into their accounts. Employers may make matching contributions and may also add a profit-sharing feature to the plan. Full taxes are paid on all pre-tax earnings plus whatever profit has been made on that money when that money is eventually withdrawn.

Asset type/asset class/asset group

An asset type, asset class, or asset group is a specific type of investment such as stocks, fixed income, real estate, cash, etc.

Bond

A bond is a loan made by a financial institution or institutions to a business or government body. Individual pieces of the bond can be sold to other institutions or to individuals who, in turn, can either hold it or sell it at some point.

Buy and hold

Buy and hold is the investment strategy of buying an investment and holding it (not selling it or trading it) for a long time.

CDs

CDs (certificates of deposit) are a fixed-income investment where money is loaned to a bank or other financial institution for a set number of months at a set (fixed) rate of return.

Commodities

A commodity is a usable and valuable physical substance, such as wheat, corn, sugar, oil, metals, water, etc. The ownership of many common commodities can be bought and sold on the U.S. and the world commodity markets just like shares of stock.

Compounding

Compounding is the effect of getting interest on your interest and profit on your profit. Compounding occurs when the money you earn on your investments is reinvested and then that larger balance earns even more money. The effects are exponential as the money grows faster and faster because of the additional money you make on the new money added.

Cookies

A cookie is a small file deposited by a website on your computer to keep track of information about your browsing history on that site. The site will then use that information to fine tune the information it presents to you. This might be good or it might be bad. For example, the site might send or show you advertising that ties to your interests based on the searching you did. If you wish to block this from happening, your browser (Internet Explorer, Firefox, etc.) has tools for doing so by clearing out old cookies.

Dividend

A dividend is a payment, per share of stock, made from the company's earnings to shareholders. Usually these payments are quarterly, set by the company's board of directors, and are taxable. For the most part they are cash payments but sometimes take other forms such as additional shares of stock.

Dollar cost averaging

Dollar cost averaging is the investment strategy of making repeated stock buys over a period of time instead of investing all at once. The purpose of doing this is to buy more shares when the price is cheaper and less at the higher prices, so you end up paying a lower average price per share.

DOW

The DOW stands for the Dow Jones Industrial Index. This stock market index is calculated using the price of about 30 U.S. companies trading on the New York Stock Exchange (NYSE) that are chosen to represent a large portion of the mainstream U.S. stock market. Over the years it has become a less accurate indicator of the overall market than other indexes such as the S&P 500 (the 500 largest companies) but it is still used by the media and the financial services industry as their primary reference number when talking about the U.S. stock market.

ETF

An ETF (Exchange Traded Fund) represents a large number of individual investments that are all in a specific business area, such as building company stocks, bank stocks, oil company stocks, corporate bonds, etc. ETFs can represent an index such as the S&P 500, or even a specific commodity such as oil or agricultural products. They can be bought and sold daily just like stocks, and will go up or down in value based on the change in value of their underlying asset group.

Fixed-income investments

Fixed-income investments are investments that provide a fixed (set) rate of return in exchange for loaning money for a set number of months. They include bank accounts, money market accounts, CDs, treasury bills, and bonds or bond mutual funds.

Home equity

Home equity is the difference between a home's fair market value and the outstanding balance of all loans against the property. It represents the true (net) ownership position of the owner.

Index fund

An index fund will own all of the stocks in a particular index—a specific portion of the overall market, such as banking, manufacturing, health care, and so on. The amount owned of each company is weighted based on its total market value. Each stock in the index is assigned a percentage of the index identical to the size of that company's total market value as compared to the combined company values of all of the companies in the index. By doing this, the fund's performance becomes the same as all of the companies combined.

Inflation

Inflation is the increase in the prices of goods and services over a period of time. When this happens, each unit of currency buys fewer goods and services and the value of the currency involved is reduced accordingly. The rate of inflation is most commonly measured by the annual percentage change of a government-generated index such as the Consumer Price Index (CPI).

Investment

Investment is resources such as money, property, your time, etc., that are placed at risk with the intent of receiving a reward of some kind in exchange.

IRA

IRA stands for individual retirement account. It is a personal investment account governed by IRS rules and regulations. There are two types of accounts, tax-deferred and tax-free. In a tax-deferred account, the money that goes into it, as well as the money earned by the account, is not taxed until the money comes out. In a tax-free account, the money is taxed before it goes in, and all of the money in the account, including the money it earns, is tax-free.

Market

A market is a place or system where you can buy, sell, or trade goods, services, and/or information. The exchange of goods or services in a market is referred to as a *transaction*. Markets exist for an endless variety of reasons. When investors use the term *the market*, they are referring to a stock market or markets that handle the selling of stocks, bonds, mutual funds, and commodities. The largest U.S. stock market, the New York Stock Exchange (NYSE), is a mixture of a place and a computer system. The second largest market, the NASDAQ, is just a computer system.

Market cycle

Market cycles are the patterns of change in the price levels of a given market. Pretty much all markets will cycle over time between being underpriced and overpriced.

Money market account

A money market account is an account at a financial institution such as a bank that usually pays a little bit more in interest than a regular savings account. Such an account may or may not be insured by the federal government like a savings account. Even if it is not, such accounts are still usually very safe as they are backed by short-term debt instruments with maturities of one year or less. They are a good temporary place for cash you expect needing access to in the short term.

Mutual fund

A mutual fund is created when someone, usually an investment company, assembles a pool of investment money that they will manage. Each fund has a specific set of investment goals (growth, income, low risk, diversification) and specifies the type of investments it will make (stocks, bonds, commodities, real estate, foreign stocks markets, etc.). The fund may just invest in one type of investment or in many, depending on the stated purpose of that fund. Each dollar invested in the fund owns a proportionate share in that fund and therefore in the things it owns.

NASDAQ

The NASDAQ (National Association of Securities Dealers Automated Quotation) is a computerized market, or exchange, for more than 5,000 stocks. This market and its index are very heavily weighted toward technology companies such as Microsoft, Intel, Dell, and Cisco.

NYSE

NYSE stands for the New York Stock Exchange, the largest of the U.S. stock markets.

P/E

Price to earnings ratio (p/e) is the relationship of a stock price to the earnings of the company involved. It is calculated by dividing the total value of all of the common stock shares of a company (its market capitalization) by its after-tax earnings over a twelve-month period (usually the most recent twelve months reported). It is the most commonly used measure of how expensive a stock is.

Rate of return

Rate of return is the percent of profit made on an amount invested for a given period of time. For example, if you invest $100 for one year and make $7, your annual rate of return would be 7%.

Real dollar value

Real dollar value is what a dollar is worth in goods and services. Over time, inflation reduces the real world value of a dollar—of the amount of goods and services it can buy. For example, if inflation has risen by 30% over an eight-year period, then the real value of a dollar has become only ¢70 in terms of its real purchasing power.

S&P 500

The S&P 500 (also called the S&P) is an index, weighted by market value, of the prices of the stock of 500 large publicly held companies actively traded in the U.S. It provides a very good representative picture of the U.S. stock markets as it represents over 70% of the market.

Shorting a stock

Shorting a stock means to bet against the stock in the belief that its price will fall. It is done by borrowing the stock shares from a brokerage house in order to sell them, in the hope that you can buy them back later at a lower price, then return the shares to their owner, and profit on the difference. At some point you have to return the stock you borrowed. If the stock price has gone down, you win; if it has gone up, you lose.

Stock

Stock is the vehicle for sharing partial ownership of a company. The stock owner is entitled to the company's earnings equal to whatever portion of the company that each share of stock represents.

Tax-deferred investment account

A tax-deferred investment account is an account where the money that goes into it, as well as the money earned by the account, is not taxed until the money comes out.

Tech stocks

Tech stocks are stock in companies involved in technology. Tech stock performance is most commonly tracked by using the NASDAQ stock market index which is dominated by the large tech companies such as Microsoft, Intel, Dell, and Cisco.

Trailing earnings

Trailing earnings are the earnings per share for a firm's most recently completed fiscal year.

Treasury bills

Treasury bills (also called T-bills) are fixed-income loans (bonds) made to the U.S. government by financial institutions or individual investors that are due for repayment in one year or less. Treasury bills are exempt from federal, state, and local taxes. Like most other bonds, individual pieces of a treasury bill can be sold to other institutions or to individuals who, in turn, can either hold or sell them at some point.

Wrap account

A wrap account is an investment account where the management fee is a flat quarterly or annual amount based on the amount of the assets under management.

Index